Names
of the
Land

Cape Cod, Nantucket,
Martha's Vineyard, and the
Elizabeth Islands

Names
of the
Land

Cape Cod, Nantucket,
Martha's Vineyard, and the
Elizabeth Islands

Eugene Green and William L. Sachse

The
Globe
Pequot
Press

Chester Connecticut

Library of Congress Cataloging in Publication Data

Green, Eugene, 1932-
    Names of the land.

    Bibliography: p.
    Includes index.
    1. Names, Geographical — Massachusetts — Cape Cod.
2. Names, Geographical — Massachusetts — Elizabeth
Islands. 3. Names, Geographical — Massachusetts — Martha's
Vineyard. 4. Names, Geographical — Massachusetts —
Nantucket. 5. Cape Cod (Mass.) — History, Local.
6. Elizabeth Islands (Mass.) — History, Local. 7. Martha's
Vineyard (Mass.) — History, Local. 8. Nantucket (Mass.) —
History, Local. I. Sachse, William L. (William Lewis),
1912-   . II. Title.
F72.C3G73 1983   917.44'92'00321   82-82167
ISBN 0-87106-971-1

Manufactured in the United States of America
Book and Cover Design by Peter Good

For Allen Walker Read

Contents

Acknowledgments

Many have assisted in the making
of this dictionary. We are especially grateful for the
aid and encouragement of Harriet Cabot, Paul
Chesbro, Barbara Conathan, George Kelley, Frederick B. Matthews, and Florence W. Ungermann [all
of Barnstable]; M. Susan Cobb [Bourne]; Marian H.
Wylie [Brewster]; Ernest J. Knapton and Joe Nickerson [Chatham]; W. Jeremiah Burke, Pauline Derick,
Mrs. Linwood Foss, Mrs. Richard Reid [all of Den-
nis]; Frederick H. Jewell and Howard Quinn [East-
ham]; Dudley Hallett and Deborah Schilling [Fal-
mouth]; Doris M. Doane and Virginia S. Doane
[Harwich]; Everett S. Allen and Henry Beetle Hough
[Martha's Vineyard]; Jim Peters [Mashpee]; Barbara
Andrews, Louise Hussey, and Edouard Stackpole
[Nantucket]; Tom Fuller [Orleans]; Thomas Kane
[Provincetown and Truro]; Russell Lovell [Sand-
wich]; Mrs. William D. Purcell and Florence Rich

[Wellfleet]; Hugh S. Clark [Yarmouth]. All have saved us from inaccuracies; whatever errors remain are our own. We are greatly indebted to the librarians at the following libraries, who directed us to many valuable sources: Bourne Public Library, Boston Public Library, Boston University Library, Cape Cod Community College, Cotuit Public Library, Falmouth Public Library, Peter Foulger Museum, Nantucket Athenaeum, the library of the New England Historic Genealogical Museum, South Yarmouth Library, the State House Library of Massachusetts, the Sterling Memorial Library of Yale University, Vineyard Haven Public Library, and the Yarmouth Port Library. We benefited from the support of Professor Frederic G. Cassidy [Wisconsin], Mrs. Harriet Lane [Boston University], Mr. Donald J. Orth [U.S. Board on Geographic Names], and Professor Thomas A. Sebeok [Indiana]. The columns of the *Cape Cod News*, the *Falmouth Times*, the Dennis Historical Society *Newsletter*, the *Vineyard Gazette*, and the *Register*, Yarmouth Port, were helpful. For research on this book Eugene Green has had support from an ACLS Grant-in-Aid, the American Philosophical Society, and the Boston University Graduate School Research Fund.

E.G.

W.L.S.

Introduction

Cape Cod and the Elizabeth Islands, Martha's Vineyard and Nantucket — these are the outermost shores of Massachusetts, scraps of earth in heavy seas, glacial remnants that long before the coming of the Pilgrims accommodated Algonquians, that gave harbor to coastal packets and whalers before the arrival of airplanes and yachts. To these many generations, the compactness of the Cape and the Islands has revealed rapid shifts in terrain: the descent along the coast, from high cliffs to white beaches and sudden shoals; farther inland, forests of pine and hemlock opening into kettle ponds and strings of boulders. Gales and tides have remade the shorelines. The summer sun, southwest winds, and the Gulf Stream have encouraged colonies of summer people to spring up by the sea. So little land, such a remarkable harvest of nature and history. Year-rounders have farmed the land and the sea: cranberries from the bogs and strawberries from sandy soil; lobsters and clams along the shores; cod and bluefish farther out; and in the past sperm whales in the great deeps. Summer people have brought roads and trains, state parks and art shows, religious revivals and shopping malls. And more and more in recent times, both islanders and off-islanders, Cape Codders and those off-Cape, have sought to reserve lands as sanctuaries of nature and to turn mills, coast guard stations, as well as salt boxes and Cape houses, into museums of local history.

This dictionary of place-names gathers together into its thousand entries the natural and the historic, the past and the present of Cape Cod and the nearby Islands. People cannot live very long on the land without naming its rivers and ponds, its hills and hollows, its coves and beaches. We name our towns and villages, our streets and bridges and canals. Swamps as well as parks, islands as well as reefs, all have their names. There are names even for places that probably

never existed: Webbs Island, Shanks Pond, and
Sheepfold Hill on the Cape and Green Hollow on the
Vineyard. Some names take us back, past history, into
the realm of Algonquian and European myths of creation and discovery. Legend accounts for the creation
of Scargo Lake, Santuit River, and the Devils Bridge.
A belief in the voyages of Vikings to the new world
produces explanations for the names Kjalness and
Nomans Land. And there are names, too, for places
that no one has ever convincingly identified. Just
where were Tuckers Terror, Shimmo, Hills Hap, and
Shoal Hope? And finally, the mysteries of such in-
triguing names as Queen Sewells Pond, German Hill,
Quaker Run, and Loagy Bay — places clearly marked
on maps — remain as unfathomable as a Cape Cod
fog.

Algonquian names are the oldest in the
dictionary but also the hardest to interpret. Very
few English settlers of the 1600s learned the Indian
language — Richard Bourne did on the Cape, the
Mayhews on Martha's Vineyard, and Peter Folger on
Nantucket — yet none of them recorded or translated
the Algonquian names for places. Instead, places
like Monomoy, Cotuit, Succonessett, Menemsha,
Chappaquiddick, Nantucket, Naushon, and Muskeget — we could go on and on — survived in old deeds
and maps and in the everyday speech of settlers and
their descendants. They wrote and said what they
heard and remembered, sometimes with unexpected
or even startling changes. So before long the townspeople of Sandwich and Bourne were saying Monument River and Beach instead of the Algonquian
Manomet. And in Falmouth the village of Teaticket
most likely had its origins in the Indian *keht-tukq-ut*
"at the big river." By and large, the settlers who
adopted Indian names for their villages — names like
Cotuit and Sesuit on the Cape, Siasconset on Nantucket, and Menemsha on the Vineyard — had no
knowledge of what they meant, but chose them because they were reminders of a romantic, natural past
and because they had liquid pronunciations. Other
communities — Hyannis on the Cape, Wauwinet on
Nantucket — bear the names of Indian sachems, otherwise long since forgotten. And other places — like

Sipsons Island in Pleasant Bay and Gibbs Pond on Nantucket — recall Indians who took English names. To learn the backgrounds and meanings of these names is like treading over the uncertain sands of a backside beach.

Still we can make some sense of the Indian place-names, because the difference between the dialects of the southern New England Algonquians was no greater than, say, the difference in the speech of New Yorkers, Los Angelenos, and Bostonians. Then, too, the Indian way of life was very much the same from tribe to tribe, and the pace of life kept rhythm with the cycles of the year, from a time to hunt and a time to fish to a time to plant. From season to season the tribes would hunt in the forests, fish in the streams, and burn off grass to plant their crops, mostly maize. The Indians' place-names helped them to identify the landmarks and waterways of their terrain, to keep familiar the space of their immediate world. So just as Katama in Edgartown signifies "a big fishing place," Kittemaug on the Thames River in Connecticut may have also been a seasonal setting for Indian fish weirs. Coatue Neck on Nantucket, Cotuit in Barnstable, and Cowassit in Canterbury, Connecticut are all names for stands of pine trees, where the Indians most likely found game. And Cuttyhunk in Gosnold is quite likely a shortened form of Mohican Poquetan'noc "lands already broken up for planting." But as these comparisons of names show, we do not have exact fits that match name to name and never will have. At best, the interpretation of Algonquian place-names remains a matter of informed guessing, a hope that we can reveal a few of the hidden meanings behind their romantic sounds.

A second mystery in the naming of places on the Cape and the Islands has to do with the maps and jottings of early explorers. When Juan de la Cosa sailed along the Atlantic coast of the Cape in 1500, he surely recorded it on his map and gave it a name. But which? Was it Cavo de Yngleterra, as some believe, or some other? Verrazano's voyage, nearly thirty years later, produced another map with other names, but no greater certainty. Some say that he named Cape Cod Pallavisino; others argue that the name was Armel-

lini. And in 1543 Vallard drew up another map that
includes the Cape, calling it Cap de Croix. What is
more, none of these names endured; none stirred the
minds of men sufficiently to encourage large emigra-
tions. Not until Gosnold sailed west in 1602 to redis-
cover and to name the Cape, the Vineyard, and the
Elizabeth Islands [some say, too, that he sailed past
Nantucket], do we find English families alert to his
explorations and willing to follow his course over the
Atlantic.

The English were the first settlers to lay out
farms and towns on the Cape and the Islands. Samuel
de Champlain sailed twice, once to Monomoy, the
other time to Sandy Neck, even before John Smith or
the *Mayflower* entered Cape Cod Bay, but he established no trading post. The Dutch in the 1620s began
to trade with the Pilgrims at Aptucxet Trading Post,
drew up a map of the Cape some years later, but never
sent any colonists to claim the land. But in the 1630s
and 1640s came families and congregations from
Plymouth and also from Massachusetts Bay Colony
and, soon after, Quakers seeking a haven from the
narrow Puritans. They incorporated towns and, as
elsewhere in Massachusetts, named them mainly in
honor of villages and parishes in England, many of
them also coastal towns: Truro and Chatham, Yarmouth and Falmouth, Harwich and Sandwich. And,
on the Vineyard, Thomas Mayhew went further and
named two towns Tisbury and Chilmark for the villages he had known back home in England. The settlers had come to practice their religion, free from
Archbishop Laud's restrictions, to acquire property in
a land far less crowded than England. But the names
of their towns reminded them, too, of the world they
had left behind, of the English coast that they had exchanged for one in America.

Within their towns the settlers and their descen-
dants continued to remember England right up to the
American Revolution. Both Cape Cod and the Vine-
yard had early roads named the Kings Highway.
Harwich and Chatham shared Queen Annes Road.
The Old Rose and Crown is a shoal off Monomoy
Point named for an intersection, probably familiar to
sailors, in Soho, London, and Bishop and Clerks took

its name from islets off the coast of Wales. The commons of English villages, open to the pasturing of livestock, account for the Old and New Commons of early Barnstable, and for Barnstable and Falmouth Greens today. And the great fish market of London spurred the oystermen of Wellfleet to name their district in town Billingsgate.

Like true Englishmen, too, early Cape Codders and Islanders had a keen sense of social standing and the importance of the ownership of land. The townspeople of Sandwich, for example, paid their first minister William Leverich in part with a parcel of land and called it, out of respect for him, Mr. Leverichs Meadow. And although much of the land granted to the early families still bears their names — say, Baker Town in Dennis, Cooks Brook Beach in Eastham, Starbuck Neck Road in Edgartown, and Swain Hill in Nantucket — the Cape and the Islands have ponds, coves, swamps, and hollows identified only by the first names of men and women. Truro had a Hectors Stubble for a black man; Sandwich a Chloes Swamp for a black woman. Peters Pond in Mashpee, Zacks Cliffs on Gay Head, Phillips Run on Nantucket, and Jobs Neck on Nonamesset Island are all names of Indians. And Aunt Bettys Pond in Hyannis, together with Uncle Barneys Road in Dennis, recall members of families long established by the 1800s. So first names for places often included slaves, servants, converted Indians, and lastly, intimate members of families. All these people, the leaders of the community and family servants, as well as favorite uncles and widowed aunts, helped to form local society and to identify local places.

Family tradition, old neighbors, and town characters like Abigail Dunham at Nabs Corner on the Vineyard also contribute, for many latecomers to the Cape and the Islands, a heightened sense of identity and closeness. To own ten acres in Truro or on the Vineyard and to have roots as old as the Hopkinses or the Daggetts — the idea has prompted some, as in the town of Dennis, to name streets for every uncle one can name, from Uncle Bill and Uncle Bob to Uncle Stanley and Uncle Zeke. And others, maybe from the Great Plains and the deserts of Arizona, have trans-

ported such Indian names to Yarmouth as Apache
Drive and Navajo Road. This romantic desire for the
past is, of course, nothing new. Old-timers on Nantucket and the Vineyard believe that Gosnold sailed
past their southern shores on the way to Cuttyhunk,
while natives of Falmouth say that he anchored off
Woods Hole on his way down Vineyard Sound. The
romance of the Cape and the Islands lies, then, in the
delight of their fresh ponds, clean beaches, and deep
blue bays; but also in the atmosphere created by their
names, by Squibnocket Pond, by First Encounter
Beach, and Lewis Bay. The history of the Cape and
the Islands authenticates for summer people the
pleasures of a holiday.

　　But after Labor Day, when school resumes and
the illusions of summer depart, the place-names of
Wellfleet and Harwich, of West Tisbury and Oak
Bluffs, of all the towns between Buzzards Bay and the
Atlantic, help to account for a history of enterprise
and failure, of bravery and patience. The early settlers, for example, were mostly farmers who kept
their sheep, as Conrad Aiken supposed, on Sheepfold
Hill, and drove them in the spring before fleecing to
Washing or Shear Pen or Sheep Ponds. For two hundred years Nantucket thrived on sheep herding, celebrating Shearing Day, and squabbled over rights to
the pastures in Plainfields. But by 1850 the Austra-
lians and the Iowans were sending sheep and wool to
market at so low a price that the Islanders could no
longer compete. The seven Flax Ponds, sprinkling
the Cape from Bourne to Harwich, once covered over
and soaked bundles of fibers, softening them just
enough until they were ready for the mills to clean
and to spin into yards of linen. Flax clothed the Cape
and was even a cash crop until the early 1800s, when
Eli Whitney's cotton gin sent the price of cotton tum-
bling and the market for linen down. Rich land in itself was never abundant. Although Forestdale is a
village in Sandwich, named for the lushness of the soil
in surrounding fields and woods, Poverty Hollow in
Falmouth and Goodie Halletts Meadow in Eastham
have unworkable acres, fruitless even in early days.
But just when cotton replaced linen as the staple cloth
and sheepherding was becoming too costly, Henry

Hall of Dennis began to grow cranberries for market
and the Hatches and Smalls of Falmouth produced
large crops of strawberries. Cranberry Highway
[Route 28] advertises the value of such farms as Lawyer Lovells and Shaving Hill Bogs, and Strawberry
Lane in Yarmouth Port makes us think of berry boxes
and plump fruit.

The search for other profitable industries began
early, too. Prospect Hill in Chilmark probably has its
name for the excellent view at its summit of Vineyard
Sound, but maybe because an iron mine close by in
the 1700s promised some rich dividends. The trouble
was that it took only from fifty to a hundred years to
exhaust the ore. Jarvesville, a name no longer in use,
identified the site of the Sandwich Glass Works, that
for about sixty years [1825-1888] hired many a hand,
brought glass blowers from Germany and England,
but closed down when the cost of material and labor
went up too high to turn a profit. Nearby, the Keith
Car and Manufacturing Company constructed the
wooden Sagamore railroad and freight cars, named
for the village, until the steel-bodied trains of Pitts-
burgh replaced them in the 1920s. In the 1800s, too,
Brick Yard Creek in Barnstable, Paint Mill Brook in
Chilmark, and Blacksmith Shop Road in Falmouth all
named industries that flourished for a generation or
two before competitors elsewhere outdid them. But
the most fortunate failure of all was on the peninsula
at Woods Hole, romantically named Penzance. Before
Penzance became a community of large estates, it regularly sent a stench across Great Harbor to Woods
Hole from the Pacific Guano Company — producers
of fertilizer. When the cost of importing guano from
the Howland Islands and mixing it with menhaden
rose too high for farmers, the company closed for
good just before the opening of the oceanographic research institutes at Woods Hole in the 1880s. So the
stench died down and in its place the waters of Great
Harbor, well-situated for scientific experiment, made
possible a renewed vitality for the old whaling village
at Woods Hole.

Whaling was, of course, the great enterprise of
Cape Cod and the Islands. The search and killing of
the leviathan had a risk and danger that exceeded the

hope of profit from sperm, blubber, and oil. Herman Melville has Ishmael, Captain Ahab, and the other sailors aboard the *Pequod* start out from Nantucket in search of Moby Dick, the fabulous whale reported in 1820 to have rammed and sunk another, actual Nantucket whaler, the *Essex*. And in his poem *The Quaker Graveyard in Nantucket*, Robert Lowell talks to us as sailors who are endlessly on the hunt beyond "tree-swept Nantucket and Wood's Hole/And Martha's Vineyard," ready to make our swords "Whistle and fall and sink into the fat," as if the chase for the whale were also a pursuit of a sea god, able both to enrich and to destroy.

The Quakers of Nantucket were among the hardiest mariners on whaling ships, but they were not alone. New Guinea in Nantucket Town names a quarter where black sailors, who joined in the hunt for whales, lived. And Angola Street recalls the west coast of Africa, where ships would dock and enlist blacks to join the crew. On Martha's Vineyard, too, the Barbary Coast, an old name for Eastville, was a district of sailors and harpooners who sailed with the captains of Edgartown like Nathaniel Jernegan [he founded Jerneganville] for three or four years at a stretch to hunt the whale. And the district of Fayal in Oak Bluffs honors in its name the Portuguese of the Azores, who first came to the Vineyard aboard whaling ships. Up-island on the Atlantic Coast, Lookout Hill took its name early in the 1700s, because from its summit spotters would signal the presence of whales. For more than a century, until the discovery of oil and kerosene, whalers and their families lived in the towns and villages of Nantucket and Martha's Vineyard, first hunting along the shores the way the Indians had done, then sailing out in ships, chancing their luck and their lives far south on the Atlantic and Pacific.

Cape Cod sent many sailors and skippers to sea. It also built the ships to render the blubber and haul the freight. And some of the boat yards and clippers, busy in the 1800s, remain still in the names of streets. Hippogriffe Road is named for a clipper of the 1850s that sailed from Boston to San Francisco and on to Calcutta; Kit Carson Way is for another clipper built in Dennis. In East Dennis, too, Shiverick Road recalls the best known shipbuilders on the Cape. The end of building clippers soon followed the decline of whaling. Steamers with steel hulls replaced the sailing ships, yet left the harbors of the Cape and the Islands open to small craft and to the construction of fishing boats. Crosby Town on West Bay is a name associated with a safe, handy boat developed on the Cape. Macmillan Wharf honors a Provincetown explorer of the Arctic and serves as the town dock for local fishermen. Finally the Cape Cod Canal, the waterway that for many summer people marks the entrance to days of swimming and fishing in Cape waters, is itself a name that suggests a safe sea lane, a protection against the dangerous tides and currents of the Atlantic farther east off the Great Beach and Monomoy Island.

The early explorers who braved the swells and storms of the Atlantic to reach Cape Cod and the Islands reported a luxuriance of flora and fauna. Gosnold gave the Vineyard its name because of its abundant vines; he described the flourishing growth of Nomans Land, which later came to be, through overcutting and spoliation, a target area for bombers and thereby suffer the fate of its name. In the 1850s Henry Thoreau began his trips to Cape Cod, Nantucket, and the Elizabeth Islands, as keen as Gosnold to appreciate the flora and fauna, but aware as well of the need for conservation. Coming upon Herring River in Orleans, he said that though the Cape had many streams called Herring River, they would "perhaps, be more numerous than herrings soon." He learned the name of Gull Pond in Wellfleet and heard from his host, Uncle Jack, that the gulls returned to them less frequently each year, because "the English robbed their nests far in the north, where they breed." On his way to Provincetown he passed Brush Hollow in Truro and saw, as its name suggests, "a low brushwood, a quarter of a mile wide, and almost impassable." Near the Highland Light the name Clay Pounds made him speculate on its origins, on the likelihood that water collects in pits or ponds of clay.

Some place-names of fauna and flora include localisms that are special to the Cape and the Islands. Wickertree Road is for the willows of Falmouth, and Popple Bottom Road is for the poplars of Sandwich.

Wrinkle Point in Dennis is for the periwinkle, and
Horsefoot Cove on the Bass River is for the horseshoe
crab. On the Vineyard, Beetlebung Corner in
Chilmark is for the tupelo, and the old name for Eel
Pond in Edgartown, Gurnet Pond, is probably a local
name for a sea robin or sculpin. Turkeyland Cove on
Edgartown Great Pond is not for gobblers but for turkey wheat, otherwise known as maize. Nantucket, by
contrast, has place-names for animals and birds that
disappeared some time ago. Brants Point on Nantucket Harbor commemorates the great flocks that no
longer return, and no one in recent memory has seen a
black racer or a puff adder near Snake Spring. Buzzards Bay, north of Gosnold and west of Cape Cod, is
not named for the turkey buzzard but rather for the
osprey or fish hawk. And on Naushon Island is Rattlesnake Neck; the snake was, according to Wait Winthrop, a gift of the devil to a powwow who found
himself rejected by local Indians.

     In the nearly four hundred years since the Eng-
lish first came to settle, some species have unfortunately disappeared. The brants and the snakes of
Nantucket are to be found elsewhere, but on the
Vineyard nothing could stop the extinction of the
heath hen. The Commonwealth of Massachusetts began to set aside acreage in 1908, calling it the Martha's
Vineyard State Forest, but not all the formality of this
official act could stop the destruction of the heath hen
by forest fires and hunters. The loss of the heath hen,
despite efforts to save it, increased the determination
of those who love the Cape and the Islands to do all
they could to preserve as much of its natural life as
possible. These efforts have resulted in the establishment of state and federal parks with somewhat bu-
reaucratic names: Shawme-Crowell State Forest in
Sandwich and the Cape Cod National Seashore, from
Chatham to Provincetown. Other sanctuaries bear the
names of private donors: Beebe Woods in Falmouth;
the Alexander Reed Bird Refuge in West Tisbury;
and Maraspin Creek in Barnstable. And some sanctuaries keep the traditional names of a place, just as they
try to preserve natural settings and native wildlife. On
the Vineyard there are sanctuaries at Felix Neck,
Dodger Hole, and in the Menemsha Hills. Naushon

Island in Gosnold has a stand of self-perpetuating oak and beech trees. The Cape has Tern Island in Chatham, the Knob in Falmouth, and Wellfleet Bay Wildlife Sanctuary.

This desire to preserve wildlife and to use mostly traditional names is characteristic of the Cape and the Islands. Local history has remained so much a dynamic part of the atmosphere that only infrequently do we come upon names that appear imported. Orleans honors events related to the French Revolution, Hadley Harbor perhaps an English inventor. New Boston in Dennis and Lynn Pond in Chatham are unusual borrowings from elsewhere in Massachusetts. Three names of towns on the Cape — Bourne, Brewster and Dennis — are for prominent citizens, although Brewster actually lived west of the Bay in Plymouth County. Emigrants to the Cape lived in neighborhoods such as Little Dublin and Little Italy. And in the late 1800s developers brought in such euphemistic labels as Aurora Heights on Nantucket, Belvidere in Falmouth, and Vineyard Haven. Sunset Hill on Nantucket and in Hyannisport is perhaps a little less cloying than Vespers Pond in Brewster. Street names sometimes suffer from too much of the nautical. Dennisport would be better off without First Mate, Second Mate, Third Mate, and Quartermaster Rows. West Yarmouth does not need Schooner Street and Yacht Avenue, Bowsprit Path and Scrimshaw Lane.

But, on the whole, the Cape and the Islands have escaped some of the boosters' names that advertise other parts of America. We have no Romes or Athenses or Parises. Foreign and domestic heroes are largely left for other towns and landscapes: no Washingtons or Lincolns, no Lafayettes, Bolivars or Kossuths. Even the names of the villages are fairly unelaborate. We have -villes in Hatchville, Eastville, and Craigsville, a -dale in Bournedale, and so far few localities or neighborhoods with -parks or -valleys. Although Americans on the Cape and on the Vineyard engaged in skirmishes against the British in the Revolution and the War of 1812, there are no communities named in honor of some fort. Later on, the arrival of immigrants from Ireland, Italy, and Portugal helped

to enrich the cultural diversity of Cape and Island villages, yet none so far bears the name of a saint.

Still, the place-names of Cape Cod and the Islands have undergone some changes. The treacherous
waters off the Backside of the Cape prompted
the settlers in the early 1700s to call their village
Dangerfield — a name as expressive of their anxieties
as Gosnold's Tuckers Terror. But before long the
danger and terror of the currents and tides subsided
enough to encourage the adoption of the name
Truro. A hope for abundant oysters, on the other
hand, made Wellfleet a name more attractive than
the earlier Poole. And a dissatisfaction with such
apparently unflattering names as Cottage City and
Holmes Hole stimulated the change to Oak Bluffs
and Vineyard Haven. Other features of the land also
underwent a change of name — especially the names
of ponds. As families sold out to newcomers, the old
names of property gave way to new. Walkers Pond
in Harwich became Bucks, just as Aunt Lizzie
Robbins Pond became Whites, and Francis Cahoons
Beach became Bush's. Commercial interests also
had their effects, as plain Salt or Oyster Pond had
its name transformed into Wychmere Harbor.

Throughout the Cape and the Islands, the place-
names uncover, after a little prodding, a rich treasure
of history and nature, of enterprise and conservation.
The emphasis on the local in the names heightens the
desire so many have to spend their summer months
by the beaches and ponds, in the narrow streets of
Nantucket and Provincetown, in dry Vineyard Haven, along the Sound at Dutchers Dock and Menemsha. The combination of summer sun, cool beach
winds over warm combers, and local lore draws us all
from California and Wisconsin, from Florida and
New York. Year-rounders and islanders have these
historic, local names as part of their legacy, reminding
them of events in the past as well as of moments in
their own lives. As one islander recalls, she and her
husband ferried from the Vineyard to Nantucket, followed the map to the Quaker Graveyard, and began to
read Lowell's poem to each other. In the midst of that
place and their reading, a gull flying overhead broke
in and splattered the page. To mention the Quaker

Graveyard on Nantucket to them is to recall a place
where nature and art joined in an arresting moment.
The aim in this book is to preserve the significance of
the historic and the natural, imprinted in so many
ways in the names of Cape Cod and Island places.

The entries in this dictionary appear alpha-
betically in four sections, one each for Cape Cod,
Elizabeth Islands, Martha's Vineyard, and Nantucket. With few exceptions the place-names are in
current use [we could not resist separate entries for
Dangerfield and Dogtown, for example, or for such
historic but no longer extant names like Jarvesville or
Strouts Creek]. The entries include names that have a
recoverable history, are part of folk-lore or legend, or
identify a characteristic or significant feature of the
terrain.

Our purpose, too, is to locate places sufficiently
to enable anyone who desires precise information to
find them on a map. Most pronunciations of place-
names are obvious, but we have also provided a guide
for the hard cases. All one need do is to use the chart
on pronunciation to help read aloud the phonetic
transcriptions that appear among the entries. The
spelling of all place-names, except for Martha's Vineyard, omits apostrophes. This practice follows the
conventions of the National Geological Survey maps.

Many entries include alternates or place-names
no longer in use. As far as possible we have accounted
for their backgrounds, as well, explaining their source
or their meaning. Only the alternate names and the
older ones appear in the index, not those that are al-
phabetized in the main entries.

Some terms among the place-names may be unfa-
miliar. A *hole* as in Woods Hole or Quicks Hole signifies "a small bay, a cove, or a narrow channel." A
hollow on Cape Cod is "a wide stretch of land that sags
toward the center." A *bottom* on Martha's Vineyard is
the same as a hollow on Cape Cod. A *bight* as in
Menemsha Bight is both "a long bend on a coast line
that helps to form a broad bay and also the broad bay
itself." A town, as elsewhere in Massachusetts, has its
own local government and may include open acreage

within its borders as well as settled localities. A village is one that has its own post office or grade school.

The analysis of Indian names is most difficult. We have tried to show plausible correspondences between forms as they appear on current maps or in earlier documents with those that appear in Trumbull's works. For example, *Tashmoo*, in our view, seems related to *keht* 'great' + *ashim* 'spring' + *ut* 'at' = "at the great spring." Obviously the correspondence is open to criticism, but we offer it, because it is the best one we could find and because it accords with what we know of the terrain. Another difficulty is that we have made correspondences between Indian names imperfectly recorded and forms that occur in Natick, a language of central Massachusetts, in Narragansett, a language of Rhode Island, in Mohican, a language of Connecticut, and even in Abnaki, a language of Maine. We have no evidence at all from Wampanoag, the language most likely spoken on the Cape. Moreover, we have not included the wide variety of glosses listed in secondary sources. Often these are given without supporting evidence, and in many instances, when we have examined the possible basis for a gloss, we have found it grammatically implausible. What we have tried to do, instead, is to provide a possible gloss for each part of an Indian name [as in *Tashmoo*]. If no reasonable correspondence seemed evident, we have simply listed the name itself.

What is historic and what is legend or folk-lore are not always clear. Accounts related to Maushop or Michabo, the Algonquian god who could transform the land, are easy enough to identify. We have tried as much as possible to limit those accounts to what is essential to a narrative. Accounts of pirates and prisoners, of lonely women and treasure hunters, may have some possible basis in fact. But to avoid giving them too much credence, we have customarily introduced the legendary or folk-loristic by such expressions as "it is said" or "some say." There is a tendency to scoff at imaginative tales. We do not, because they often divulge the desires and anxieties that color a particular place and its name. And it is our hope to join feeling and fact as an essential part of place-names.

Guide to Pronunciation

In the columns below phonetic symbols for vowels
and consonants appear on the left. The italicized
letters of the familiar words in the central column are
keys to the pronunciation of the symbols. The italicized letters of the place-names in the right-hand
column have the same sounds as the italicized letters
in the corresponding familiar words. Each place-name
also appears in phonetic script.

Phonetic Symbol	Familiar Word	Place-name
ə	tomato, done, bluff	Gull Island [gəl] ['aɪlənd] Oklahoma [ˌoklə'homə]
æ	pack, canal	Sampson Hill ['sæmsən] [hɪl]
a	pond, chop	Swan Neck [swan] [nɛk]
aɪ	line, side	Bryants Neck ['braɪənts] [nɛk]
aʊ	mountain, town	Icehouse Pond ['aɪs,haʊs] [pand]
b	beach, bulb	Jim Browns Creek [jɪm] [braunz] [krik]
č	branch, church	Mitchell River ['mɪčel] [rɪvər]
d	dike, leader	Muddy Creek ['mədɪ] [krik]
ɛ	pen, neck	Pleasant Bay ['plɛzənt] [be]
e	cape, bay	Quaker Road ['kwekər] [rod]
f	fog, bluff	Raycroft Beach ['re,krɔft] [bič]
g	gull, tug	Sagamore ['sægə,mɔr]
h	hole, behind	Schoolhouse Pond ['skul,haʊs] [pand]
ɪ	city, inner	Shiverick Pond ['šɪverɪk] [pand]
i	stream, peak	Wellfleet ['wɛl,flit]
j	yeast, yell	Yarmouth [jarmuθ]
ǰ	join, bridge	Jobs Neck [jobz] [nɛk]
k	creek, cove	Quicks Hole [kwɪks] [hol]
l	lake, dale	Black Brook [blæk] [bruk]
m	marsh, farm	Chilmark ['čɪlmark]
n	new, run	Hines Point [haɪnz] [pɔɪnt]
ŋ	spring, sink	The Kings Highway [ðə] [kɪŋz] ['haɪ, we]
o	rode, boat	Nomans Land ['nomɪnz] [lænd]
ɔ	raw, port	Norton Point ['nɔrtən] [pɔɪnt]
ɔɪ	point, royal	Oyster Pond ['ɔɪstər] [pand]
p	place, rip	Paine Hollow [pen] ['halo]

Phonetic Symbol	Familiar Word	Place-name
r	ra*il*road	*R*ock Ha*r*bor [rak] ['harbər]
s	*s*ea, gra*ss*	*S*arahs *S*wamp [særəz] [swamp]
š	*sh*eep, mar*sh*	*Sh*awme Pond [šɔm] [pand]
t	*t*unnel, s*t*a*t*e	*T*rou*t* Brook [traʊt] [brʊk]
ө	*th*ick, mou*th*	*Th*umpertown ['өəmpər,taʊn]
ð	*th*ere, hea*th*er	Smoo*th* Hummocks [smuð] ['həmɪks]
u	sch*oo*l, f*ue*l	Lag*oo*n Pond [lə'gun] [pand]
ʊ	w*oo*d, br*oo*k	Atw*oo*ds Corner ['æt,wʊdz] ['kɔrnər]
v	slee*v*e, *v*alley	Ta*v*ern Field ['tævərn] [fild]
w	*w*ind, be*w*are	*W*atch Hill [wač] [hɪl]
z	*z*ero, *l*ose	*Z*acks Cliffs [zæks] [klɪfs]
'	this mark appears before syllable with strongest stress	
		Telegraph Hill ['tɛlə͵græf] [hɪl]
•	this mark appears before syllable with next strongest stress	

Cape Cod

A

Acapesket [ækə'pɛskət]

An Algonquian name in the 1600s for a tribe near Woods Hole and for a small pond: *ukque* 'at the end' + *paug* 'pond' + *es* 'small' + *ut* 'at' = "at the end of a small pond." The modern Acapesket, laid out in 1923, is on Lewis Neck between Great and Green ponds.

Agawam Point ['ægəwam]

Agawam means "on the other side" in the local Algonquian dialects. Agawam Point is in Bourne and faces Onset Bay on the other side of Buzzards Bay, in Wareham. In early days the point was known as Frenchmans Point, for two seamen whom Captain Thomas Dermer ransomed from the Indians in 1619. The French sailors had escaped a shipwreck in 1616, had become the prisoners of Cape Cod sachems, and although hard-worked and regarded with contempt, remained in good health during their captivity.

Airline Road

So called because this road between Routes 134 and 6A in South Dennis runs over much of its course in as direct a line as possible. Side streets connected to it include Propeller Lane, Pilot Drive, Wing Lane, and Jet Drive.

Allen Harbor

A boating center in Harwich Port, off Lower County Road. It is named for John Allen, who acquired land in the area in 1756. It has also been known as Grays Harbor or Pond.

Amos Pond

About half a mile west of Santuit in Mashpee, the pond is named for an Indian family of religious and political leaders. Blind Joe Amos preached early in the nineteenth century. Daniel B. Amos helped Mashpee in 1833 regain its rights as a district; Israel Amos served as a selectman.

Amrita Island [æm'ritə]

Amrita is a Hindu name for an island and appears in Robert Southey's poem *The Curse of Kehanna*: it means "a drink of immortality." This island, in Squeteague Harbor near the village of Cataumet in Bourne, was named by Thomas A. Baxendale, the designer and producer of the box-toe shoe. Baxendale bought the island in the 1890s — it was earlier known as Great Island — and in 1914 established a foundation to advance an understanding and concern for bird and animal life. The Animal Rescue League accepted trusteeship of the island in 1934 and conducted summer sessions for youngsters and teachers. In 1951 the League moved to the mainland, and the island became private property.

Andrews Pond

For Andrew Clarke, one of the petitioners in 1694 for the incorporation of Harwich. Clarke lived near the pond, a mile north of Harwich Center, east of Pleasant Lake Avenue. It has also been known as Clarks and as Katys Pond.

Aptucxet [æpə'təksɪt]

Possibly from Algonquian *wapwa* 'strait, narrow' + *tuk* 'tidal river' + *s* 'little' + *ut* 'at' = "at the narrow, little tidal river." The stream flowed into Buzzards Bay, part way along the course now followed by the Cape Cod Canal.

The Pilgrims opened a trading post here in 1627, not far south of the stream, but abandoned it in 1635 when a hurricane ripped through its planks of hewn oak. At the post they began a brisk trade with the Dutch, which continued even after the hurricane. By the 1660s the Pilgrims had sold enough pelts of otter and beaver for so high a profit that their debts to London creditors were discharged. The abandoned trading post was a landmark for some time, and prompted such new names in Bourne Village as Trading Post Field, Trading Post Landing, and Trading Post Corners. Aptucxet Trading Post is now a museum of local history.

Areys Pond ['ɛriz]

For the Areys of Orleans, who were ship captains in the 1800s. Captain John Arey was master of the clipper *Spitfire*; Captain James H. Arey made "fruit voyages" to the Mediterranean, ran a grist mill, and served as selectman. A tidal pond fourteen feet deep, it lies at the head of Namequoit River at the west end of Little Pleasant Bay. It was also known as Potonumecot Salt Water Pond, where John Sipson, the last of the Nauset chiefs, lived.

Ashumit Pond [æ'šumɪt]

The pond's Algonquian name is probably from *ashim* 'spring' + *ut* 'at' = "at the spring." The Indians living at this pond on the Falmouth, Mashpee, and Sandwich lines supposedly drew water from a nearby spring.

Atlantic White Cedar Swamp

For the white cedars that stand along a trail in the swamp near Marconi Beach in Wellfleet. The swamp is a part of the Cape Cod National Seashore. The marked trail passes through clumps of scrubland, pitch pine, and mixed oak, as well as swampland.

Atwoods Corner

For the Atwood family, who first settled on the Neck in Chatham in the 1700s. Captain Atwood built a house at the corner [near Cedar and Stage Harbor streets] in 1752. It is one of the oldest in town and is the headquarters of the Chatham Historical Society.

Aunt Bettys Pond

For Betty Bearse, wife of Lot Bearse, who in 1830 had an orchard on the pond. In the early 1800s it was also called Bearses Pond. It is at North and Main streets in Hyannis.

Aunt Julia Anns Road

For Julia Ann, a hardy woman of the 1800s, who was the third wife and young widow of Captain Levi Baker. After his death she kept Levi's Chandlery as a supply store for the town's fishermen. The road, passing the chandlery, ended at Bass River Wharf, not far from Aunt Julia Anns Beach in West Dennis.

Aunt Lydias Cove

Probably named for Lydia Eldridge [there were three in the nineteenth century], this Chatham cove is actually a channel that lies between Tern Island and the mainland. At the south end of the cove is the Chatham Fish Pier, constructed in the 1940s. It was once called Morris Cove, for Morris Farris, an eighteenth-century settler.

Avalon Point

So called for a girls' camp located on Crows Pond. It is an extension of Nickersons Neck, named for a family long resident in Chatham.

B

Back River

So called because the river takes a course "back" of some land that faces Phinneys Harbor near the village of Bourne. In the days of early settlement Back River was plentiful in fish, the lands nearby plentiful in quail. By the 1700s Deacon Elijah Perry had laid out near the river a cordwood road that led to his market. In the 1800s the river was a center for wharves and saltworks. At the close of the century a railroad bridge at the river provided passage to Falmouth and villages near the south shore.

The Backside of the Cape

The shoreline along the Atlantic Ocean from Provincetown to Orleans has from early times suggested a curved spine braced against the force of high waves. Strong currents off the Backside, treacherous to ships, have helped to form what is called the Graveyard of the Atlantic. The Backside is also known as the Great or Outer Beach. Running along the Backside is the Edge, a line, on charts, denoting twenty fathoms of water.

Baker Pond

In the 1700s William Baker lived at this pond [28 acres] on the Brewster - Orleans line, just south of Route 6A. Its supposed Algonquian name is *poponnesset*, related to *popon* "winter" or *paponaumsu* "tom cod," but of course one does not expect a marine fish in a fresh pond. Actually, the pond is stocked with trout.

Baker Town

So called for the old family of Bakers, residents of South and West Dennis, on and around Main Street. In the days of whalers and clippers the Bakers sent twenty-nine captains to sea; to quote the Sandwich bird carver, Peter Peltz,

> The English were prolific
> On Cape Cod's sandy shore,
> And if you don't believe it
> Look at all the Bakers.

Within Baker Town are located the Ezra Baker School and the Francis Baker Memorial Park.

Balance Rock

So called because the rock seems precariously balanced on its perch. Actually it is a heavy boulder firmly lodged on a low, circular rock close to Signal Hill on the Bournedale Road.

Ballston Beach

For Sheldon W. Ball, who in 1891 built some cottages on the beach that faces the Atlantic. The beach is 1000 acres in all, from Brush Hollow to Longnook in Truro. The cottages, rented to summer visitors, were continually in danger from storms off the ocean. Both the beach and Ballston Heights are now part of the Cape Cod National Seashore. In the 1950s sunbathers in the nude began using the south end of the beach.

Barley Neck

So called for the crops of barley grown on the neck at the north end of Little Pleasant Bay in Orleans. This area is unusually fertile for the lower end of the Cape, and large harvests of barley produced sufficient malt for cattle feed and beer. Until 1900 it was known as Deacon Rogers Meadow, for Joseph Rogers, who came on the *Mayflower* and settled on the Cape. Old Field Point at the southern tip of the neck was probably one of the first fields he planted.

Bar Neck

For a narrow stretch of land between Penzance and the village of Woods Hole in Falmouth. During the 1800s shipyards at Bar Neck launched, among others, *Uncas, Bartholomew Gosnold, Commodore Morris,* and *Elijah Swift.* The Candle House, erected at the Neck in 1836, has walls two feet thick made of well-fitted boulders. It was at first a supply house for whalers and a factory for making spermaceti candles. Since 1903 the Candle House has become a storehouse for the Marine Biological Laboratory.

Barn Hill

An old name of West Chatham, the hill is at the intersection of Barn Hill Road and Barn Hill Lane.

Barnstable   ['barnstəbl]

This town is named for Barnstable, Devonshire, possibly the birthplace in England of some of the first settlers on Cape Cod. As in England, so on Cape Cod the two towns share similar features. At ebb tide in both towns large flats and narrow creeks emerge from the retreating sea, and in both towns, too, broad uplands rise high over the shore. Barnstable on Cape Cod was incorporated in 1639, and from its beginnings as a small settlement near the Great Marshes it expanded within fifty years to become the largest of the county towns. After the establishment of the town by settlers from Weymouth and Scituate, Indian sachems nearby sold large tracts of land to Barnstable for very little. A parcel of land [from Centerville to Hyannis] sold by the sachem Yanno to Barnstable cost, for example, twenty pounds and two pairs of breeches. The acquisition of these large tracts prompted the townspeople to subdivide them after 1700 into manageable areas. At first the division of the town resulted in two districts for training local militia and two parishes. During the nineteenth and twentieth centuries divisions have mostly resulted from the founding of villages. Toward Cape Cod Bay are the villages of Barnstable and West Barnstable. Toward Nantucket and Vineyard Sounds are Cotuit, Osterville, Centerville, and Hyannis. At the west end of Barnstable, near Sandwich and Mashpee, is Marstons Mills.

Barnstable County

The county was organized in 1685, the same year that the Plymouth Court also established Plymouth and Bristol Counties. Although the county has always included the entire Cape, it lost Wareham, Marion, and Rochester to Plymouth County in 1707. The village of Barnstable has served as county seat from the days of the first court sessions in 1686.

Barnstable Green

In its early days the Green was a training ground for the local militia. At the outbreak of the American Revolution the Barnstable patriots accused their Tory neighbors of chopping down the Liberty Pole on the Green. Soon after, some of the patriots dragged Miss Abigail Freeman, a Tory and an outspoken defender of the English cause, from her grocery onto the Green and there tarred and feathered her. They made her ride a rail and did not relent until she promised to say no more about politics. Two centuries later, in 1974, Barnstable dedicated a new liberty pole at the Green. The Green is at the foot of Rendezvous Lane in Barnstable Village.

Barnstable Harbor

The harbor lies between Sandy Neck and the north shores of Barnstable and West Barnstable Villages. From Slough Point eastward, it extends over tidal flats, channels, and shoals to Beach Point, where there is more than twenty feet of water. At ebb tide the flats are good for clamming. Champlain's name for the harbor was Le Port aux Huistres, an anchorage that gave his ship five or six fathoms and his crew a great quantity of excellent oysters.

Barnstable Village

The village is as old as the town of Barnstable, and once extended from Calves Pasture Point to the bounds of Yarmouth. In later years the village itself was divided into smaller communities, among them Cummaquid on the east, Cobbs Village at Barnstable Harbor, and Pond Village on the west, near Hinckley Pond. From the 1600s on, the village has been the county seat. As early as 1690 prisoners stayed in a lockup on Jail Lane to await trial at the nearby court house. In the 1800s the village was a station on the Underground Railroad.

Barrel Hill

A barrel hoisted to the top of a flagpole erected at the summit of this hill would inform townspeople that a packet had arrived or was about to sail to Boston. The barrel was a village signal during the first half of the 1800s. The hill stands within view of the ships at Maraspin Creek in the village of Barnstable.

Bassett Island

For Colonel William Bassett, a selectman and marshall of Sandwich, who in the early 1700s helped fix the town's boundaries with Falmouth. It was first known in the 1600s as Newmaks Island, for William Newmak, who sold it to Bassett. A three-cornered island, it lies in Red Brook and Pocasset harbors, opposite Patuissett Village in Bourne.

Bass Hole

This is a tidal inlet on Cape Cod Bay near Chase Garden Creek in Yarmouth. Its Indian name Hockanom means "hook shaped." It is said that the Algonquians fought a pitched battle with Thorvald Ericson, the brother of Leif, at the hole in the year 1003 and killed him. In the 1700s the Grays of Yarmouth built ships at the hole. Grays Beach at the hole is now open to public bathing, and a wooden causeway nearby runs over extensive salt marshes. Another Bass Hole on the Cape lies at the east end of Pleasant Bay.

Bassing Harbor

The *Century Dictionary and Encyclopedia* defines a "bassing ground" as a place for catching bass. Bassing Harbor, known in the 1800s as the Bassing Place, lies between North Chatham and Nickersons Neck.

Bass River

The river is the largest on Cape Cod. Its source is Weir-mill Brook at Weir Village, whence it follows the Yarmouth - Dennis line southward, and becomes a tidal estuary as it approaches Nantucket Sound. Although it has been called a "great salt creek," it nearly cuts the Cape in two, and some have proposed, over the years, that it be made into a canal. In the 1800s the river harbored coastal packets at its mouth and had several mills along its banks. Today its lower reaches abound with pleasure craft.

Bass River Village

The village is on the west bank of Bass River, not far from its mouth, where one finds Bass River Beach. A century ago it was known as Quaker or Friends Village; it was then centered near the surviving Quaker meetinghouse in South Yarmouth.

Katherine Lee Bates Road

This road in Falmouth Village commemorates Miss Bates, who taught at Wellesley College and wrote "America the Beautiful."

Baxters Neck

Probably named for Sidney Baxter, a resident of Cotuit in the 1800s. The neck lies half a mile north of Osterville Grand Island, across North Bay. During the second World War it served as the site for Camp Can-Do-It, under the direction of the Army Engineers, who trained men to run amphibious landing craft.

Baxter Wharf

Probably for Alexander Baxter, Jr., a prominent shipowner and entrepreneur in Hyannis during the 1800s. As a young man of seventeen Baxter dodged British privateers throughout the War of 1812 in his sloop *Polly*. In 1829 he switched from smuggling to religion and helped found the Universalist Society. Before the wharf was named for Baxter it was known as Gage Wharf, for Lot Gage, who supervised from 1827 to 1837 the construction of the Hyannis Breakwater. Not far from Baxter Wharf there once stood the house of Edward Coleman, the first house built in Hyannis during the seventeenth century.

Beach Point

Until 1854 the point lay at the entrance to East Harbor on Cape Cod Bay. Thereafter, the Commonwealth first had a bridge and then a dike with a surface road installed from the point northward to Provincetown [some 1600 feet away] over the mouth of the harbor. The construction of the dike made East Harbor a lake [Pilgrim Lake]. Villagers in Truro once grew cranberries at the point, set out fish weirs, and processed trash fish into fertilizer at a local plant.

Bear Hollow Pond

This pond may have been close to a den of black bears or it may have had large boulders on its shores that from a distance suggested a family of bears. It is now drained, however, and is a part of Otis Air Force Base in South Sandwich.

Bearse Shoal   [bɪrs]

The shoal is probably named for George N. Bearse, a Chatham fisherman of the mid-1800s. East of Monomoy Island, it sometimes lies in shallow water no more than six to eight feet deep.

Beebe Woods   ['bibɪ]

A tract of 500 acres, named for James M. Beebe, a Boston dry goods merchant of the nineteenth century. Beebe's son Frank built a mansion in the woods [its carriage house is now a theatre] and called the family estate Highfields. In the 1970s Mr. and Mrs. Josiah K. Lilly donated the woods to the town of Falmouth, to be kept as a sanctuary for wild life. The woods are northwest of Falmouth Village, toward Sippewisset.

Bells Neck

For John Bell, who owned a large tract at the neck in the later 1600s. Surrounded by marsh, the neck lies at the end of Bells Neck Road, east of Herring River in West and North Harwich.

Belvidere Plains

Marcus Starbuck of Nantucket helped plan this residential area in 1915. He chose the name Belvidere to suggest that the houses he had built on the plains [between Shore Street and Falmouth Harbor] would offer a "beautiful view" of Vineyard Sound.

Billingsgate

An old name for the northern district of Eastham which in 1763 became the town of Wellfleet. Early settlers found fish and oysters so plentiful near their lands on Cape Cod Bay and Wellfleet Harbor that they took the name Billingsgate from London's main fish market and fish wharves. The lands of Billingsgate cost the settlers nothing: as soon as they learned from the Nauset sachems who lived at a village called Pononakanit that the property was no one's, they said, "It is ours." But although the abundant Billingsgate oysters soon overtopped all others for their flavor and brought great profits, within a hundred years they nearly disappeared from overfishing and an excessive harvesting of shells for lime. By the time Thoreau arrived in the 1850s fishermen had to import oysters and lay them down in the harbor; so he says of Wellfleet that a part of the town "is still called Billingsgate from the oysters having been formerly planted there; but the native oysters are said to have died in 1770." Billingsgate Island and Point on the southwest edge of Wellfleet Harbor once had thirty houses, a school, and a lighthouse. Miles

Standish and a party of men from the *Mayflower* stopped at the point during their survey of the coast in 1620. But the force of the sea has eroded Billingsgate Island so extensively that it remains no more than a sliver of ground washed over most of the time.

Bishop and Clerks

['bɪšəp n klərks]

This ledge, about three miles off Point Gammon, was named in the 1700s possibly for the Bishop and Clerks Islands off Pembrokeshire, Wales. According to a local writer, Ted Frothingham, "two especially huge boulders" on the ledge may have also suggested the name. A lighthouse stood at the ledge from 1858 until 1952.

Black Ball Hill

In the 1800s a large, black ball, hoisted to the top of a pole on the hill, announced the arrival of Boston packets to the residents of Dennis. As Thoreau said, "Every higher eminence had a pole set up on it, with an old storm-coat or sail tied to it, for a signal, that those on the south side of the Cape, for instance, might know when the Boston packets had arrived on the north." Black Ball Hill is about half a mile southwest of Scargo Lake.

Blackfish Creek

So called for the blackfish or grampuses stranded at the mouth of the creek in Wellfleet Bay. In 1793 Levi Whitman, a local minister, counted four hundred of them, and two thousand were beached at Provincetown in 1884.

Blacksmith Shop Road

In the 1800s several forges built along this road produced the iron work needed for the construction of whaling ships at Woods Hole. The road runs eastward from West Falmouth to Shallow and Crooked ponds.

Blish Point

For Abraham Blush, an early settler, whose descendants spelled their name Blish. In the 1800s the point was known as Bacons Point, for Isaac Bacon, the owner of the packet *Somerset*, who shipped his own farm produce to the markets in Boston. Once, it is said, Isaac Bacon had no straw to wrap about his bunches of early onions and instead blanketed them with green bulrushes. Arriving in Boston, he said to his buyers, "Gentlemen, these are 'tarnity onions; they'll keep to all eternity." Isaac sold his onions, but every buyer was soon holding his nose and tossing them out. Blish Point stands at the mouth of Maraspin Creek in the village of Barnstable, the creek where packets in the Boston trade docked in the first half of the 1800s.

Blue Rock Road

So called for a large boulder, probably hard sandstone, set on the west bank of the Bass River in Yarmouth near the Great Western Road. The road is near the river, and so are Blue Rock Golf Course and a new subdivision also called Blue Rock. Some maintain that the Vikings drilled holes in the rock in order to moor their ships.

Bluff Point

So called for the bluff that rises west of the point at the entrance to Cotuit Bay, Barnstable. West of the bluff was a house built by a veteran of the Civil War, Colonel Charles R. Codman. Cotuit Highlands [known as Cotuit Highgrounds in the 1800s] is even farther west of the bluff. The Bluff Point Oyster Company had beds of oyster seed near the point in Cotuit Bay. For several decades the Company brought the seed from Long Island, New York, raised it in the Bay, and sold the oysters in the markets of Boston.

Boat Cove Creek

Farmers living near the Great Marshes of Barnstable in the later 1600s kept their boats in the creek. The creek runs out of Mill Pond and empties into Scorton Creek.

Boiling Spring Pond

The pond is fed by the waters of the fresh springs nearby, pouring up from the ground at irregular intervals throughout the year. At the shores of the pond, east of Sandwich Village near Route 6A, are a pumping station, the Greenbriar Jam Kitchen, and a natural preserve of fifty-two acres, Briarpatch Park. The Thornton W. Burgess Society bought the Kitchen and worked with the town of Sandwich to establish and manage the park.

Bone Hill Road

Not far from this road north of Cummaquid, David Davis and Patrick Hughes were out plowing a field one day, when they overturned a brass kettle and discovered a human skeleton sitting underneath it. It is said that the skeleton is the remains of Sachem Iyanough, buried on a hill in 1623. The Cape Cod Historical Society gave Iyanough's bones to Pilgrim Hall in Plymouth and marked the site of his discovery with a tablet: "Sachem Iyanough — the friend and entertainer of the Pilgrims, June, 1623." Gustavus Swift started his first meat packing plant on this road in 1875.

Bound Brook Island

In Cape Cod at the bounds of Wellfleet and Truro. Although once surrounded on all sides by water, it is now a tombolo connected to the mainland by a bar of sand and gravel.

Bourne [bɔrn]

This town on the border of Plymouth Colony was in 1884 the last on the Cape to be incorporated. Some say that the name of the town commemorates Richard Bourne, an early settler and minister to the Indians, but the greater likelihood is that it honors Jonathan Bourne, a whaling merchant of the late 1800s who left funds for the area to build a memorial library. Once a part of Sandwich, the town wanted its own selectmen in order to guarantee a fair distribution of taxes. The Indians called a large part of

Bourne Manomet, possibly from *móunumóonk* "a gathering ." There was a community of Christianizing Indians nearby at Great Herring Pond. The town includes several villages, among them Bourne, Bournedale, Buzzards Bay, Sagamore, Monument Beach, and Pocasset.

Bournedale

This village had its name changed from North Sandwich after the incorporation of Bourne as a town in 1884. Bournedale is north of the Cape Cod Canal, not far from Great Herring Pond and the early site of an Indian village called Comassekumkanet, probably related to Narragansett *acawen* 'on the other side of ' + *sachim-maacommock* 'prince's house' = "on the other side of the prince's house." The Indian settlement was so large that Thomas Tupper, an early settler, felt compelled to preach and to convert, although he was not ordained.

Bourne Mill Pond

Halfway between Mashpee Village and Pond, Bourne's mill began to grind grain in the 1700s. The mill was probably Joseph Bourne's, pastor of the Mashpee church in the 1730s and the great-grandson of Richard Bourne, who helped the Indians establish their rights to the land. The mill is now the site of the Mashpee Indian Museum.

Bourne and Sagamore Bridges

These two highway bridges span the Cape Cod Canal. The Bourne Bridge carries traffic on Route 28; the Sagamore Bridge, farther east, leads to the Mid-Cape Highway. Both bridges have a span of 616 feet and rise 135 feet over the canal. They opened for traffic in 1935 and replaced drawbridges that had been built in 1913.

Bourne Village

The history of this village on the south side of the Cape Cod Canal begins with the Indians, who had a large settlement long before the arrival of the Pilgrims. A number of trails still mark the district where the Indians probably lived, in the village known as Manomet [it means "a gathering"] and later called Monument by white settlers. In early days wood cutters had plentiful stretches of forest for supplying cordwood and logs to ready markets at Woods Hole and Nantucket. In the 1800s some of the villagers were captains aboard such coastal vessels as the *Fruitful Vine*, the *Greenport*, and the *Speed*. In the 1850s Bourne Village was a station on the Underground Railroad.

Breakwater Beach

So called for a breakwater of the 1800s, now scarcely visible, constructed to protect packets docked at Brewster. The beach is at the end of Breakwater Road, running north from Route 6A.

Brewster

Carved from the northern part of Harwich in 1803, this town is named for William Brewster, a leader of the Pilgrims. Although Brewster had many descendants who wished to honor him, Thoreau claims that they chose the name for fear that he "would be forgotten else." Edward Kendall, who traveled over the Cape in the early 1800s, wrote that the politics in the new town was anti-federalist and opposed to the views of those living in Harwich. To oppose the Federalist Party was to stand against its efforts to establish local authorities to support its program of national solutions for political and economic problems. The western part of Brewster was first known as Setucket; the eastern region was called Namskaket.

Brick Kiln Road

The road crosses from Oyster Pond in West Falmouth to the mouth of the Coonamessett River. From the early 1700s, there was a kiln near the road to fire clay into bricks. Josiah Thompson, the last to make bricks, had his kiln in the 1800s on Forest Hill just off the road.

Brick Yard Creek

The West Barnstable Brick Company [opened in 1878, closed in 1929] gave the creek its name. Near the creek were claypits, sand, and the waters of Garretts Pond. The company had to bring in wood for its furnaces. Garretts Pond is the source of the creek; Broad Sound is at its mouth.

Bridge Creek

The bridge over the creek was once part of the early post road that ran through the north side of Barnstable. The creek begins at Spruce Pond, flows north through cranberry bogs, and empties into the Great Marshes and Broad Sound.

Broad Sound

The sound is a shallow body of water between Huckins Island and Calves Pasture Point in the southwest corner of Barnstable Harbor. Broad Sound is an early name in the history of the town.

Bryants Neck

For Solomon Briant, an Indian pastor at Mashpee from 1742 to 1758. Mr. Briant preached in the local Wampanoag dialect, and his parishioners said of him that "he grows better as he grows older." The neck extends into Santuit Pond. The Old Indian Meeting House on the neck is the oldest of all the churches on Cape Cod. It was built in 1684 and has undergone repair and remodeling, but the Indians of Mashpee could never afford to replace it.

Bucks Creek

For the old Buck family of Chatham. The creek begins east of Taylor Pond and empties into Cockle Cove.

Bumps River

Probably for Samuel Bumps, who lived by the river in the early 1700s. Bumps is a French name, from "Bon Pas," quite like the English name "Goodspeed." Other early names for the stream were Trout Brook and Phinneys Mill Brook. Salterbrook trout would run up from the sea to the stream — the word "salter" is the name for the fish when it is about to enter fresh water. Eli Phinney, also a resident by the side of the stream in the 1700s, built a grist and carding mill on its shores. Dirty Hole, at the head of the stream, was once low marshland, but is now a cranberry bog. The Algonquian name for the stream was Skunk-ko-mug, from *ous-chankamaug* "fishing place for eels or lampreys." Bumps River runs south into Scudders Bay on the west side of Centerville.

Burtonwood Beach

In the 1700s a man named Burton sold his property near Eel Pond in Bourne to the Perrys. They cleared the land of underbrush and woods and built a saltworks. Years later, in 1927, the property became a bathing beach named for the first owner, Burton, and for the woods that once grew on it.

Burying Hill

About 150 feet above sea level, it is the oldest graveyard in Chatham, located just west of Ryders Cove. The graveyard served the Indians before the whites. The oldest gravestones are those of Zenas, John, and Elizabeth Ryder, who all died of smallpox in 1766.

Buttermilk Bay

A local meaning of buttermilk is "wet or marshy land," just the condition of the bay's shoreline at the bounds of Wareham and Bourne. The muddy water along the coast also suggests the texture of buttermilk. The Indian name for the bay was Waquonscott, from Algonquian *wiquaesket* "the end of the marsh or swamp."

Buttonbush Pond

The buttonbush grows by streams and ponds, and is covered over in summer with white button-like flowers. The pond in Eastham is just down the trail from Salt Pond. Buttonbush Trail is the work of the Cape Cod National Seashore, designed especially for the blind, with markers posted in Braille.

Buzzards Bay Village

This village is in Bourne at the west end of the Cape Cod Canal. It was until the onset of the 1800s the farm land of the Bourne family, who were early settlers. But the Sandwich Glass Company, after its opening in the 1820s, bought the Bourne property and converted it into a port for ships bearing sand and coal from New Jersey and elsewhere. Later in the century the village became busy enough to have a railroad junction and shipyards at Scow Cove [so called because scows would deliver timber for the building of ships from the head of Buttermilk Bay]. In the 1800s the village became a summer resort and the home of the actor Joseph Jefferson, a friend of Grover Cleveland's. In the 1930s the Corps of Army Engineers established a traffic control center for the Cape Cod Canal at the village. And in 1948 the Massachusetts Maritime Academy moved its campus from Hyannis to Taylors Point, just at the head of the village on Buzzards Bay. The first name of the village was Cohasset, for nearby Cohasset Narrows. Buzzards Bay became the village name in the 1880s, after Bourne was incorporated as a town. "Buzzard" here does not mean a vulture, but an osprey.

C

Cable Road

So called for the telegraph cable laid across the Atlantic in 1879 from Brest to Eastham, where the road comes off Nauset Beach. Eleven years later the cable station was moved from Eastham to Orleans, where it remained in business until 1959. At Cove Road and Route 28, it is now a museum.

Cahoon Hollow and Cahoon Hollow Beach

For the Cahoons, a family long resident on the Cape, especially in the towns from Harwich to Wellfleet. The hollow and the beach are on the backside of Wellfleet, in the Cape Cod National Seashore. The hollow is typical of the valleys in the lower Cape, which, as Barbara Chamberlain says, "cut east-west . . . and, opening into the beach, scallop the sea cliffs."

Cahoon Pond [kəˈhun]

Probably for Francis Cahoon, who lived near the pond on the border of Harwich and Brewster. It has also been called Bushy Beach Pond. The Cahoons were early residents, and two of them, James and William, helped to incorporate the South Precinct of Harwich in 1746.

Calves Pasture Point

The Calves Pasture, fenced off quite early in the history of Barnstable, was also the first burial ground. Its first grave was that of Timothy Dimmock, who in 1640 died six months after his baptism. The point is at the northwest corner of the pasture, across from Huckins Island in Broad Sound. In 1851 John Barker Crocker proposed building a dike from the point across the harbor to Sandy Neck. He hoped in vain to increase the value of the land, to develop oyster and herring fisheries, and to provide greater water power.

Camp Edwards

An army camp east of Pocasset, Bourne, opened shortly before World War II, but closed to regular use in 1953. The camp is named for the commander of the Yankee Division during the first World War, Major General Clarence R. Edwards.

Camp Grounds

A station opened in the 1870s by the Old Colony Railway in South Yarmouth near the Methodist revivalist grounds at Great Western Road. The Methodists came to Yarmouth in 1863 and erected their tents on the grounds that were soon known as Camp Station.

Candlewood Lane

So called for the small splits of pine once used in the place of candles for lighting rooms. The street runs south from Upper County Road in Dennisport.

Cannon Hill

The Cape has three Cannon hills, one in Wellfleet Village, one in Brewster, and one in North Chatham. The cannons atop these hills fired reports to the townspeople on the arrival of packets from Boston. The hill in Wellfleet Village overlooks Duck Creek and once had two cannons mounted on it, the older one dating from the Revolutionary War. The hills in Brewster and North Chatham had poles as well as cannon. After the gunners fired a round, they would hoist an empty barrel and leave it at the top of the pole for as long as the ship was docked.

Cape Cod

Locally, people call it the Cape. Cape Cod did not at first include the entire peninsula from Bourne to Provincetown, but only the headland between Race Point and Wood End, where in 1602 Bartholomew Gosnold and his men aboard the *Concord* had anchored and hauled in a large catch of codfish. It took more than a century for the name to spread westward through the towns, but by the end of the 1700s correspondents were writing about Barnstable on the Cape, and travelers like Timothy Dwight were describing the Cape Cod houses located on the road from Yarmouth to Provincetown. In 1616 John Smith named the headland where Gosnold had anchored Cape James, for King James of Scotland and England. Samuel de Champlain called the entire cape Le Cap Blanc, for its white beaches and dunes. Some years later the Dutch called the peninsula Nieuw Hollant. Before Gosnold's voyage the Cape may have had other names. Some say that the Vikings landed on the beaches near Bass River and called the peninsula Kjalness, "keel point." Giovanni de Verrazano apparently found the shoals of the Cape treacherous and so named it Armellini for a papal official, Cardinal Francesco Armellino of Perugia, who was "the most subtle and resourceful tax gatherer who ever lived."

Cape Cod Bay

The bay is a large bowl shaped by the north shore of Cape Cod and by the east coast of Plymouth County. In 1602 Bartholomew Gosnold skirted its rim and called some corner of it Shoal Hope [*hope* is an old word for an inlet or small bay]. On John Smith's map of 1616 it appears as Stuards Bay, for the English royal family. Samuel de Champlain named it Baye Blanche, for the white sands of its shores. The Dutch called it the Noort Zee, and added the name Staten Bay for the waters near Sandy Neck and the name Fujc Bay [in Thoreau's gloss "bow net"] for what is now Provincetown Harbor. The English settlers in the 1600s first called it Barnstable Bay, for the largest town on the Cape. In the 1700s Cape Cod Bay came into common use, although Barnstable Bay still remained as the name for waters off Sandwich and Sandy Neck.

Cape Cod Canal

The canal is more than eight miles long, cutting through the north sections of Bourne and Sandwich to connect Buzzards Bay with Cape Cod Bay. Over seven hundred feet wide at the surface, it is the widest of all sea-level canals and flows beneath two highway bridges and a single-span railroad bridge. Although deepened and broadened by the Army Corps of Engineers, the canal was initially the work of August P. Belmont and his company, who opened it to shipping in 1914 after five years of digging and dredging. In the 1600s Governor Bradford of Plymouth Colony was among the first to propose a canal recognizing the need for a sea lane in order to by-pass the treacherous passage around Race Point and the backside of the Cape. The Massachusetts General Court passed a resolution in 1697 to support the building of a canal, and during the Revolution General Artemus Ward and Thomas Mechin examined the possibilities. In the 1800s a number of plans failed because of inadequate support or direction. In 1880, for example, more than four hundred Italian immigrants recruited for digging rebelled after they went payless and hungry. The town of Sandwich opened kitchens for the men and had the state pay their fare back to New York. Ships have benefited from the use of the canal, and some Cape Codders say that somehow it has brought milder weather. [For another canal on the Cape, see Jeremiahs Ditch.]

Cape Cod National Seashore

A national park embracing about 27,000 acres on the lower Cape. It was established in 1961, with headquarters in South Wellfleet. The park extends from Nauset Beach off Chatham along the Atlantic coastline to Long Point Light at Provincetown; in some places it covers the width of the Cape. Within it lie parts of six towns: Chatham, Orleans, Eastham, Wellfleet, Truro, and Provincetown. The area includes six public beaches: Coast Guard, Head of the Meadow, Herring Cove, Marconi, Nauset Light, and Race Point. There is a museum and visitor's center on Nauset Road in Eastham.

Captain Daniels Neck

For an Indian, Wieomoncacom, whom the English of the 1600s called Captain Daniel. Wieomoncacom was actually a member of the English militia and served under Major Church in 1689 against the French and Indians in Maine. The neck is at the Upper Millpond, West Brewster, and became in 1715 the property of John Wing and Lieutenant John Dillingham.

Carsley Neck ['karzlɪ]

The Carsleys lived in Barnstable before the 1700s. The neck helps divide Mystic Pond from Middle Pond, both in the village of Marstons Mills. The Cape Cod Airport is about a quarter of a mile northeast of the neck.

Cataumet [kə'tamɪt]

A locality in Bourne on Red Brook and Squeteague harbors, just north of Falmouth. Cataumet is from Algonquian *kehte* 'great' + *amaug* 'fishing place' + *ut* 'at' = "at the great fishing place." From early on, quahogs have been plentiful in the harbors nearby and Buzzards Bay has always had schools of cod and sea bass. The soil at Cataumet is also rich. Early settlers called it Old Indian Orchard.

Cedar Lake

More than a hundred stones mark the graves of Indians on a hill beside the lake. It is near Megansett in North Falmouth.

Centerville

The village took its name from the Centerville Post Office, opened in 1834, and is midway between Hyannis and Osterville. But in 1796, when the local congregation erected its first meeting house, the village name was Chequaquet or Wequaquet, from *wehqu-auk* "end of the land."

Centerville Harbor

The harbor is on Nantucket Sound, from Squaw Island to Craigville Beach and East Bay. In the early 1700s the harbor lay "under the school lot," because settlers had set aside lands at Squaw Island for "the maintenance of a school." Its name in the 1800s was New Harbor. Spindle Rock sits in the harbor, a half mile south of Craigville Beach, and is named for its shape.

Centerville River

The river flows south and west past Craigville and Long beaches to East Bay. Its name in the 1700s was Great Brook. In the 1800s, when Long Beach was known as Chequaquet Beach, James Crosby, Jonathan Kelly, and

Samuel Crosby had at least two coastal schooners built on the sands and launched in Centerville Harbor.

Chamber Rock

So called because the shape of this rock near Signal Hill, Bournedale, suggests a dilapidated room. The large cracks and divisions of the rock resemble a house of fallen walls and a collapsed roof. In early days some called it Sacrifice Rock. It was said that whenever Indians passed by they would lay dry sticks on the rock as an offering. But it was also said that in the distant past the rock was a setting for ceremonial dances, chants, and ritual sacrifice, sometimes human sacrifice. So, when Richard Bourne came to preach and minister to the Indians, he warned that among the dangers of such sacrifice was the vengeance God could take. Still the Indians persisted in their rituals until one night a flash of lightning struck the rock and split it apart.

Chapin Memorial Beach [ˈčepɪn]

For George H. Chapin, a real estate broker, who gave land for the beach to the town of Dennis soon after World War II. The beach borders extensive tidal flats on Cape Cod Bay in the northwestern end of Dennis. Long before it became a public beach it was called Black Flats, for the color of its sand.

Chappaquoit Rock [ˈčæpəˌkwɔɪt]

Chappaquoit is possibly from Algonquian *chappa* 'separated' + *auk* 'land' + *ut* 'at' = "at the separated land." At one time the boundary between Falmouth and Sandwich ran "from the edge of one hill to another," right down to Buzzards Bay. But the word "edge" touched off a controversy. Some said that "edge" meant the summits of the sloping hills; others said that the "edge" intended was at the bottom. But John Horton, an old Indian of Falmouth, gave to "edge" an unexpected meaning that satisfied everyone. "The edge," John said, "is neither at the top nor at the bottom of the hills, but runs over Chappaquoit Rock, about half way between." Where was Chappaquoit Rock? Only John Horton knew. So they all followed him up a hill near Buzzards Bay and stopped half way as he pointed and said, "Here is the rock where people set the boundary, where they laid down a bough every time they passed." Those with John Horton pulled away the brush and found the rock. The controversy was over.

Chase Garden Creek

A boundary between Yarmouth and Dennis. It bears the name of a pioneer family. William Chase [d. 1659], who emigrated from England with John Winthrop, was in the Barnstable area by 1638; by 1654 he was described as "of Yarmouth."

Chatham [ˈčæt,hæm] or [ˈčætəm]

At the elbow of the Cape, Chatham became a town in 1712 and is named for Chatham, England, an old Kentish seaport where Queen Elizabeth I installed her royal dockyards. In the 1600s the first English settler, William Nickerson, bought much of the land at Chatham, then called Monomoit, and at once antagonized the magistrates of Plymouth Court. The magistrates, having reserved the lands of Monomoit for the families of the Oldcomers [those who had come to Plymouth aboard the *Mayflower*, the *Ann*, and the *Fortune*], fined Nickerson 200 pounds as a trespasser. But Nickerson repudiated the fine and refused any compromise with the magistrates. Finally, in 1672 he bought out the competing claimants for ninety pounds, purchased another large tract from John Quason, the son of the sachem Mattaquason, and owned more than 5000 acres. Early Chatham had two divisions: the Inlands were reserved to the Indians; the Outlands or Commons were the lands that Nickerson had bought. From the mid-nineteenth century Chatham has included the town center and four villages — North Chatham, West Chatham, South Chatham, and Chathamport. Chathamport has the safest harbor in town. Older residents pronounce the name of the town with two full syllables — "chat" and "ham." Some say that train conductors after 1887 were the first to shorten the second syllable.

Chatham Harbor

South of Pleasant Bay between the mainland and Nauset Beach, it was until about 1870 a navigable channel, lined with wharves and warehouses. The upper part of the channel also had the name Old Harbor and had direct access to the ocean by means of a deep cut through Nauset Beach. But in the later 1800s gales shifted the sand bars so extensively that the harbor lay bare at low tide, and the cut through Nauset Beach became clogged.

Chatham Lighthouse

Opened in 1808 on James Head in Toms Neck, the lighthouse had a north and a south tower, together with the keeper's quarters, all built near the edge of a cliff overlooking Chatham Harbor. The original purpose of the towers was to flash two beacons in contrast to Monomoy Light [one beacon] and Nauset Light [three beacons] and so help seamen to locate their position near the treacherous shoals and beaches of Chatham. After the gale of 1871 and the opening of a breach through Nauset Beach, the sea began to batter and erode the cliffs at the foot of the lighthouse, until the south tower collapsed in 1879 and the north tower in 1881. The present lighthouse was built in 1877 farther from the cliff on the west side of the road. Near Chatham Lighthouse is the Mack Monument, erected in 1908 to commemorate twelve men drowned during an attempted rescue from the coal barge *Wadena:* the captain and his four men [including William Mack] and the seven men from the Monomoy Lifesaving Station who failed in the effort.

Chequesset Beach and Neck
[čəˈkwɛsɪt]

Chequesset is possibly from Algonquian *keche* 'large' + *ques* 'land or place' + *ut* 'at' = "at the big place or land." Both the beach and neck are on the north shore of Wellfleet Harbor.

Childs River

For the Childs of East Falmouth, a family of seamen and farmers. The river flows from Johns Pond in Mashpee to Eel Pond, west of Waquoit Bay. The bed of the river was the work of a flash flood at the close of the Ice Ages. But the river is mostly an overflow from Johns Pond with a current that never was strong enough to cut its own channel. Whites Landing, built in 1896, is a fisherman's dock on the river.

Chip Hill

In the western part of Provincetown, it was graded down seventeen feet for the purpose of building a saltworks in 1805. Its name is due to the wood chips taken from Nathaniel Hopkins's spar-yard to cover and harden the levelled suface. The saltworks were last in use in 1855. In 1853 workmen digging beneath a cellar on the hill hit a stone wall. Its origin remains a mystery, though some call it the Norse Wall, as if to suggest that a thousand years ago Vikings had remained long enough to build it.

Chloes Swamp

Chloe was a slave of Elisha Bourne in the 1700s. A merchant and Tory, Bourne hid in the swamp after the outbreak of the Revolution for several months and had Chloe bring him food. Bourne made it to Connecticut, escaping his hostile neighbors, but lost much of his land. The swamp was not far from Bournedale.

Chopcheag Woods [ˈčap,ček]

Chopcheag is probably related to Narragansett *Chip'pachaug* "a place apart or separated." The woods were in Marstons Mills, not very far north of Santuit Pond. Once, it is said, old Nye Jones and his four grandsons went deer hunting with their dog Sukey on a cold December day. Near sundown the grandsons quit, too cold to go on tracking deer, but Nye stayed on. "Whale on, " Nye said, "don't ye hear old Sukey sing it off up toward Conaumet? She'll be certain to drive the deer down to Chopcheag right quick. We'll get him before the moon is an hour high." The women at home fretted and scolded the four boys for leaving their grandfather behind. One hour, then another, went by. The nail heads on the door cleats became rimed with frost. But before the boys could pull their boots back on to go fetch their grandfather, he thumped on the door and staggered in, his flintlock in one hand, a 120-pound doe on his shoulder. He had carried it home, a mile and a half, old Sukey whimpering at his heels with frozen paws. He threw the doe down and said to his grandsons, "Now see if you can stand the cold in the barn long enough to dress the deer while I have my supper."

Christian Hill

For the Christian Camp Meeting Association, which in 1872 erected a summer chapel called the Tabernacle at the top of the hill in Craigville. Before the arrival of the camp meeting the hill was commonly known in Barnstable as Strawberry Hill.

Christophers Hollow

For Christopher Holder, who preached to the Quakers of Sandwich in 1657 and 1658 at the houses of William Newland and Ralph Allen, and also in the hollow, somewhere between Sandwich Village and Spring Hill. Trees bordered the hollow, and at its center near a spring the Quakers would sit on felled logs and listen to their minister preach from atop a large rock.

Clapps Pond and Clapps Round Pond

Probably for William Clapp, who in 1705 wrote to the Governor in Boston, Joseph Dudley, that marauders were seizing ships, smuggling goods, and claiming beached drift whales that by rights belonged to the Crown. In response, Dudley appointed Clapp as a lieutenant and gave him the duty of inspecting "drift whales at the Cape." The ponds are just beyond Provincetown Village, heading toward the Atlantic.

Clay Pounds

On the Atlantic coast in the Highlands of North Truro, these high, solid cliffs [rising more than 100 feet straight up] have been the backdrop for many shipwrecks. Some say that the name comes from the incessant pounding of sunken ships against them. Others note that within the crevices of the cliffs many pockets or holes contain pools of water, shaped into basins by the firm clay. The clay of the cliffs has been used in laying road beds; a cone of blue clay 200 yards wide stands at the midpoint of the cliffs. Bank-swallows nest by the thousands among the cliffs each year. The Indians called the place Tashmuit, from *keht* 'great' + *ashimu* 'spring' + *ut* 'at' = "at the great spring."

Cleveland Island

This island in Wakeby Pond, Mashpee, once belonged to President Grover Cleveland, who spent summer holidays fishing for trout, shooting ducks, and collecting tales from his guide John Attaquin. In *Fishing and Shooting Sketches* Cleveland says that, according to John Attaquin, Daniel Webster once landed a large trout near the island and then "talked mighty strong and fine to that fish and told him what a mistake he had made, and that he would have been all right if he had left the bait alone."

Cliff Pond

There are cliffs at the west end of this large pond in Nickerson State Park, Brewster. The pond has brown and rainbow trout, replenished after each fishing season. It almost runs into Little Cliff Pond, farther east.

Coast Guard Beach

So called for a coast guard station long since out of service and now a memorial to the Lifesaving Service on the Cape. Its exhibits of lifesaving equpment are on display at the end of Nauset Road, Eastham.

Cobbs Pond

For the Cobbs of Brewster, descendants of Jonathan Cobb, born 1694. A century later Captain Elijah Cobb persuaded Robespierre to release his ship, seized by the French, and then saw him subsequently beheaded at the guillotine. At the outset of war with England in 1812 Cobb sailed his ship, filled with cargo, out of Norfolk Harbor, Virginia, the very hour that the Embargo Act went into effect. The pond is off Breakwater Road, Brewster.

Cobbs Village

Now a year-round community, it began in the late 1800s as a cluster of cabins, built by George Cobb for summer people. North and east of Maraspin Creek, it borders on Barnstable Village. In the 1600s the lands of Cobbs Village were known as the Old Common Fields, granted to early settlers by the magistrates of Plymouth Court. Eastward along the shore of Barnstable Harbor, near Mill Creek and the Yarmouth line, were the New Common Fields. The Algonquian name for these fields was Mattakeese, from *matta* 'bad' + *askaki* 'wetlands' = "bad meadows or wetlands."

Cockle Cove

Probably named for cockles found along its shores by early settlers in what is now South Chatham. At one time shacks for shucking oysters stood near the cove. Mill Creek, which flows into Cockle Cove, was once known as Bucks Creek [for a family of that name] and Cockle Cove River. In 1750 Moses Godfrey had coal kilns near the cove, where there were also beds of peat.

Cohasset Narrows [ko'hæsɪt]

Cohasset is probably from Algonquian *koua* 'pine' + *s* 'little' + *ut* 'at' = "at the small pine trees." The narrows are a twisting channel between Wareham and Bourne connecting Buttermilk Bay and Buzzards Bay. Railroad tracks, Route 6, and Route 28 span the Narrows on the way to Cape Cod.

Cold Harbor

The name given by the Pilgrims in 1620 to the mouth of the Pamet River, Truro.

Cold Storage Beach and Road

So called for the storehouses in the early 1900s that kept cool and fresh the fish that were hauled in from weirs along the shore. The beach and road are in East Dennis, near Sesuit Harbor.

Conaumet Neck [kə'nɔmɪt]

The neck resembles a quail, its bill pointed southward into Mashpee Pond, its tail gliding to a tip in Wakeby Pond. Except for a narrow channel on the east shore, the neck separates the ponds entirely. Conaumet probably stems from Algonquian *quannamáug* "lamprey" or from *quinn'amaug* "long-fish place." Directly opposite the neck is Pickerel Cove, named for a popular game fish. Abbott Lawrence Lowell, President of Harvard University [1909-1933], owned the neck until his death in 1943. Thereafter the Trustees of Reservations assumed responsibility for its stands of native American holly, beech, red maple, and mountain laurel. The neck is now known as the Lowell Holly Reservation.

Cooks Brook Beach

For the old Cook family of Eastham. Josias Cook helped prepare a survey of the land in the late 1600s for prospective settlers from Plymouth. In 1876 E. P. Cook began to grow oysters from seed. The beach is in North Eastham, but the brook now lies covered with sand and salt grass. In Wellfleet, at Cahoon Hollow Road, there is another Cooks Beach.

Coonamessett River
[ˌkunəˈmesɪt]

An early variant of Coonamessett
was Quanaumet, possibly from
Algonquian *quinn'amaug* 'long
fish or lamprey' + *ut* 'at' = "at
the place for lampreys." Until the
1800s the river had large runs of
herring, but by 1885 the town of
Falmouth banned fishing on
weekends and from dusk to
dawn. In recent years Falmouth
has tried to substitute Lake Supe-
rior trout in the river for the
diminished runs of herring. In
the 1700s the river was known as
Dexters River for Philip Dexter,
who had a grist mill on it. It was
also called Five Mile River for the
distance from its source at Coonamessett Pond to its mouth at
Great Pond. Until 1735 [when
Falmouth annexed lands extending to Waquoit Bay] the river was
the east boundary of Falmouth.

Corn Hill

So called in November 1620 by
the Pilgrims who in their search
for food found a supply of corn
stored by the Pamet Indians on
the side of the hill. Located not
far from the former mouth of the
Pamet River [the river now empties farther south into Cape Bay],
the hill stands as a bluff or cliff
overlooking the coastline. During
the 1800s it had the names Captain Sams Hill and Hopkins Cliff.
Hopkins Cliff is probably for Caleb Hopkins, an early proprietor
of Truro, and for his descendants.
In 1730 Caleb and two other
townsmen were chosen "to prevent cattle and horses going upon
the meadows and beaches
adjoining."

Corporation Beach

For the Nobscusset Point Pier
Corporation, established in 1814
by Henry Hall and the Howes
brothers. Old-timers in Dennis
called the beach at the east side of
Nobscusset Point "Co-operation
Beach." It is also known as
Nobscusset Beach.

Cotuit   [kəˈtuɪt]

Two villages in Barnstable have
had the name Cotuit. In the 1800s
Old Cotuit was a village on the
Santuit River in southwest
Barnstable. About 1875 the village changed its name to Santuit
to conform with the name of a
new post office. The second village in Barnstable called Cotuit is
farther down Main Street on Cotuit Bay. Known as Cotuit Port in
the 1800s, this second village
shortened its name to please Au-
gustus Perkins, a local resident.
The village on Cotuit Bay was
called Little Harvard in the early
1900s because of its attractiveness
to Harvard faculty members and
their families. It was also labeled
the "oyster center of New England," because of the demand
for Cotuit oysters. The name Cotuit is possibly Algonquian *kowaw* 'pine' + *tugk* 'wood' + *auk*
'land' = "pine wood land."

Cotuit Bay

Cotuit Village is on the west shore
of Cotuit Bay. On the north shore
of the bay, near a channel called
the Narrows, a Barnstable convict
many years ago dug for a chest of
gold which Captain Kidd, it is
said, had left behind. Watched
closely by his jailor, the convict
dug until he was tired. Then the
jailor had the turnkey dig. The
convict rested for a few minutes,
then suddenly came up to the
jailor. Pointing down into the pit
where the turnkey was digging,
he said that he was sure that the
gold was within reach. The jailor
bent over to look, saw the turnkey lift his shovel, and was struck
by a sudden blow. The convict
fled. Some believe the pit is still
there.

Crab Ledge

During the 1700s this ledge, covered with cedars, stretched southward into Chatham Harbor from James Head. But in the nineteenth century the tides of the harbor drowned the roots of the trees and submerged the bank under two feet of water. The eastern end of the ledge came to be called the Stump Ground.

Craigville

For Dr. J. Austin Craig, President of the Christian Biblical Institute until his death in 1881. Before then Craigville was known as Camp Christian. The Camp began in 1872, when twenty-four ministers pitched their tents and conducted prayer meetings on a bluff known as Strawberry Hill, south of Centerville.

Craigville Beach

On Centerville Harbor, Barnstable. It is a bayhead bar, gathering sands from the currents and waves, and is one of the best beaches on Cape Cod for bathing. Summer people began coming to the beach soon after 1900.

Cranberry Highway

A boosters' name for Route 28 which runs from Bourne to Falmouth and then along the south side of the Cape to Orleans. Henry Hall of Dennis began growing cranberries for market in 1816. Since then local farmers have planted 3500 acres of bog. The largest and most productive bogs are in Barnstable and Harwich.

Crosby Landing

Albert Crosby, who built the mansion "Tawasantha" in the 1880s, lived near the landing. It is now a public beach, at the end of Crosby Lane off Route 6A in Brewster. Crosby had gone over-land to California in the gold rush of 1849 and became a rich man.

Crowell Village [krol]

For the large Crowell or Crowe family of the mid-Cape. It was located on Grand Cove in West Dennis. Thoreau crossed Bass River at a toll bridge and recalled that he walked "through Crowell Village, Grand Cove, to Isaiah Baker's in West Harwich." Crowell Village was also known as Crowe Town and Crowes Neck.

Crowes Pasture

For many years the pasture was simply known as Indian land. Crowe was a common surname for families with white and Indian spouses. The land is now a reserve for fauna and flora; it is in East Dennis at the end of South Street.

Crow Hill

For the crows frequenting this hill, north of Woods Hole near Quamquisset Harbor. In the 1800s Cape Codders returning from the California gold rush called the hill San Diego Heights. Farther up Buzzards Bay at Wild Harbor is Crow Point, also a haunt for birds.

Crows Pond

So called for the descendants of Thomas Crow or Crowell, an early settler. This saltwater pond in Chatham opens directly on its east side into Bassing Harbor.

Crystal Lake

The Osterville Land Company of the 1870s gave this pond in Wianno Village its name. The Company also named Sea View and Ocean Avenues and called its summer houses Pine and Sweetbriar cottages. There is also a Crystal Lake near Route 28, Orleans.

Cummaquid   ['kəməkwɪd]

The Algonquian name for a post office and village in northeast Barnstable, near Yarmouth. The meaning of Cummaquid may be similar to that of Mohican *acomeques*, from *acomes* 'on the other side [of the water]' + *ques* 'land or place' = "land or place on the other side of the water." In the 1800s, before the opening of a post office, the village was called East Barnstable. In the early 1600s Indian settlements at Cummaquid were called Iyanoughs Town. The Sachem Iyanough and his tribe would return yearly to this part of the Cape, and in 1621 offered hospitality and assistance to Edward Winslow, on his way to Nauset to recover a youngster named Billington. Close by this area, in 1637-38, the Reverend Stephen Bachiler and his congregation had a settlement that soon gained the name Old Town from those who came with Lothrop two years later. Cummaquid's golf course, first opened in 1895, is the oldest on the Cape. Directly after the Second World War, local planners developed the neighborhood of Cummaquid Heights next to the golf course.

D

Dangerfield

This early name for Truro (in use 1705-09) is possibly due to the risk that the shoals and treacherous waters off the Atlantic coast presented to ships sailing the backside of the Cape. Dangerfield Road near the Pamet River commemorates the old name.

Daniels Island

This island is actually a peninsula, named for a Mashpee seaman of the 1800s, Daniel I. Amos. It is at the bounds of Ockway and Popponesset Bays.

Davis Beach

For Charles Henry Davis, who sold the beach in West Dennis to the town in the early 1900s. The beach is at the mouth of the Bass River on Nantucket Sound. Across the river in South Yarmouth, Davis had several houses carted to a single lot, assembled, and joined together into one mansion, topped by seven large chimneys. Neighbors who knew their Hawthorne called Davis's house the House of Seven Chimneys.

Davisville

The Davises of Falmouth went to sea on whalers. James Davis built the first house in the locality in 1825. After the decline of whaling the locality did not thrive until the summer people bought up the seamen's houses. Davisville is on Bournes Pond and Vineyard Sound.

Dead Mans Hollow

In North Truro, it faces the Atlantic and the Peaked Hill Bars offshore. The British frigate *Somerset*, engaged in the Battle of Bunker Hill in 1775, struck the Bars on November 3, 1778, went over them, and beached itself not far from the Hollow. Many crewmen died, but hundreds survived, fell prisoners to the local Truro militia, and were marched under armed guard to Barnstable and then to Boston. The remains of the *Somerset* soon disappeared, only to reemerge in 1886 after a severe storm had altered the shape of a dune under which they had lain for nearly a century; another storm in the 1970s again exposed parts of the ship.

Deep Pond

Falmouth has two Deep Ponds. The pond west of Hatchville and Coonamessett Pond is twenty-eight feet deep at its center. The other pond, half as deep, is east of Sippewisset in Beebe Woods, and has a sweep of encircling hills, some of them seventy feet high. It is also known as the Punch Bowl, because it sits at the bottom of a steep, bowl-shaped hollow, surrounded by slopes.

Delap Hill ['di,læp]

For James Delap, who at fourteen crossed from Dublin on the *George and Ann* and came to Barnstable after a harrowing voyage (see Wreck Cove). Delap became a blacksmith and the master of a packet between Barnstable and Boston. The hill was in the village of Barnstable.

Dennis

A mid-Cape town, incorporated in 1793 and named for its first minister, Josiah Dennis. In the days of Josiah's ministry, the town was a part of Yarmouth and was known as the East Precinct. The Indians called its northmost sections Nobscusset, Sesuit, and Quivet. The town of Dennis purchased Josiah Dennis's house in 1968, restored it, and opened it to public view. The old District Schoolhouse, built in the early 1800s, stands on the same grounds on Nobscusset Road. Dennis Village, in the northeastern end of the town, is also known as North Dennis.

Dennis Pond

For Robert Dennis, a settler in early Yarmouth who lived by the pond. The pond is not in Dennis, but in Yarmouth, near the Barnstable line. It has a public beach.

Dennisport

In 1850 Thomas Howes, the first postmaster, gave the village its name. Its earliest name had been Crooks Neck, for Samuel Crook, an Indian who deeded his land to the English settlers in the 1600s. Later residents probably did not remember Samuel, nor did they care for the connotations of *crooks*. So they changed the name to Crockers Neck. The village is near the Herring River and Swan Pond, in the southeastern part of Dennis.

Depot Pond

The pond, once called Long Pond, is near a former Old Colony Railroad station in Eastham Village. The coming of the railroad also prompted Depot streets or Station streets in such Cape communities as Dennisport, Brewster, East Harwich, and South Yarmouth.

The Devils Dumping Ground

This is a broken chain of boulders dispersed in shallow hollows on the south side of a low ridge near the Sandwich and Bourne bounds, along the Pocasset-Forestdale Road. It is said that the devil himself hurled the boulders over the tops of trees on the ridge into the bottoms of the hollows.

Devils Foot Island

The shape of the island suggests the name. Its big toe hooks into Woods Hole Passage close to the shores of Penzance. The Devil in the name is probably due to the many shipwrecks on the coast of the island, the result of treacherous currents and strong winds in Woods Hole Passage. In the 1800s it was also known as Bluff Island.

Discovery Hill

The word *discovery* here means "to have a view, to enjoy a prospect"; it does not mean "to find something new." This hill in Sandwich, east of Route 130 on the Mid-Cape Highway, became in 1974 a part of a memorial for Thornton W. Burgess. A native of

Sandwich, Burgess wrote stories of the old briar patch, of Sammy Jay, Old Mr. Toad, Johnny Chuck, and Peter Rabbit. His memorial is a natural setting of hill and valley, of grape vines, black locusts, and white pine.

Doane Rock

For the Doanes of Eastham, stemming from Deacon John Doane, a settler in 1644. It has also been called Enochs or Enos rock, for the deacon's son, as well as Great Rock. The rock, possibly the largest boulder in southern New England, was left by a glacier between what is now the Salt Pond Visitor Center of the Cape Cod National Seashore and Coast Guard Beach.

Doanes Field

Probably for Abiathar Doane, a shipmaster of Harwich in the mid-1800s. The field is east of Allen Harbor, Harwich Port, and is also known as Mattacheesett Field [see Cobbs Village] and Wyndemere Bluffs.

Dogfish Bar

A shoal in Nantucket Sound, named for the dogfish, a member of the shark family commonly found near the coasts of New England. The bar is several miles long, between the mouth of Bass River and Point Gammon.

Dogtown

This settlement of the past is recalled in the doggerel of the Reverend A. J. Church:

> The railroad cars are coming, let's all get up and crow.
> The little dogs in Dogtown will wag their little tails;
> They'll think that something's coming, a-riding on the rails.

Dogtown was named for its obscure, impoverished residents, eking out their lives somewhere between the villages of Wellfleet and South Wellfleet.

Donnelly Pond

For First Lieutenant Ralph E. Donnelly, killed in action during the first World War. The pond is in the Camp Edwards-Otis Air Force Base section of Bourne.

Dowses Beach [dausəz]

On East Bay, Osterville, this town beach is named for William B. H. Dowse, a lawyer and businessman. The Dowse family sold the beach to the town of Barnstable in 1946. It was once known as Dry Island.

Drift Highway

An early road, laid out in 1705, twisting and turning its way past the "best watering places" from East Harbor through Great Hollow to the Head of Pamet, Truro. Local residents nowadays report some difficulty in identifying the exact course of the old road.

Drummer Cove

The drummer is a local name for the squeteague or weakfish, and is also known on Cape Cod as a spotted boy or silver fish. The cove is near Wellfleet Harbor in South Wellfleet.

Duck Harbor and Creek

The harbor is a marshland between Bound Brook Island and Griffin Island in northwestern Wellfleet. Nearby is Duck Harbor Beach, just off Chequesset Neck Road. Duck Creek, farther east, is a part of Wellfleet Harbor. Before 1869, when the Old Colony Railroad built a bridge across the creek, it provided most of the anchorage for the town's fishing boats and for coastal traders.

Dunbar Point

For James Dunbar, an early resident. In 1950 Dr. Herbert T. Kalmus, who helped to develop color photography, donated forty acres at the point for use as a public beach. The point is a boundary marker between Lewis Bay and Hyannis Harbor.

Dutchmans Brook

Possibly for Hessian soldiers, taken prisoner during the Revolution, who settled in Mashpee and married Indian girls. The brook runs southeast and empties into Hamblins Pond on Waquoit Bay.

Dyer Pond

For an old family of the lower Cape. William Dyer arrived before 1700 and probably lived close to the pond in central Wellfleet, at that time part of Eastham. It was once a good place to go skinny-dipping.

E

Eagles Neck

This small strip of land, so called since the 1700s, juts out into Pamet River, Truro, just south of the Pamet Yacht Club. Early records also refer to Eagles Neck Meadow.

East Bay

So called because it is east of Osterville. Schooners and coastal packets of the past would anchor outside the bay to load and unload cargo.

Eastham ['ist,hæm]

Incorporated in 1651, the town may have been named for an English Eastham [one is in Cheshire, another in Worcestershire] or for its location at the east end of the Cape. It was first known as Nauset, the name also for the local Indians. In its early history, Eastham extended west to Yarmouth and north to Truro, but gradually became the third smallest town on the Cape after the establishment of Chatham, Orleans, Harwich, and Wellfleet. A windmill built in Plymouth, shipped to Truro, and finally erected in Eastham in 1793, still grinds corn sometimes. When the town celebrated Windmill Weekend in September 1980, the federal government issued a commemorative stamp. Much of Eastham, nearly a third, is now within the federal reserve.

East Harbor Creek

The creek flows from the south end of East Harbor into the Salt Meadow, Truro. In November 1620, the Pilgrims apparently entered the creek aboard a shallop. Thoreau notes in *Cape Cod* that at the head of the creek "the Atlantic is separated but by half a dozen rods of sand from the tidewaters of the Bay."

East Harbor Village

A community of twenty-three houses during the Revolution, it became in the 1800s a deserted village. Of the young men who left to fight for independence twenty-three died, and the village never recovered. It stood near High Head, south of Pilgrim Lake in Truro.

Eel Grass Cove

For the eel grass that grows near the shore of this cove, north of Broad Sound and Sand Island in Barnstable Harbor. In season hunters would go out with shotguns in search of ducks.

Eel Pond

The Cape has three saltwater Eel Ponds, one in Bourne, two in Falmouth. The pond in Bourne is in the village of Monument Beach. It was earlier known as Calebs Pond, for Caleb Perry, who had the first salt-works in the locality. The two ponds in Falmouth are in Woods Hole and Menauhant. The pond in Woods Hole flows under a drawbridge into Great Harbor and has the Marine Biological Laboratory at its southwest shore.

Egg Island

Shaped like an egg and once a popular beach for clambakes, the island dwindled into a sand bar by 1940. It was in Lewis Bay.

Elbow Pond

Named for its shape, this pond in southeastern Brewster has a good stock of pickerel.

Elephantback Hill

The shape of this hill [south of Sandwich Village] suggests the name. In the 1800s, before the division of Sandwich, it was Bournes Hill, for the Bourne family.

Ellis Landing

For the Ellises of Harwich and Brewster, beginning with Jacob Ellis, a settler in the 1720s. The landing is on the Bay, East Brewster, just off Ellis Landing Road and Route 6A.

Englewood

North of Lewis Bay in West Yarmouth, this district is named for a former hotel. Englewood Beach is at the bay, at the end of Berry Avenue.

Lief Erickson Drive

A developer's name for a street running from Old Bass River Road toward Kellys Bay in South Dennis. This drive [*drive* is itself a euphemism for the word *street*] takes its name, as do Thorwald and Freydis Drives all in the same locality, from the supposed arrival of Vikings on Bass River in the year 1000. The Norse sagas, however, spell Erickson's name *Leif*, not *Lief*.

F

Factory Village

In West Brewster near Stony Brook. Although the first mill opened in the 1660s, the village did not begin to thrive until a hundred years later, when clothmakers, tanners, ironmongers, and tin-stampers all had factories beside the brook. Sidney Winslow's factory, for tanning leather and making shoes, was the forerunner of the United Shoe Machinery Corporation. Nowadays there remains a grist mill on the brook, open in the summer as a museum. The village was also known as Winslows Mills and Brewsters Mills.

Falmouth ['fælmʊə]

The town borders Vineyard Sound and Buzzards Bay at the southwest corner of the Cape. Many of its localities on the sea, from Waquoit on the east to Falmouth Village, Quisset, and Megansett on the north, look each year for the return of summer people. Farther inland, localities such as Teaticket, Smalltown, and Hatchville are close to freshwater ponds [the town has more than thirty], to cranberry bogs, and to sandy fields of strawberries. For some the town is "Naples by the Sea"; for others it is the "Eden of the Cape." The Indians spoke of the area as *suckanesset* "where there are black shells or shell fish," from *sucki* 'black' + *anawsuck* 'shells' + *ut* 'at.' Suckanesset was the name of the white settlement in 1686 when it became a town. The name Falmouth first appears in 1694, probably for Falmouth in Cornwall, from which Bartholomew Gosnold sailed for America in 1602.

Early settlers in the 1660s came from Barnstable and Sandwich, many of them Quakers seeking refuge from the intolerant orthodoxy of Plymouth Colony. During the Revolution and the War of 1812, the townspeople withstood assaults by the British navy. They broke a blockade in 1779, when under the leadership of Major Joseph Dimmick they recovered a schooner laden with corn, seized by the British on its way from the Connecticut River and held in Tarpaulin Cove. In 1814 the British frigate *Nimrod* bombarded Falmouth Village after the townspeople refused to surrender the privateer *Retaliation*, captured at Tarpaulin Cove by Captain Weston Jenkins and his thirty-two men. For thirty years after 1820 the town built whaling ships. In the 1870s, when the "dude" train from Boston first arrived bearing summer visitors, the building of hotels and cottages by the sea began. And from the 1880s on, studies of the ocean and of marine life at Woods Hole have made it one of the world's renowned centers of science.

Falmouth Green

The Green, more than two hundred years old, comprises an acre and a half in the center of Falmouth Village. In 1749 it had eight houses, a meetinghouse and a whipping post, all unfenced and surrounded by dirt roads.

Falmouth Heights

A developer's name of the 1870s, Falmouth Heights was earlier called Great Hill. It was to Great Hill that Daniel Webster came for fish chowder picnics. On the hill, too, Dr. Hugh George Donaldson and Dr. Francis Wicks opened a smallpox hospital shortly after the Revolution and began to vaccinate. In the 1600s, it is said, Queen Awashonks of the Narrangansetts would stop at the hill during her stay in Sacconessett, before crossing Vineyard Sound to Gay Head. The Heights overlook the sound from Inner Harbor, east of Falmouth Village.

Falmouth Inner Harbor

The harbor has the shape of a finger pointing northward from Vineyard Sound toward the outskirts of Falmouth Village. General George W. Goethals, the builder of the Panama Canal, advised local planners on how to open the harbor to the sea. Until the late 1800s the harbor was known as Deacons or Bowermans Pond. Joseph Davis, a land owner at the pond, was a deacon of the First Congregational Church in the 1790s. The Bowermans, an old family in Falmouth, came

with the first settlers. In 1804 Abram and Lois Bowerman sold their land at the pond to Deacon Davis.

Farmersville

So called for the farmers in southeast Sandwich, who lived near the village on Lawrence Pond.

Faunces Mountain [fɔnsɪz]

The hill, the only one on Cape Cod to be called a mountain, is named for the Faunces, who first came to Sandwich from Plymouth in the 1700s. It is in the Shawme-Crowell State Forest, west of Sandwich Village.

Fawcetts Pond [fɔsɪts]

For Dr. Thomas Fawcett, a doctor of the 1800s, who wrote his own epitaph: "I have practiced on the eclectic option in Mass., Ohio, and Mich., over 50 years, and have never lost that number of patients. I conversed with the spirits of the dead for forty years, as with the living." The pond was first known as Tar Pit Pond, because early settlers distilled turpentine and tar from the resin of nearby pine trees. Also, the large stand of pine trees was known as Tar Pit Valley. The pond is in the west end of Hyannis.

Fay Bluff

For Joseph S. Fay, a Boston merchant of the 1850s, who came to Little Harbor near Woods Hole and bought the land at the bluff. Fay later deeded land to the town of Falmouth and had the Church of the Messiah built in Woods Hole.

Featherbed Swamp

In southeast Truro. So called because of its soft, grassy cover.

Samuel Fessendens Pickle

A *pickle* is a local word, of North English origin, that means a "small plot of land surrounded by a hedgerow." In the early 1800s Samuel Fessenden lived in Monument Village, now a part of Bourne.

Fiddle Head Rock

Those who named the rock believed that it resembles the carved spiral or volute on the neck of a fiddle or on the prow of a ship. The rock is in Lewis Bay, nearly midway between Hyannis and Yarmouth.

Fiddler Cove

A basin on the south side of Megansett Harbor on Buzzards Bay, Falmouth. The cove is probably named for the fiddler crabs that herd together at the shoreline. The male fiddler digs a burrow with his huge right claw that sweeps in front of him like a bow. Charles Rand, a manufacturer of file cards, had the basin dug out in the 1920s.

First Encounter Beach

In 1620 William Bradford, Miles Standish, and a group of Pilgrims from the *Mayflower* explored the terrain near the beach just north of Bees River on the bay side of Eastham and for the first time encountered hostile Indians. A tablet on Mulfords Cliff close by commemorates the Pilgrims' search for a suitable harbor and settlement.

Flashy Pond

The word *flashy* has the obsolete meaning "over-moist" or "watery" to describe the grass that springs up in a pond, especially after heavy rains, but does not dry well enough to make fodder. Grassy Pond is another name in common use; in the 1800s it was Deborah Bottles Pond. The Massachusetts Audubon Society has forty-five acres of holly trees, magnolias, heaths, dogwoods, franklinia, and beds of lady's slipper near the pond. Wilfrid Wheeler brought the holly trees to the site of the pond from all over the Cape, Martha's Vineyard, and Nantucket. He also developed hardy strains of his own. In 1962, with the aid of Mr. and Mrs. Josiah K. Lilly III, Wheeler's collection became part of a sanctuary, where visitors can see catbirds and kingfishers overhead and look for black bullhead, ribbon snakes, and painted turtles in the pond. Flashy Pond and the surrounding Ashumit Holly Reservation are in Mashpee, just north of Hoophole Road and south of Ashumit Pond.

Flax Pond

Before the invention of the cotton gin, linen made from flax was a common cloth on the Cape. Farmers would ret their bundles of flax in these ponds until the fibers soaked free from the woody pulp of the plant. So widespread was the growing of flax that farmers took their bundles to ponds in seven towns on the Cape: Barnstable, Bourne, Brewster, Dennis, Harwich, Falmouth, and Yarmouth. The largest, in Brewster, is also called Flat Pond. [The name *flat* is possibly due to a play on the pronunciation of *flax*.]

Flintrock Pond

The pond has deposits of flint-rock in and about its shores. It is near Barnstable Village, not far from Flint Rock and Mary Dunn roads.

Flume Pond

Near Gunning Point on Buzzards Bay in Falmouth, the pond was once a source of salt hay for cattle. Farmers would drain water from the pond through a flume before harvesting the marsh grass and making hay.

Follins Pond

For Thomas Folland, a settler in the 1600s near the pond on the Dennis - Yarmouth line. A fairly large pond, it forms with Weir Pond the head-waters of Bass River.

Ford Swamp

This swamp, now drained, was at Liberty and Main Streets in Sandwich Village. It was so called because, in the absence of a bridge, villagers had to ford it.

Forestdale

So called because of the rich growth [nurtured by twenty inches of topsoil] in the fields and woods near this village in the south end of Sandwich. Forestdale replaced the earlier Greenville in 1887, after the village requested a local post office. In the 1700s the name for the district was simply the Woods.

Fort Hill

The Cape has three Fort hills [in Yarmouth, Eastham, and Orleans], and Sandwich has a Fort Hill Road. Atop these hills the settlers are said to have erected houses that had walls of oak thick enough to serve in forts. The hill in Yarmouth is near the town's first meetinghouse. The hill in southeastern Eastham, overlooking Nauset Marsh, is at the end of a trail which skirts the marsh and descends into Red Maple Swamp. At the head of the trail is the mid-Victorian house of Captain Edward Penniman, a shipmaster of Eastham in the 1800s. Two great whale bones stand as a gateway to the entrance. The hill in Orleans was supposedly the home of Atta-cospa, the last of the Nauset tribe. It is near a boiling spring, one of the very few in the Lower Cape. Indians once said that a great whale swam in under the hill, found himself short of air, and attempted to blow. The weight of the hill was too much, so that all he could do was to start the spring flowing. Then he swam west until he lay under Hosey Swamp. There he let go a full spout that formed a little pond, ever since called the Whale Hole.

Freeman Pond

For the Freeman family, who owned land at the pond near the Pocasset River and Bennets Neck in Bourne. Edmund Freeman came to the district in 1637. Frederick Freeman of the same family, a minister and historian of the 1800s, wrote a two-volume account of Cape Cod, its traditions, people, and towns.

Freemans Pond

For Major John Freeman, who lived at the pond in the late 1600s. The pond is in West Brewster, near Cape Cod Bay.

Fresh Brook Village

Sometimes called Brook Village, this settlement is located in the southern part of Wellfleet. Fresh Brook empties into Wellfleet Harbor near the Massachusetts Audubon Society Bird Sanctuary.

Friends Village

For a community of Friends who lived near their meetinghouse in South Yarmouth during much of the nineteenth century. In 1809 David Kelley gave half an acre of his land to the Society to have the meetinghouse built and a graveyard laid out. But Thoreau says that in his excursion of 1857 - when he stepped out of a stagecoach "on the northwest edge of Yarmouth . . . [he] inquired of the ticketmaster the way to Friends village in the southeast part of the town. He never heard of it." The graveyard and meetinghouse on North Main Street still mark the site of the community, which was also called Quaker Village.

Frostfish Cove

The tom-cod is called a frostfish because it is most abundant in New England waters when the frost comes. The cove is off Little Pleasant Bay, Orleans.

Frostfish Creek

The frostfish or tom-cod is quite common in New England waters. The creek is in Chathamport and flows into Ryders Cove. In the 1700s it was known as Covels River, for the early settler William Covel and his family. The stream flows southward under Orleans Road [Route 28] and changes its name to Stepping Stone Creek. At one time townspeople stepped over stones to cross the creek; in the late 1800s they built Stepping Stone Bridge. The Indian name for the area was Quassaqueesett.

Fuller Point

Probably the property in the late 1600s of Captain Matthew Fuller, a physician and officer in the Plymouth militia during King Philip's War. The point is at the east end of Scorton Neck, Barnstable.

Funn Pond

Funn is a shortening of the word *funnel* and a name for charcoal burners. These were used near the pond which is in Dennis, southeast of the intersection of Routes 134 and 6A. A local name for the area at the pond is Fun Town, though it has never had a roller coaster or casino.

G

Gages Hill

For Lot Gage, the first superintendent of the Hyannis Breakwater. In the early 1800s Gage built the Red Cottage on the hill overlooking Nantucket Sound; it is now known as the Loutrel Cottage.

Gansett Point

Gansett is a short form of Narragansett. The point is at the entrance to Quisset Harbor, Falmouth. The Marine Biological Laboratory bought Gansett Woods in 1916 for the benefit of its research staff.

Garretts Pond

For Andrew Garrett, a lietutenant in the Continental Army during the Revolution, who lived beside the pond after the war. During the war he was a prisoner of the Indians for four years, followed their customs, and may have taken a wife. On his return he learned that the woman he had married before the war had found another husband [she thought he had died]. So, shortly after, Garrett married a Barnstable girl, Miss Blish. At the turn of the nineteenth century the pond was known as Stewards Pond, for a local family. In earlier times it was known as Annables Pond, for Goodman Anthony Annable, who came to New England on the *Ann*. Not far from the Great Marshes, the pond is a source for Brick Yard Creek.

Georgetown

For George Baker, the "King of Georgetown," who lived in this locality on the west side of Bass River, South Yarmouth, in the earlier 1800s. The Quaker David Kelley erected a chapel in Georgetown for his daughter Rose, soon after she lost her baby in 1872; she died in 1874. Nearby on the river, Georgetown Flats is good for clamming.

Gibbs Narrows

For the old Gibbs family of Bourne and Sandwich, who lived by the narrows between Buttermilk and Little Buttermilk bays.

Gingerbread Lane

For Gingerbread House, a nickname for Captain Hawes's summer home in Yarmouth Port, constructed in the 1800s and adorned with ornate woodwork. The house, now a restaurant, stands near the lane which runs north off Route 6A.

Glendon Road Beach

For Hubert Glendon, a Marine officer in World War II and a rowing coach at Columbia University from 1927 to 1947. Glendon gave the village of Dennisport land for a beach, which is close to where he lived on Glendon Road.

Governor Prence Road

The Cape has three roads named for the third governor of Plymouth Colony: one in Eastham [where he lived], a second in Brewster, a third in Yarmouth [spelled Prince]. There is a Prince Way in Dennis and a Prince Valley in Truro, just off Cape Cod Bay. Governor Prence held office from 1657 until 1673 and preferred to rule from his home in Eastham rather than to move to Plymouth.

Grand Cove

Grand is an exception to the typical use of *Great* to name waterways. The cove covers seventy acres and is a part of Bass River, lying between South and West Dennis. The Judah Baker Windmill now on Willow Street, South Yarmouth, once overlooked the cove and was used to grind corn until 1891. Charles Henry Davis, its next owner, deeded it to Yarmouth when he died.

Grass Pond

So called because of the grass that grows near the shores of the pond. In the past the pond has also been known for its size — Long Pond — and for its shape — Crooked Pond. Its Algonquian name was Wonkapit, probably from *wonki* 'crooked' + *pe* 'water' + *ut* 'at' = "at the crooked pond." The pond is north of Harwich Port, halfway to Harwich Center.

Gray Gables

This village at the west end of the Cape Cod Canal takes its name from a summer house owned by President Grover Cleveland. The President and his wife Frances bought the house in 1891, called it Gray Gables, and spent holidays there during his second term. In those years, too, the New York, New Haven and Hartford Railroad provided a depot for the growing village. The house itself, which burned down, stood at Gray Gables Point on the south shore of the canal. In earlier days Gray Gables Point was known as Tudor Haven, for the family who owned the land.

Grays Beach

For the Grays of Yarmouth. John Gray, the first of the family, had a grant of land near Nobscusset Neck in 1642. The beach, sometimes called Bass Hole Beach, is at the northern end of Center Street in Yarmouth.

Great and Little Harbors

Great Harbor is to the west and Little Harbor to the east of Juniper Point at Woods Hole. The salinity of Great Harbor is unusually stable [no brooks empty into it] and so provides an excellent setting for scientific experiments at the Marine Biological Laboratory, the National Maritime Fisheries Service, and the Woods Hole Oceanic Institute. The Coast Guard maintains a buoy depot next to Fay Bluff at Little Harbor.

Great Hill

So called from the first days of settlement in the 1600s, it rises 130 feet in Chathamport, a familiar landmark to coastal seamen. The hill's two summits are easy to recognize. On clear days they provide a view of Nantucket, twenty miles off. Stands of oaks growing on the hill were cut down by settlers in the 1700s to build houses. In 1821, to prevent erosion and to keep sand from covering the village, the selectmen had pines and beach grass planted. This effort is the first instance of reforesting in America. During World War II the hill served as a radar station.

Great Hollow

A wide, sagging stretch of land north of Corn Hill, this hollow served as a burial ground for the Pamet Indians. When the Pilgrims first happened on the Indian burials in November 1620, they also discovered a large iron kettle, some reed baskets, the remains of an old hut, and a few planks from the ship *Friendship* [run aground in 1617 or 1618, some of the crew killed by Indians, others ransomed by their chief officer, Captain Dermer]. The hollow is in Truro.

Great Island

The Cape has two Great islands, one at the southeastern end of Lewis Bay, the other on the western side of Wellfleet Harbor. Great Island in Lewis Bay became a promontory in 1831, linked to the shore by a gravel bar. Great Island in Wellfleet Harbor is also no longer a true island, but instead borders on The Gut, a marshy strip that runs off the mainland. In the early 1700s fishermen would trap whales close to the shores of the island in Wellfleet. Nowadays it is part of the Cape Cod National Seashore and is open to visitors, who may follow the Great Island Trail, more than eight miles long. The trail passes Great Beach Hill, overlooking the harbor.

Great Marshes

The marshes stretch from Sandwich to Barnstable, 4000 acres bordered by the beaches of Cape Cod Bay. Wells, Scorton, and Eel creeks flow in and out of the marshes, great spawning grounds for fish. And birds migrate to the marshes to nest in the grasses. Early settlers called the Great Marshes the Hay Ground, because they would cut fox grass and salt thatch for cattle feed. Scanton, the Indian name for the area, is not for the marshes themselves, but for the creeks; it is possibly a variant of *scauton* or *scata'cook*, "the place where the stream branches."

Abner Hersey, a doctor of the 1700s, bought farm land in Barnstable and tracts in the Great Marshes with the fees he collected from his patients everywhere on the Cape. In 1787, ill from smallpox, the Doctor bequeathed his holdings in the Marshes to thirteen parishes on the Cape. He provided larger shares of land to the parishes where most of his patients lived. His hope was that the deacons of these parishes would rent the marshes, buy equipment to keep the land fertile, and prepare sermons to keep parishioners devout. His will also promised that he would return in a hundred years, to witness "the immortality of his fields." The deacons convened each year at Sturgis Tavern in Barnstable to plan the management of the fields at the Great Marshes. Within ten years they found that income from the marshes was about equal to the cost of lodging and board at the tavern. Within twenty-nine years the marshes, fields and woods had become a wasteland. By 1816 the deacons had sold out; the provisions of the Doctor's will were no longer enforced. On January 9, 1887, the year of the Doctor's promised return, a townsman swore he had heard the hoofbeats of a horse clattering by Barnstable graveyard, and had seen old wheels fading across the bare, brown flats, where Hersey once had had stands of pine and oak trees. And just when the wheels had almost passed beyond hearing, there came forth a voice shouting at the horse, "Thunder of Jehovah, what have they done! Ah, I'd as lief be chained to a galley-oar as look at this again! Giddap, giddap, Mehitable! Oh, for a spot of wilderness!"

Great Pond

Six ponds of the Cape — in Eastham, Falmouth, Bourne, Provincetown, Wellfleet, and Truro — are called *great*. The smallest is in Bourne [4 acres], the largest in Eastham [109 acres] on Great Pond Road. Wiley Park, a beach on the pond in Eastham, has a bathhouse and picnic grounds; it is named for Maurice W. Wiley, who until 1962 served Eastham for many years as a selectman.

Great River

A saltwater river on the east side of Waquoit Bay, Mashpee, that turns northward to Jehu Pond.

Great Rock

The Cape has many large boulders, but two, especially, have had the name Great Rock. One was a landmark at Hyannis Inner Harbor, planted in 1749 at the south boundary of Shubael Gorham's land to designate the right-of-way he was donating to Barnstable. Eighty years later, long after the town had built a road along the right-of-way, hardly anyone recalled Gorham's rock as a landmark. So it simply became another boulder, thrown in together with all the others needed for the construction of the Hyannis Breakwater.

The second Great Rock is southeast of Bourne Village and weighs four hundred tons. It is said that the Indian giant Maushop was once carrying several boulders in his apron on his way to the south shore to build a causeway from the Cape to Nantucket. But as he was stepping over hills and uplands, a chickadee saw him balancing his burden and laughed. Suddenly angry, Maushop hurled one of his rocks at the bird and missed. He then caught his foot in Bourne Pond, stumbled, and dropped his load.

The boulders fell helter-skelter out of his apron, the largest one — Great Rock — falling not too many miles from the pond. The bird flew off and the causeway remained unbuilt.

Great Sippewisset Swamp

[ˌsɪpəˈwɪsɪt]

Sippewisset is probably related to Natick *sepaw* 'stream' + *es* 'little' + *ut* 'at' = "at the little stream." Great Sippewisset Creek is a tidal estuary that reaches northward to the center of the swamp from Buzzards Bay. In the 1600s Quakers at West Falmouth Harbor called the section of the swamp close to their settlement Hog Island, because they put their swine on it to feed and root.

Great Western Road

An old road that runs northwesterly from Harwich Center to Weir Road, Yarmouth.

Greenough Pond   [ˈgrino]

For Thomas Greenough, an Indian who lived in Yarmouth Port during the late 1700s. It has also been known as Taylors Pond, after an old family long resident near the West Yarmouth Road.

Grews Pond

For the Grews, a family in Falmouth since the 1700s. The pond is north of Falmouth, just south of Long Pond and Pumping Station Road. In 1894 Joseph S. Fay gave some land at the pond to Falmouth for use as a park. He chose the name Goodwill Park to commemorate his gift.

Griffiths Pond

For William Griffith, an early settler on the Cape. The pond is south of Brewster Village, near Great Fields Road. It has also been known as Snows or Whites Pond, and its Indian name was supposedly Wishoea.

Gross Hill

The Cape has two Gross hills, one in Truro, the other in Wellfleet. The hill in Truro Center, named for the Gross family of Castle Road, is the site of the First Congregational Church, for which, perhaps, Paul Revere cast a bell. The second Gross Hill is named for a family of early Wellfleet settlers. Many of them were long-lived; in the 1800s the combined age of ten sisters and two brothers totalled more than a thousand years. The hill is northeast of Wellfleet Village, just below Gull Pond.

Gull Pond

Although Thoreau wrote that innumerable gulls *once* flocked to this pond and others nearby, they are still to be found resting on the waters. The pond [more than a hundred acres] fills a hollow formed by a glacial ice-block. It is in the northeastern part of Wellfleet. There is another Gull Pond in the Wellfleet Bay Wildlife Sanctuary in South Wellfleet.

Gunning Point

On Buzzards Bay near Sippewisset in Falmouth. Hunters would come to the point for shooting ducks over the bay.

The Gut

The gut is a low-lying, narrow stretch of marsh that connects Griffin and Great islands in Wellfleet Harbor. Apparently the tides running between the islands have shifted enough sand to create this thin passage or gut.

H

Peter Haigis Beach   ['hegəs]

Mrs. Haigis gave the land for the beach to the village of Dennisport in commemoration of her husband. It is west of Glendon Road Beach.

Halfway Pond

This pond is halfway between West Yarmouth and Yarmouth Port, just off the West Yarmouth Road. [See Little Halfway Pond.] Barnstable also had its Half Way Pond. [See Mary Dunn Pond.]

Halletts Hole and Meadow
['hælɪts]

It is said that in the 1600s the town of Eastham accused Goodie Hallett of witchcraft, stoned her, and drove her out of town. She went to live near a graveyard [now the South Wellfleet Cemetery] on a waste of sand called Halletts Hole and Meadow. Travellers on the Old Kings Highway rode at a gallop past her hut, especially after sundown. Some say that she buried her faithless lover, the pirate Sam Bellamy, beneath the poverty grass and sand of her meadow and that she married her soul to the devil, who gave her the sand dunes for a home, also called Satans Harvest and Lucifer Land.

Hamblin Plains ['hæmlɪn]

For the Hamblin family of Marstons Mills in Barnstable, who lived on the plains. In 1819 their neighborhood was the first on the Cape to welcome Methodism. The Cape Cod Airport occupies part of the plains. Each year from 1954 until 1972 the Barnstable County Fair had its fairgrounds on the plains at the end of July.

Hamblin Pond

The Hamblins have lived by the pond for nearly three hundred years. The pond is a kettle hole, the bottom link in a chain of four ponds: Hamblin, Middle, Mystic, and Little ponds. In the late 1800s all four ponds were simply known as Hamblin Ponds. In the early 1800s they were all called Cotuit ponds. And in the 1600s and 1700s the settlers knew them as the Indian ponds. Some villagers in the 1800s also called it South Pond and Grigsons Pond. The ponds are all in the village of Marstons Mills. Hamblin Pond itself, sometimes called Clear Lake, has had the Clear Lake Duck Farm on its shores since 1931. Since 1946 there has been public bathing at the pond.

Hammonds Bend

A curving arm of Nantucket Sound on the west side of Monomoy Island, named for the Hammond family of Chatham. Inward Point, also on the west side of Monomoy Island, is a stretch of land that hooks "inward" into Hammonds Bend.

Handkerchief Shoal

The sandbanks and rocks in this shoal southwest of Monomoy Point, Chatham, probably looked from the deck of a ship like a waving handkerchief. Charts and maps since the 1700s show that some of the banks and rocks in the shoal lie under very little water.

Handy Point

The Handys were an early family in Cotuit. Azubah Handy, married to Bethuel G. Handy, was buried near the point in 1819 at Little River Cemetery. Mark Antony DeWolfe Howe, long an editor of the *Atlantic Monthly,* once owned Handy Point. Handy Point is on the west side of Cotuit Bay. Barnstable oystermen a century ago found the water at the point excellent for their seed beds.

Happy Hollow

The hollow is near Sherman Square, Hyannis, the district in the village where blacks lived in the 1800s. The name Happy Hollow is in memory of Gentle Annie Gould, who would say to her neighbors, "Do I like it here? Oh, I'm so happy." Gentle Annie lived in the hollow with her husband Barney, whom she would periodically thrash. Nearby lived her neighbors, Three-Fingered Ruth, Black Jane, Uncle Phi, and Tamsey Ann. Sherman Square is named for Paul Hosland Sherman, a veteran of the First World War.

Harbor Bluff

The bluff stands at the entrance to Hyannis Harbor from Lewis Bay. In the 1800s the land behind the bluff was known as Fish Hills and had many boulders and knolls. But the builders of the Hyannis Breakwater stripped the hills of their glacial boulders, and the owners of real estate levelled almost all the knolls.

Hard Digs

Also known as Hard Scrabble, this run-down neighborhood of the 1890s near Hyannis Inner Harbor suffered from losses in the maritime business after a crash of the market.

Harding Beach

This beach on Nantucket Sound near Stage Harbor commemorates the old Harding family of Chatham. Stage Harbor Light, also called Harding Beach Light, stood as a beacon from 1880 until 1935. Thereafter the federal government installed an automatic light at the top of an iron framework.

Hardy and Gould Wharves

For Josiah Hardy and Leander Gould, the owners of the wharves north of Chatham Light in the 1800s. Packets from Nantucket docked regularly at their wharves until the catastrophe of November 1871, when a gale ripped out the supporting piles and turned the harbor into a treacherous channel.

Harwich   ['harwič]

Incorporated in 1694, Harwich is named for a seaport in Essex, England, familiar to many early voyagers who were bound for New England. It is said that Patrick Butler chose the town's name while walking from the Cape to Boston. When he arrived, he urged its adoption by the General Court. In 1772 southeastern Harwich became what is now South Orleans. Until 1803 the town continued to straddle the Cape from the Bay to Nantucket Sound. Thereafter it lost its northern lands to the newly incorporated town of Brewster.

Hatch Beach

More fully, the Paulina B. Hatch Bathing Beach. It was given to the town of Eastham in her memory by Aylmer Hatch in 1953. It is located on the Bay, just south of First Encounter Beach.

Hatches Creek

For the Hatch family of Eastham, descendants of Moses Hatch, a settler of the 1600s. At one time the creek was large enough to give anchorage to dories. Until the late 1700s the Hatches kept the creek wholly within their property, but thereafter it became the dividing line between Eastham and Wellfleet.

Hatches Harbor

Named for Jeremiah Hatch, a resident of Provincetown in the 1700s. It lies on the tip of the Cape, between Herring Cove and Race Point.

Katy Hatchs Hill

For Aunt Katy Hatch, who with her husband Benjamin farmed this hill near Falmouth Village in the mid-1800s.

Hatchville

Jonathan Hatch, who differed with the church at Barnstable, fled to the area of Falmouth in 1660. The village is not far from the Sandwich line, at the northernmost reaches of the yellow aster that grows throughout the nearby fields. In the 1700s, before Hatchville had a post office, it was known as the East End because of the East End Meeting House, built for local families of farmers who could not easily travel to Falmouth Village to worship. Nowadays the New Alchemy Institute near Hatchville practices farming and conservation with the use of natural fertilizers, windmills, and solar heating.

Hathaway Ponds

In the 1700s the first of the Hathaways at the ponds was James, who spelled his name Heddeway. In the 1600s the ponds had separate names: Rowley Pond [on the south for Henry Rowley] and Lewis Pond [on the north for Edward Lewis]. The ponds are on Phinneys Lane, north of Wequaquet Lake, near Barnstable Village.

Hawksnest Pond and Hawksnest State Park

The hawks most common to the Cape are the red-tailed hawk and the rough-legged hawk. The pond and the park are in northeastern Harwich near Long Pond. An earlier name for the pond was Wolf Hill Pond.

The Head of Pamet   ['pæmɪt]

A marsh land bordering on the Pamet River near the Atlantic Ocean. In the 1700s Truro village stood near the edge of the marsh. In later times parts of the marsh have become cranberry bogs and swamp gardens.

Hectors Bridge

There were also Hectors Nook [a meadow] and Hectors Stubble [a field], named for a slave sold when he was three to Benjamin Collins, an owner of meadows, woods, and marsh lands at the Head of Pamet near the ocean. Hector received baptism in 1747 [he was then twenty-four] in the Truro church. He was a lonely, devout man without family, who recited his prayers aloud as he worked in the fields. Buried without a gravestone, he remained something of a legend to local residents during the nineteenth century.

Hedge Fence

A shoal in Vineyard Sound northeast of Oak Bluffs. Hedge Fence is a fanciful name suggesting a barrier placed near Martha's Vineyard.

Herring Brook

The alewives coming up the brook from Buzzards Bay probably attracted such early settlers of the 1600s as Isaac Robinson and Jonathan Hatch. The brook runs close to Falmouth Cliffs and Old Silver Beach.

Herring Cove

Between Race Point and Wood End, Provincetown, it is three miles long and marks the northeast edge of Cape Cod. Thoreau says in *Cape Cod* that early maps identify the beach of the cove as Bevechier [maybe related to an Old French form *bevier* 'measure of land']. Herring were once so plentiful in the waters of the cove that in 1714 Governor Dudley considered calling Provincetown, Herrington. In the 1880s when the herring fisheries declined, local "mooncussers" and "beachcombers" — they looted shipwrecks — carried out their raids so often that their settlement had the name Hell Town. According to George Washington Ready, the Provincetown crier in 1886, a sea serpent 300 feet long and 12 feet wide with a head the size of a 200 gallon cask came ashore from Herring Cove. The scales of the serpent [green, red, blue] were each the size of a barrel head. The serpent crawled to Pasture Pond, leaving behind it a burned-out path smelling of sulphur. It plunged into the pond and drew all the water with it. At the center of the pond there remained a hole 20 feet around and 1500 feet deep, so far down that no one could find the bottom.

Herring River

The Cape has several Herring rivers and brooks: in Barnstable and Bourne, in Brewster and Falmouth, in Harwich and Mashpee, in Orleans and Wellfleet. The river in Bourne flows down from the Indian cemetery at the south end of Great Herring Pond to Foundry Pond and then becomes the Bournedale Herring Run that ends at the fish ladders on the Cape Cod Canal. The fish ladder draws thousands of alewives in the early spring. They swim up the canal, squirm up the ladder, and spawn in Foundry Pond. In the 1600s Herring River had so many alewives that the people of Sandwich divided them annually into shares. They were good for smoking, for fertilizing [to spread the fields with "fish corn," settlers said] and for trade. In the 1800s Thoreau noted that there "are many Herring Rivers on the Cape. They may soon be more abundant than herring."

Higgins Crowell Road

For Captain Higgins Crowell, postmaster of West Yarmouth in the 1870s. The road connects Route 28 with Willow Street.

Higgins Pond

Located in the northeastern corner of Wellfleet, immediately north of Gull Pond. Richard Higgins was one of the original settlers of Nauset [later Eastham] in 1644, prominent in local affairs, and patriarch of a numerous clan. According to Savage there were more families of this name in Eastham in 1801 than of any other except Smith.

Highbank Bridge and Road

So called for the high banks of the Bass River at the bridge and road, which connect South Dennis and South Yarmouth. The road is a continuation of the Great Western Road and lies halfway between Route 28 and the Mid-Cape Highway. The bridge was once known as the "upper" bridge to distinguish it from the "lower" bridge in West Dennis.

High Cedar Island

A hill near Pilgrim Lake once covered with cedars. For ships sailing west toward the Cape, the hill in Truro looked from a distance like an island.

High Head

A high plateau just south of Pilgrim Lake in Truro. A lifesaving station, High Head Station, once stood toward the east on the Atlantic. In early days the soil at High Head was the richest in the town, but farming declined after the Revolution. High Head is now also called Pilgrim Heights; the new name is spelled out with large letters on the face of the plateau.

High Land

Gosnold called it a "mighty headland," a stretch of hills and plateaus along the Atlantic coast of Truro. It includes Clay Pounds and Highland Light. During the

Second World War the federal government took the lands for the 762nd Air Craft Warning Station. Along the shore runs Highland Beach.

Highland Light

The light is in the High Land of Truro, on what Levi Whitman in the 1790s described as a "mountain of Clay." He noted that this mountain would make an excellent foundation "for a lighthouse which would save the lives of thousands, and millions of property." In 1798 the light was constructed, the first on Cape Cod. The federal government has rebuilt it periodically; it now stands 183 feet above sea level, with 300,000 candlepower. Near the light the sea has washed away seven acres of the shore. The light is one of the first landmarks for ships headed toward Boston. It is also known as Cape Cod Light.

Hill of Storms

Also called Storm Hill, it was the site in North Truro of the first meetinghouse, constructed in 1711 but dismantled in 1740. The meetinghouse also served as a landmark for ships years before any light was erected in Truro. It is said that a red-heeled witch darkened a seaman's light in the meetinghouse and so caused the wreck of six ships, with twenty lives lost. Peters Hill, the current name, is for a family of Portuguese descent.

Hinckley Pond

For Thomas Hinckley, Governor of Plymouth Colony [1680-92], who had a house on the pond. In the 1600s it was known as Coggins Pond, for Henry Coggins, an early sea captain and an owner of land on the east shore. In the 1800s it was known as Great Pond and Ice House Pond, for the shed that stored harvested slabs of ice. The pond is north of Pond Village, Barnstable.

Hinckleys Pond

For Thomas Hinckley, who lived at the pond in the 1700s. It has also been known as Herring Pond. In northern Harwich toward the Brewster line, the pond is a source of the Herring River.

Hippogriffe Road

For the clipper ship *Hippogriffe*, 678 tons, built in 1851-52 at the Shiverick yards in Dennis. Designed for speed and long voyages, the ship bore a hippogriff [half horse and half winged griffin] as its figurehead. Skippered by Captain Anthony Howes, it sailed around the world to San Francisco, Calcutta, and then home by way of the Cape of Good Hope. In 1858, in the Java Sea, it ran upon an uncharted rock, ever since called Hippogriffe Rock. The sunken vessel has been described as a "notoriously crank ship and unlucky one." Hippogriffe Road runs off Beach Street in Dennis.

Hog Island

This island of sand and marsh is just south of Sampson Island in Little Pleasant Bay, Orleans. Some say that at Money Head, on the north end of the island, Captain Kidd stored his treasure in "a box, lockt and nailed, corded and sealed." In early days farmers would graze their livestock, sheep, and hogs, on the island. There were other Hog Islands on the Cape: in Provincetown [it was submerged by a tidal wave in the 1700s] and in Buzzards Bay, Bourne.

Hog Ponds

These two ponds [sometimes called Lower and Upper Hog ponds] are near Farmersville in the east end of Sandwich. They were also known in the late 1800s as the Percival ponds, for the Percivals, a family of farmers. The Hog Ponds, together with Triangle and Spectacle ponds on the north, form a chain of kettle holes.

Hogs Back

A hill located south of the Pamet River near Cape Cod Bay and once covered by a ridge of pine trees, it very early suggested the back of a hog. Fishermen used the hill as a landmark; in 1725, for example, John Lewis testified that he had struck a whale "near or at a place called Hog's Back." A later tradition ascribes the naming of the hill to British sailors engaged in the American Revolution. The Truro records of 1806 refer to a "hogsback valley."

Hokum Rock

Actually a cluster of rocks, the largest shaped like a wedge or hook and possibly called by the Indians, *hoccanum* "bend back." It is said that an old brave once lived among the rocks and greeted all passers-by with a suspicious "Ho kum?". He would have been unhappy, were he alive now, to see cars race by his wigwam on their way to the nearby drive-in theater on Hokum Rock Road, Dennis.

Honey Bottom

The bottom lies on the slope of Scorton Hill in Barnstable, and

was once a burial ground for Indians. No water, it is said, ever gathers at the bottom. The sides of the bottom have the shape of a bowl; the rim of the bowl is lined with pine trees. Developers from Sandwich, however, have dumped their land fill into the bottom.

Hoopers Landing   [hupərz]

For Samuel Hooper, the first of the summer visitors in Cotuit, who returned each year in the 1840s with his wife Anne Sturgis [herself a native of Barnstable]. Congressman Hooper had the landing built for the village on Cotuit Bay, between Bluff and Handy Points. In the early 1900s packets made the landing a regular port of call in order to pick up loads of cordwood.

Hope Spring

The spring was once Charles Hope's, an Indian who lived in Cataumet, Bourne.

Hopkins Island

For Giles Hopkins, a passenger on the *Mayflower*, who settled near the island in Orleans in 1648. The island is in the Town Cove.

Horsefoot Cove

A *horsefoot* is a localism for a horseshoe crab. The cove is on the eastern side of Bass River in West Dennis. Dennis also has a Horsefoot Road and a Horsefoot Path.

Hosey Swamp

Hosey was born about 1730, the daughter of John Sipson, the last of the Nauset sachems. The swamp is now an overgrown cranberry bog, northeast of Paw Wah Pond in Orleans.

Hospital Cove

So called, according to local huntsmen, because ducks wounded in flight would come down into the cove and supposedly remain there until they had recuperated. The cove is at the south end of Red Brook Harbor, near Cataumet, Bourne.

Hoxie Pond ['haksɪ]

For the Hoxie family, residents near the pond on the Old County Road near East Sandwich since the early 1800s. Joseph Hoxie bought land at the pond in 1822 and was a shoemaker. For a time he was the town's representative at the General Court in Boston. In 1914 the Commonwealth opened a game farm of 135 acres near the pond for breeding and raising pheasant and quail.

Hyannis [ˌhaɪ'ænɪs]

For Iyanough or for Yanno of the South Sea, both Algonquian sachems of the 1600s. Iyanough's lands were northward in Barnstable, near Cummaquid and Sandy Neck. Yanno's lands were largely near Hyannis Village. Edward Winslow describes Iyanough in *Mourts Relation* as a hospitable sachem, a friend to a party of Pilgrims on the Cape in 1621 who were in search of a lost

youngster named Billington. Two years later, at the age of twenty-six, Iyanough died in a swamp in flight from Miles Standish and his militia. Yanno died in peace. He and his son John sold tribal lands to the proprietors of Barnstable in 1664 and 1680. Nicholas Davis built a warehouse near Hyannis in 1666; Edward Coleman built a house in 1690. The village has flourished in commerce and has a number of handsome houses. It was known as Lovelyville in the early 1900s and as the Metropolis of the Cape in 1932, a name given to it by the editor Arthur Tarbell.

Hyannis Harbor

Hyannis Breakwater is at the west end of the harbor; Dunbar Point is at the east end. The construction of the breakwater began in 1826 and took nearly a hundred years to complete. Even in its early years the breakwater provided ships with a barrier against stormy seas. In the 1700s the harbor was often called Hyannis Roads. The public beach at Hyannis Harbor is named for Orrin F. Keyes, a veteran of the Second World War.

Hyannis Inner Harbor

Settlers at the harbor in the late 1600s were among the first in Hyannis. The harbor is on the Barnstable -Yarmouth line, next to Lewis Bay.

Hyannis Park

A locality in West Yarmouth, between Hyannis Harbor and Glenwood Street.

Hyannis Port

The best known houses in Hyannis Port and West Hyannisport are those in the Kennedy Compound. The area of Hyannis Port along Ocean Avenue affords a fine view of the harbor and sound.

I

Icehouse Pond

So called for a shed beside the pond, where slabs of ice were stored. The pond is in Tonset, a locality in Orleans; another pond of that name is in Barnstable, and still another is on Martha's Vineyard.

Île Nauset   [ˌilˈnɔsɪt]

Henry C. Kittredge gave this vanished island on the coast of Eastham its French name. In his view it was a headland projecting eastward from Nauset Light. In 1602 Bartholomew Gosnold named its coast Point Care, possibly because of the treacherous tides his ship *Concord* had to endure. Tuckers Terror, for one of the men aboard the *Concord*, was apparently a stretch of bars north of Point Care. In 1620, according to Kittredge, "the surf breaking on . . . [Point Care] . . . caused the *Mayflower* to turn back to Provincetown, instead of continuing her voyage to the Hudson." Some years later in 1659 Point Care came to be known as Sluts Bush, possibly related to the Dutch *sloot* "ditch." The Dutch *sloot bloempjes* is the name of a shrub. Nowadays some regard Île Nauset, like Webbs Island, as a "lost Atlantis of the Cape."

Indian Burying Hill

The Herring Pond Indians buried their dead on the hill. In 1637 they began to worship at a meetinghouse near a spring on the south slope [it was known as Meetinghouse Spring]. In 1924 the town of Bourne dedicated a flag pole and a memorial tablet at the hill to honor Thomas Tupper and Richard Bourne, who were missionaries to the Indians. The hill is just outside Bournedale.

Indian Neck

The Cape has two Indian necks, one in Truro, the other in Wellfleet. The Indian Neck of Truro divides the Pamet River into two branches, close to what was Jonathan Paine's wharf of 1755. The neck was also known as Old Toms Hill, for a Pamet Indian. The Indian Neck of Wellfleet is a marshland stretching into the harbor near Pilgrim Spring Road. It was a treasure trove of Indian relics, of arrow heads, stone tools, and bones. There is a public beach nearby.

Indiantown

For a settlement of Indians on Bass River, established in 1715 but abandoned by the end of the century. The Indians called it Pawkanakut, possibly from Algonquian *pauquun* 'cleared' + *auk* 'land' + *ut* 'at' = "at the cleared land." The Rev. Timothy Alden said in 1797 that "within the memory of some, the Indians . . . [in South Yarmouth] were nearly as numerous as the white people," but at that time only one wigwam remained.

Inman Road Beach

The beach, open to the public, is at Lower County Road in Dennisport. The Inmans lived on a corner of the road; Isaiah Inman was the sheriff of Barnstable County in the late 1800s.

Israel Pond

For Israel Hamblin, who lived beside this pond in East Barnstable until the early 1700s. In the 1800s it was also known as Small Pond.

J

railroad tracks on Factory Street in Sandwich Village.

Jackson Island

Possibly for Samuel Jackson, an early settler who in 1644-45 was "excommunicated and cast out of ye church for Lyeing and sundry suspitions of stealing, as pinnes . . . and divers other things from others." This marshy land is close to the entrance of Scorton Creek in Barnstable Harbor.

James Head

For Little James, an Indian from Orleans who in the early 1700s married Wawhanana, a daughter of the sachem John Quason. Chatham Lighthouse stands on the head, facing Nauset Beach.

Jarvesville

In 1825 Deming Jarves, a merchant of Boston, had his Flint Glass Manufactory built in the village of Sandwich, together with row houses and stores. Jarvesville, also known as Glass Factory Village, produced Sandwich glass for more than sixty years until the factory closed in 1888 because of declining profits and labor disputes. After Jarves had opened the factory, bought and leased about 2000 acres of woodland for fuel, and brought in many workers, Daniel Webster said that game "had thinned out . . . to such an extent that the neighborhood ceased to supply good sport." Webster soon after built a mansion in Marshfield, but in 1850 accepted from Jarves a large, molded glass, produced at the factory, called the Union Bowl. Jarvesville was north of the

Jefferson Island

For Joseph Jefferson, a friend of Grover Cleveland and an actor especially known for his role as Rip Van Winkle. The island, once known as Stayonit, is near the north shore of Wakeby Pond, Mashpee.

Jenkins Pond

Falmouth has two ponds named for the Jenkins family. One is south of Hatchville; the other is closer to Falmouth Village on Sandwich Road. The first Jenkins to come to town in the late 1600s became an agent and helped distribute land to settlers.

Jeremiahs Gutter

This stream [now only a ditch in the Eastham-Orleans marshes] was large enough in the 1700s to carry vessels from the head of Boat Meadow Creek near Cape Cod Bay to the Town Cove, an arm of the Atlantic. The gutter was named for Jeremiah Smith, a settler of the late 1600s in Eastham; it was also known as Jeremiah Smiths Gutter and Jeremys Dream, a misinterpretation of the word *dreen*, which is a localism for the more common *drain*. In 1717 Cyprian Southack, under orders from Governor Shute in Boston, crossed over Jeremiahs Gutter on his way to Nauset Harbor to recover for the British Crown what he could from the broken-up ship *Whidaw*. But by the time he arrived local residents had left him little to salvage. The brief distance from Cape Cod Bay to the Town Cove has from time to time prompted notions of digging a canal along Boat Meadow Creek and Jeremiahs Gutter. In 1804 Eastham and Orleans actually completed a make-shift canal that had scarcely any use until the War of 1812, when, in an effort to evade a British blockade of shipping, local boats carried salt produced on Cape Cod Bay to privateers waiting in Nauset Harbor, ready to sail for harbors along the Atlantic coast. As late as 1844 heavy ocean tides periodically crashed over the land and created a natural channel between the lower and middle parts of the Cape.

Jeremy Point

Possibly for Jeremy, an Indian of the late 1600s, who lived in Truro. The point itself is at the tip of Great Island, west of Wellfleet Harbor, and is accessible at low tide over the Great Island Trail.

Jericho Path

A road north of Falmouth Heights, once surrounded by a tract of woods. An early owner called the woods Jericho soon after he had paid for them. "Why Jericho?" he was asked. "Was it not to Jericho, " he replied, "that the man in the Good Book was travelling when he fell among thieves?" Grover Cleveland also mentioned Jericho in a talk that he gave to his neighbors one July Monday in 1891 at Gray Gables, Bourne. "I see no similiarity," he said, "between my situation and that of the man who went down from Jerusalem to Jericho and fell among thieves." At the end of Jericho Path near Little Pond, is Elysian Avenue, known as Elysian Fields in the 1870s, but now bordered by tennis courts. For a time Little Pond was itself called Lake Leman, the traditional name for the Lake of Geneva.

Jim Browns Creek

Named for Jim Brown, the owner of a boat house. The creek was once the south branch of the Pamet River, but now serves as part of a boat basin on Cape Cod Bay, Truro. It was also known as Eagles Nest Creek.

Johns Pond

Maybe for John Hammond, who came to Mashpee from Sag Harbor, Long Island in the early 1800s. His son Watson F. Hammond was the first Indian to sit in the Massachusetts House of Representatives. Johns Pond is fairly large [243 acres] and is close to the Sandwich and Falmouth line.

Jones Pond

For Thomas Jones, who came to Falmouth in 1750, contributed most of the funds for a new schoolhouse in 1798, and bought a bell cast by Paul Revere for the First Congregational Church. The pond is at Falmouth Village near Jones and Gifford Roads.

Josephs Pond

Also known as John Josephs Pond, for an early resident of Harwich. Two miles northeast of Harwich Center, it was called in early days Okers or Briggs Pond. Joanna Oker was a poor woman of the early 1700s who suffered the fate of being warned out of town and who lived on charity in Chatham.

Joshua Pond

For Joshua Lambert, an early settler in Osterville. Until the days of refrigeration the pond would regularly yield crops of ice. Nowadays it is a public beach.

Juniper Point

Charles R. Crane had the junipers planted on his estate at the point dividing Great and Little harbors near Woods Hole. Crane, a minister to China and the "patron saint" of the Marine Biological Laboratory, bought his estate in 1907. Woodrow Wilson had a summer house on the point, and so did the Whitneys, who called their cottage the "Airplane House" because of its flat roofs and wings. In the late 1800s the area was known as Butlers Point, for a shoe manufacturer from Lynn. In the 1700s it was Parkers Point, maybe for Lieutenant Joseph Parker, who skippered a ferry between Woods Hole and Martha's Vineyard.

K

Keeters Great Field

The field belonged to the widow Keeter in the late 1600s. It lay east of the Santuit River and was bequeathed to her grandsons Elisha, James, and Joseph, all of whom died fighting in the Revolution.

Keith Island

For Benjamin Franklin Keith, who owned the Gaiety Theatre in Boston and in 1883 began to popularize vaudeville. The island, once known as Cometoit, is on the west side of Wakeby Pond, Mashpee.

Kelleys Pond

Probably for David and Elihu Kelley, who lived by the pond in the early 1800s. The pond is in West Dennis, near Pond Street.

Kellys Bay

For David O'Kelia, who in the late 1600s emigrated from Northern Ireland and settled beside the bay. His descendants had a drawbridge built in 1805 over Bass River. The bay itself is a widening in the river [it is sixty acres in all] just north of the Mid-Cape Highway. O'Kelia became Kelly or Kelley.

Kings Highway

This shore road near Cape Cod Bay [now Route 6A] was once the only direct connection between Sandwich and Provincetown. In 1684 a jury of overseers appointed by Governor Hinckley had the road laid out from Plymouth to Barnstable, following the path of Indian trails and wagon tracks. Sometime later the road reached Provincetown, and in 1920 the General Court made the name Kings Highway official. Seventeen years later, after the Cape towns voiced some displeasure, the General Court changed the name again to the Grand Army of the Republic Highway. Since 1950 the Grand Army of the Republic Highway has been the name not for Route 6A, but for Route 6, most often called the Mid-Cape Highway.

Kit Carson Way

Not for the frontiersman, but for a clipper ship built by the Shiverick yards in East Dennis during the 1800s and christened for him. The street itself is in nearby Yarmouth Port.

The Knob

A small round hill that looks like a corn on a big toe sticking out into Buzzards Bay from the peninsula on the north side of Quisset Harbor, Falmouth. The word *knob* to designate a hill came into use in the late 1700s. Cornelia Carey, who lived at the Knob, left her land as a sanctuary.

Knowles Crossing ['nolz]

Once a grade crossing on the New York, New Haven and Hartford Railroad, it offers a full view of Provincetown harbor and village. Close to the Provincetown Water Pumping Station, Beach Point, and Knowles Heights in North Truro, the crossing is probably named for the family of Howard Knowles, a resident of Truro who was famous at the turn of the twentieth century as a dwarf circus clown. It was also known as Calebs Crossing for the head of the family.

L

Lake Elizabeth

For Elizabeth Barry, wife of the Reverend Joseph Barry of Boston. In the late 1800s Mrs. Barry often served as the hostess for benefits at Christian Hill for the Craigville Improvement Fund. The lake is in Craigville, north of Craigsville Beach Road. The north part of the lake is sometimes called Red Lily Pond or Pink Lily Pond because of the flowers that once floated on the water.

Lawrence Pond

For the Lawrences, who came to Sandwich in the late 1600s. The pond is in the east end of town near Farmersville.

Lawyer Lovells Bog

So called for "Lawyer" Lovell, born in New Hampshire and trained for the law in Boston. Lovell came to Cotuit to catch trout. Out fishing one day with a friend, he boasted that the mussels in the stream contained pearls. To his delight he broke open a mussel, plucked out a pearl, and sold it for forty dollars. From that time on Lovell was a pearl fisherman until at last he came down with rheumatism from frequent wading through brooks. Lovell lived on the Santuit River and grew cranberries in his bog.

LeCount Hollow

For the LeCounts of Wellfleet; Azubah LeCount lived in the hollow as late as 1872. Now a part of the Cape Cod National Seashore, the hollow contains a small community and opens onto Maguires Landing [a public beach on the Atlantic] at the end of LeCount Hollow Road. It is also known as Snows Hollow.

Mr. Leverichs Meadow

['lɛvərɪks]

The meadow had this name for some time in the seventeenth century, even after William Leverich, the first minister of Sandwich [1638-1654], departed for Oyster Bay, Long Island. Leverich had displeased some members of his church, not least because he wanted to hold the Lord's Supper every Sunday at night. The meadow of five acres was in the village of Bourne near today's Cape Cod Canal.

L'Hommedieu Shoals

[lə'hamɪ,dju] or ['lemɪ,dju]

This shoal in Vineyard Sound is a hazard for ships en route between Falmouth and the offshore islands. Elizabeth L'Hommedieu, from an old Huguenot family of Southold, Long Island, married Samuel Bourne of Falmouth in 1739.

Lewis Bay

For Jonathan Lewis, who lived in Hyannis during the 1700s and built the first two-story house in the village. The bay swerves outward from the neck of Hyannis Inner Harbor to Yarmouth on the east and Harbor Bluff and Dunbar Point on the west. Since 1966 the John F. Kennedy Memorial, a monument of fieldstone, has stood on Ocean Street atop the west shore of the bay.

Lieutenant Island

Probably for Lieutenant Anthony, an Indian of the 1600s who lived at Billingsgate on Wellfleet Harbor. It was also known as Horse Island in the 1800s although it mostly attracted duck hunters, among them President Grover Cleveland. The island is largely marshland, now almost a headland on Loagy Bay at the southeastern end of the harbor.

Lighthouse Road

For the Bass River Light [in service until 1914] which is now a part of Lighthouse Inn. The road is in West Dennis and runs from Lower County Road to Davis Beach Road.

Linnell Landing and Beach

For Jonathan Linnell, a proprietor of the Seventeen Share Purchase [1713]. Now a part of East Brewster, the landing and beach border on Linnell Road near Route 6A.

Little Dublin

A settlement of Irish immigrants who lived on North Street, Hyannis, during the 1800s.

Little Halfway Pond

So called because the pond is halfway between Phinneys Harbor on Buzzards Bay and Turpentine Road, the Sandwich-Bourne line. It is also halfway between the Plymouth and Falmouth lines.

Little Italy

A locality in Dennis, so called because many of the settlers were Italo-Americans, who had come from Taunton, Massachusetts, in the late 1800s to help build roads and lay railroad tracks. There is a Taunton Avenue in the district, as well as Squadrilli Way, Dr. Bottero Road, Spadoni Road, and Angelo Road. Nearby is Lombardi Heights. Little Italy has also been known as Little Taunton.

Little Pamet

Also known as Pamet Little River and North Branch. In the 1700s it was called Hopkins Creek for Caleb Hopkins, a resident of Truro. The stream is north of Pamet River and extends eastward from Cape Cod Bay toward Longnook and Higgins Hollow.

Little River

The source of the river is Lovell Pond; its mouth is at Handy Point on Cotuit Bay. Little River is also the name of a residential area at the Old Post and Little River roads in Cotuit, Barnstable.

Longnook

So called because it was a large stretch of meadow at some distance from the village center. In the 1700s villagers in Truro laid out farms, grew orchards, and built schoolhouses. Nearby, Longnook Beach on the Atlantic is a part of the Cape Cod National Seashore; it was once known as Will Rich Beach, for a member of an old, local family. Also near Longnook is Higgins Hollow, named for an old Truro family; it is sometimes called T'Other Hollow, because it takes a different path.

Long Point

At the "true" tip of the Cape, this narrow strip of land stretches into Cape Cod Bay on the west side of Provincetown Harbor. Long Point Light has been a landmark since 1826. During the Civil War the Army installed two batteries at the point, later called Forts "Useless" and "Ridiculous." In the earlier 1800s villagers at the point made large catches of fish and sold barrels of sea salt. Within forty years the size of the catch had become too small and the cost of making salt too expensive to enable the village to thrive.

Long Pond

The Cape has six Long ponds: in Barnstable, Bourne, Falmouth, Wellfleet, Yarmouth, and the largest, covering more than seven hundred acres, on the Harwich-Brewster line. The Indians called this last pond Mashpee "big water." The pond in Yarmouth, near Station Avenue and Indian Memorial Drive, bordered the last settlement of Indians in the mid-Cape, who perished of neglect and disease in the later 1700s. Farther west in Falmouth, it is said that Indians once camped on the pond not far from the Saconesset Hills, and that a young girl, who spurned a brave for a white man, shortly after found herself also deserted. In the 1700s this Long Pond in Falmouth was a washing pen for sheep, and at the close of the 1800s a reservoir. It is sometimes called Falmouth Reservoir.

Lookout Hill

From this hill in 1782 militia men in North Chatham hoisted a flag and fired an alarm to warn townsmen of a British privateer that had slipped into Chatham Harbor to seize the American brigantine *Joseph* and also a schooner and a sloop. But the militia and the town mustered quickly and drove off the British.

Loop Beach

The road along the beach "loops" southward from Bluff Point at the entrance to Cotuit Bay. During the 1800s the wives and children of whaling captains and crewmen would stand on the bluff above the beach, awaiting the return of ships on Nantucket Sound.

Lothrop Hill [ˈloθrəp]

For John Lothrop, the minister who led his parishioners from Scituate to Barnstable in 1639. The town's first meetinghouse was built on the hill in 1646. John Lothrop lies buried on the hill in the graveyard beside the meeting-house. The hill is at Main Street, in the west end of Barnstable Village.

Lovers Lake

The only pond in Chatham to be called a lake [from the mid-1800s on], it was earlier known as Lords Pond, probably for the second minister of the town, Joseph Lord. The Indian name for this pond and the one nearby was Nespoxet, from *neese* 'two' + *paug* 'pond' + *s* 'little' + *ut* 'at' = "at the two little ponds." Other ponds in Chatham have names related to the ministry: there is a Ministers Pond in northwest Chatham, near the Harwich line, and Emery Pond, for the Reverend Stephen Emery, the third minister, located just south of Lovers Lake in Chathamport. The name Lovers Lake may be due to the arrival of the railroad in Chatham and to an effort to attract summer visitors to newly constructed hotels.

Lower Cape

The stretch of the Cape from the elbow at Chatham to the wrist at Long Point, Provincetown. The other towns on the lower Cape include Harwich, Orleans, Eastham, Wellfleet, and Truro.

Lumberts Pond

The family of Bernard and Thomas Lumbert, early settlers in Barnstable, owned a farm and ran a mill near this pond on the west side of Centerville. Lumbert Mill Road passes south of the pond and crosses Falmouth Road [Route 28] to Bumps River Road. Jones Pond is an earlier name, probably for Horace Jones, one of the Centerville founders in the

early 1800s. In the 1700s it was also known as Claghorns Pond, for Robert Claghorn, who owned some land nearby.

M

MacGregor Road

Possibly for Mercy MacGregor, who in the 1800s lived near the road, owned forty-three acres of woodland, and had her swamp cleared. The road is in South Mashpee, between Sage Lot and Flat Ponds.

MacMillan Wharf

For Donald B. MacMillan, honored by his birthplace Provincetown in 1948 after a lifetime of exploration in the Arctic. MacMillan first sailed north with Admiral Peary in 1908 and subsequently returned fifteen times, sometimes leading expeditions of his own. He wrote books and essays, including *Four Years in the White North* and *How Peary Reached the Pole*. The wharf is the town dock in Provincetown Harbor.

Maguires Landing

For Dr. Frank Maguire, who donated the landing on the Atlantic to the town of Wellfleet in 1947. It is now a public beach, at the end of LeCount Hollow.

Manomet River [ˈmænəmɛt]

Once a tributary of the Herring River in Bourne, the Manomet became a part of the Cape Cod Canal. It emptied into Buzzards Bay and in the 1600s provided a harbor at its mouth for Dutch and French ships that came to trade with the Pilgrims and Wampanoags. The Algonquian name for the river was *pimsepoese*, from *pemi* 'crossing' + *sipi* 'river' + *s* 'little' = "little, crossing river," suggesting that at the mouth of the river the channel cutting across the current was longer than the channel accompanying the current. During the War of 1812 American naval ships would take cover at the mouth of the Manomet beyond the reach of the British fleet. Manomet is a name of Algonquian origin, but the Pilgrims were the first to use it for the river. Later on, the townspeople reshaped Manomet into the name Monument River.

Maraspin Creek [məˈræspɪn]

For Francis Lothrop Maraspin, a landowner at the creek in the early 1900s. Earlier names were Little Creek and Huckins Creek. Thomas Huckins had a wharf on the creek in the 1600s and traded with Boston and the West Indies. In the 1800s local caulkers and carpenters called the upper reaches of the creek Shipyard Creek. The brig *Cummaquid*, launched in 1836, was, at 186 tons, the largest built in the creek. Fishermen kept their craft moored at the foot of Rendezvous Lane on the creek from 1850 on, close to where the Barnstable Harbor Marina now is. The Audubon Society manages some of the wetlands as a sanctuary for wildlife.

Mara Vista [ˈmærəˌvɪstə]

In 1906 the Falmouth Land Company began constructing houses for this locality between Great and Little ponds and coined its Latin name as a translation of "sea view, " but soon went bankrupt. In the 1800s the land at Mara Vista was known as Lawrence Neck, for Shubael Lawrence, a representative on the General Court and a benefactor of a private academy in Falmouth Village. Lawrence High School, which succeeded the academy in 1870, commemorated his name for a hundred years, but it is now called Falmouth High School.

Marconi Beach

For Guglielmo Marconi, who established a transatlantic wireless station near the beach in Wellfleet in 1903 and had an exchange of greetings sent between King Edward VII and President Theodore Roosevelt. The station stood on the high ground above the beach until the force of erosion from the Atlantic caused it to disappear after 1930. Marconi Beach is at Wireless Road, off Route 6, and is part of the Cape Cod National Seashore.

Mares Pond

It is said that the pond takes its name from a horse that drowned in it. At the intersection of Locustfield and Brick Kiln roads in Falmouth, this pond of twenty-nine acres has a dock for freshwater sailors.

Marstons Mill River

For Benjamin Marston, a miller of the 1700s. Marston's mill cleaned, carded, and dressed cloth. In the 1600s the stream was called either Herring or Goodspeeds River. Roger Goodspeed owned large tracts of land on the river in the 1650s. The head of the river lies in cranberry bogs near Middle Pond; its mouth is at Princes Cove near Cotuit in the town of Barnstable.

Marstons Mills

For Benjamin Marston, who came to Barnstable in 1716 from Salem. He ran a woolen mill, first built by Thomas Macy in 1653. It is said that Macy's mill, used for treating or fulling cloth, was the first of its kind on the Cape [quite possibly the first in America]. The mill remained productive until the 1880s and then collapsed during a gale in 1930. The Indians called the area of the village *mistick* = *mis* 'big' + *tuck* 'river' = "big river." The village has had three subdivisions. Marstons Mills is the principal subdivision on Little River, north of Princes Cove. Newtown, near the cranberry bogs of Long and Muddy ponds, is another. Pondsville was, in the early 1900s, a small neighborhood north of Hamblin Pond.

Mary Dunn Pond and Road

For Mary Dunn, a black woman who before 1850 lived near the pond on the east side of Barnstable. It is said that Mary won her freedom by hiding herself aboard a southern coaster about to sail to Barnstable and by gaining support from the ship's captain, George Lovell of Osterville, an abolitionist. In Barnstable Mary was known for her "yarb beer" [an herb tea] and for her kindness to the dispirited. Mary Dunn Road, originally an Indian trail, runs from the pond to Barnstable Harbor. The pond was earlier known as Half Way Pond, possibly because it is about half way from Hyannis to the village of Barnstable.

In the 1700s another Barnstable woman lived by the pond — Elizabeth Blatchford [nicknamed Liza Tower Hill]. It is said that Elizabeth was a witch, and that she would do the Devil's dance and set out glowing lights in the forest. A Mister Wood of West Barnstable once complained that Liza had bridled and saddled him and had ridden him to Plum Pudding Pond in Plymouth. When Elizabeth died in 1790, stories of her and the pond persisted. Dr. Richard Bourne reported in 1810 that on his way home from a Christmas party in Hyannis he began to sing "Old King Cole" to keep up his spirits and to keep his mind off the bone-chilling cold. When he reached Half Way Pond he was sure he saw a red light aglow on a rotten stump. He thought it was a camp fire where he could warm his feet. So he slipped out of the saddle, led his mare to the light, and set his boots on the stump. After a while, when the doctor had warmed up, he mounted his horse again, but forgot his boots. All night long the doctor kept circling the pond, unable to find his way. Finally at sunup on the road, he met some townsmen and said, "Gentlemen, can you tell whether I am in this town or the next?" Elizabeth's nickname — Liza Tower Hill — is for the London district where her husband's family, the Blatchfords, had once lived.

Mashnee Island [ˈmæšni]

The island is at the head of a causeway [built in the 1930s] that hooks down past Hog Island into Buzzards Bay from Gray Gables Village in Bourne. In early years farmers tried grazing sheep on the island, but soon gave up because of the ticks that carried disease. Mashnee Island also had saltworks until the hurricane of 1815 destroyed them. In the late 1800s townspeople had fishing parties, clambakes, and picnics on the island. It is now a residential community.

Mashpee   ['mæšpi]

This town's Indian name is from *massa* 'great, big' + *pe* 'water' = "great water." Some say that Mashpee and Wakeby ponds in the north end of the town are the most beautiful on the Cape. Incorporated at last in 1870, Mashpee had for many years sought to become a town. The first efforts to establish a separate community began in the late 1600s, when Richard Bourne succeeded in having 10,500 acres reserved for the Indians of the Cape. In 1762 Reuben Gognehew travelled to the Court of St. James and induced King George III to make Mashpee a district in the province of Massachusetts. Although more than seventy Indians lost their lives in support of the Revolution, the General Court rescinded the rights of the district in 1788. In 1834 Mashpee once again became a district and thirty-six years later a town. In the 1970s the Indians of the town sued unsuccessfully in federal court for control of Mashpee's undeveloped lands.

Mashpee Pond

From *massa* 'great, big' + *pe* 'water' = "great water." Early settlers did not distinguish Mashpee from Wakeby Pond, but called both Great Pond. Together Mashpee and Wakeby ponds contain 770 acres. On the south shore of Mashpee Pond is Attaquin Park, a bathing beach named for an old local family.

Maushop Village   ['mɔ,šap]

A community of the twentieth century, the village fronts Nantucket Sound between Rock Landing and Succonessett Point in Mashpee. According to tradition Maushop was a protective giant of the Wampanoag tribe. He lived on the south shore, loved children, and inadvertently brought the first fogs to Cape Cod. In his role as guardian Maushop protected Indian youngsters from a predatory eagle, that from time to time would snatch a child and carry it up over the ocean. Once, when the eagle had swooped off with a boy gripped in its talons, Maushop heard an outcry and set out in pursuit. The giant ran through the waters of the ocean and came upon an island unknown to the Indians, yet strewn with the bones of many children [it was Nantucket]. Saddened and helpless, Maushop pulled some weeds and poke, stuffed his pipe, and sent billows of smoke drifting northwards. The smoke hid the sun and rolled in over the Cape. It was the first foggy day. Ever since, Indians say in foggy weather that Maushop is smoking again. But in other accounts of Maushop, or Michabo [as he is more accurately known], the Algonquians described him not as a giant, but as a god of nature, a white rabbit. Herman Melville tells a version of this tale in *Moby Dick*.

Mayflower Beach

For the Mayflower Beach Condominiums, an investment that failed because of a lack of funds. The town of Dennis acquired this bayside beach by eminent domain in 1977.

Mayo Beach

For the Mayo family of Wellfleet and their founder, the Reverend John Mayo, who arrived in 1646. The beach is on the northern shore of Wellfleet Harbor, where there was once a lighthouse.

Meeting House Pond

For a meetinghouse of Orleans, opened in 1718. The pond is an arm of Little Pleasant Bay and has one of the smaller saltwater beaches in town as well as a dock. It is near Barley Neck Road. In the early 1800s it was known as Zebs Pond. At the west end of the pond is Lucys Point, for Lucy Snow, who would row across each morning with her cats to fetch her mail; Lucy died in 1920, in her late seventies.

Megansett [mə'gæn,sɛt]

This Indian name for a locality is possibly related to Nipmuck *mayanexit*, from *mayano* 'there is a path or road' or from *miyana* 'he gathers together.' The Indians were at Megansett on Buzzards Bay when the Quakers arrived from Sandwich in the late 1600s. Summer people found this Falmouth locality in the 1880s.

Menauhant [mɛ'nɔnt]

This Algonquian name for a locality in the east end of Falmouth is possibly from *munnuhan-auke* "island place" or "place on the island." Today the locality is on a neck just east of Washburn Island. In 1870 it was a camp meeting site for Universalists in search of a place "away from the mundane world." Four years later the Menauhant Land and Wharf Company built some summer houses and then went bankrupt. After the Menauhant Hotel opened in 1900 the community began to thrive.

Merrick Island

For the Merricks of Eastham, settlers of the 1600s. The island lies just east of Bound Brook Island, Wellfleet.

Millers Pond

Probably for John Miller, minister at Yarmouth in 1647, and for his descendants. It is a kettle hole, formed by a glacier, near Strawberry Lane in Yarmouth Port.

Mill Pond

About half the towns on Cape Cod have a mill pond. The Mill Pond in Chatham is a saltwater branch of Mitchell River and once had a tide mill for grinding corn on its north shore. In early days it was also known as Toms Cove and Naxtouweest. Not far away at Chase Park and Bowling Green is the Old Grist Mill, built by Colonel Benjamin Godfrey in the late 1700s. Another mill pond [sometimes called Halletts Mill Pond] straddles Yarmouth and Barnstable. The Upper and Lower Mill Ponds of Brewster are sources of Stony Brook. Most mill ponds are small [two to twenty-four acres]. The only one now running a mill is in West Brewster.

Millennium Grove

A revivalist campground in Eastham for Methodists. In 1828 the church bought the grove [ten acres of woods], held yearly meetings until the Civil War, and then moved to Yarmouth when the railroad arrived. Thoreau says in *Cape Cod* that "sometimes one hundred and fifty ministers [!], and five thousand hearers, assembled" at the Grove. Many were women whose husbands and sons were away at sea or had drowned. Near the grove is Campground Landing, once associated with the Methodist revivals, but now a public beach on Cape Cod Bay.

Mitchell River

For Lieutenant William Mitchell, a Pilgrim and a member of the militia, who had a farm of forty acres in the late 1600s on the north shore of the river. Mitchell River was also known as Salt Water River and Mill Pond River. It has a short channel and runs south of Chatham Village between Mill Pond and Stage Harbor.

Money Hole

It is said that the hole was not far from Popponesset Beach on Nantucket Sound in Mashpee. One night in the distant past some Mashpee Indians began to dig near the pine tree at the center of the hole, but suddenly fled at the flash of a strange light. The Indians never returned to their digging, nor did they pass by the hole at night. Though no one knows what they were digging up, some say that it was gold and therefore called the place Money Hole.

Monomoy Island and Point

['manɔˌmɔɪ] or [ˌmaneˈmɔɪ]

Possibly related to Algonquian *munumuhkemoo* "there is a rush-

ing [of mighty water]." The local name is Sandy Point. Early explorers and mapmakers gave the point several names. In 1606 Samuel de Champlain sailed around the point and called it Cape Batturier, "the cape where rocks and shoals lie close to the surface." In 1614 Admiral Adrian Block named the point Vlacke Hoecke, Dutch for "flat hook or cape." But in 1640 another Dutchman, the cartographer of the *Atlas Novus*, misread Champlain's map of Cape Cod and misnamed the point Cape Malabar "bad bar." Malle Barre on Champlain's map actually identifies a dangerous inlet into Nauset Harbor at Eastham. From 1835 until the 1860s fishermen lived in Whitewash Village [so called for the color of the shacks] near the point, where they dried cod and haddock on stages. Earlier in the century the federal government had constructed Monomoy Light Station. About the same time the Massachusetts Humane Society erected a shelter on the point for shipwrecked sailors. The east shore of the island, facing the Atlantic, is known as Monomoy Beach. In the past it was called Monomoit Great Beach. Monomoy Island is now a National Wildlife Refuge and part of the Cape Cod National Seashore.

Monument Beach

Monument is a word reshaped from the Algonquian *manomet*. The village of Monument Beach at Phinneys Harbor, Bourne, became a summer resort after the New York, New Haven and Hartford opened a depot in 1881.

Monument Hill

For the monument commemorating the site where the Pilgrims spent their first night on shore, November 11, 1620 OS. The earliest name of the hill was Mount

Aldworth, so called by Martin Pring in 1603 to honor Robert Aldworth, a benefactor and active supporter of his voyage to Massachusetts Bay. The hill has had other names because of the structures built on it. Before the 1800s it had the name High Pole Hill because of a large windmill, identified by sailors at sea who used it as a landmark of Provincetown Harbor. In the mid-1800s it became Town Hill, because of the town hall erected on it in 1853 [the building burned down in 1877]. Methodists in 1795 built a church at the summit, but not before they had overcome a mob of townsmen who dragged the beams and timbers over the hill and set afire an effigy of the minister, Jesse Lee. The Methodists were not to be daunted, for they brought in fresh lumber and, under guard, built their church.

Monument Neck Road

The road turns westward from the village of Bourne toward the mouth of Back River. It runs past the Aptucxet Trading Post at the end of the village and farther west cuts across the tracks leading to the Buzzards Bay Railroad Bridge. In the early days of the road Methodists held yearly camp meetings nearby, until they found themselves too crowded because of "easy access" and so moved to Martha's Vineyard. Before the railroad came, the first of the summer visitors travelled the road to Monument Neck to spend the holidays bathing and fishing.

Moon Pond

Earlier called Moonpoon or Moon-poon Pond, this is bottom land near High Head and Eastern Harbor, Truro. During the 1700s Moon Pond was also known as Anthonys Bottom.

Moonakiss River ['munəkɪs]

This is a small arm of Waquoit Bay west of Hamblin Road in Mashpee. Moonakiss is probably related to *munnohquohteau* "he manures or enriches the earth," an expression used by Indians for fertilizing a field with menhaden.

Morris Island

For Morris Farris, who owned a tavern below Inward Point on Monomoy Island in the early 1700s. The Indian name for the island was Quitnesset, from *ahquedne* 'island' + *s* 'little' + *ut* 'at' = "at the little island." In the 1700s a spur of sand cut across a channel north of the island and connected it permanently to Toms Neck. On Morris Island there is a large stretch of wetlands in the northwest corner. From those wetlands rises Stage Island, not far from Stage Harbor. The wetlands also have a rare stand of white cedar. The federal government built a lifesaving station on Morris Island in 1880, one of the first on the lower Cape. Morris Island, Toms Neck, and Monomoy all form the southeast corner of Chatham, bordering on the Atlantic.

Morse Pond

For Robert M. Morse, a nineteenth-century lawyer and member of the Massachusetts General Court. Morse had a summer house near the pond in Falmouth Village. Before he bought the land the pond was known as Davis Pond for an old Falmouth family.

Mount Ararat

So called by the seamen of Provincetown in honor of the first sailor of the world, Noah, who moored at Mount Ararat after the flood subsided. Mount Ararat is a large dune near Route 6 not far from Truro.

Mount Gilboa [gɪl'boə]

A large dune near Route 6 on the Provincetown-Truro line, so called because it suggested to the townspeople the Biblical mountain overlooking the Mediterranean. The storms and heavy seas at Provincetown brought to mind David's words in Samuel: "Ye mountains of Gilboa, let there be no dew or rain upon you nor upsurging of the deep."

Muddy Creek

Also Muddy Cove and Muddy Cove River. In 1825 the towns of Harwich and Chatham built a bridge at the "wading place" on the stream high enough for scows laden with salt marsh hay to pass under. Wading Place Bridge, according to some readers of Bradford's *Plimoth Plantation*, is just west of Squanto's grave. A friend to the Pilgrims, Squanto traveled with them by boat to Pleasant Bay and Monamesset River [the old name of Muddy Creek], took suddenly ill, and died.

Muddy Hole

Early villagers of Bournedale said that the hole was bottomless. They tried draining it, but only the western half was firm enough for a cranberry bog. In 1909 Clarence Eldridge poured wagons full of sand into the north end of the hole to build a bog, but had to quit after two years. When the Army Corps of Engineers began to build the Bourne Bridge, they set out to construct a road over the hole. After four years of draining and settling, road building and road repair, they completed the work. The Algonquian name for hole was *wapoompunksett*, probably related to Mohican *wâb* = 'white' + *ompsk* 'rock' + *ut* 'at' = "at the white rock" or else to *wepe* 'narrow passage' + *ompsk* 'rock' + *ut* 'at' =

"at the narrow passage of rocks." The dredgers of the Cape Cod Canal dug up many large rocks near the Bourne Bridge.

The Mudhole

For the especially muddy bottom of the basin near Hinckley Pond and Barnstable Harbor. The muddy sediment is due to the run-off from springs on the uplands near the marshes.

Mystic Pond

Mystic is an adaptation of the Algonquian *mistuck*, from *mis* 'big' + *tuck* 'river' = "big river." The pond is a kettle hole, formed from a retreating glacier. It is in Marstons Mills, at the west end of Barnstable. Thomas Fullers Point on the pond is not far from Cape Cod Airport. In the 1890s the point was the property of William Richardson, an English actor, who built a cabin by the shore and called his land a "spot of green."

N

Namequoit River [ˈnæmeˌkwɔɪt]

Namequoit is probably from *nam'e-auke* 'fishing place' + *ut* 'at' = "at the fishing place." The stream runs between Little Pleasant Bay, near Namequoit Point, and Areys Pond in South Orleans.

Namskaket [ˌnæmˈskækɪt]

Probably from Algonquian *na-mohs* 'little fish' + *auk* 'land or place' + *ut* 'at' = "at the place of little fish." This is the Indian name for a locality bordering Brewster and Orleans, a fishing ground for the Nauset tribe, and in the 1700s a center for shipping grain to Boston. Nowadays it is a subdivision of Orleans. Namskaket Creek flows into Cape Cod Bay between Brewster and Rock Harbor.

Nauset [ˈnɔsɪt]

Probably from Algonquian *nashaue* 'the place between' + *ut* 'at' = "at the place between." The lands of Nauset were near the elbow of the Cape, from Dennis eastward to the Atlantic. The Indians had a large settlement, thrived on fish and maize, and seemed to the Pilgrims a nation of their own, "the kingdom of Nauset." Before long, however, the English began to settle in Nauset and soon after incorporated themselves as the town of Eastham. The name Nauset still persists in Nauset Harbor, Nauset Heights [northern Orleans], Nauset Marsh and Nauset Beach [North Eastham to Chatham].

Nauset Beach

The Indians and their chief Aspinet dwelt along the beach from Eastham southward to Chatham on the Backside of the Cape. According to maps and reports, the beach has undergone several transformations during the past two hundred years, mostly from the impact of gales. In 1891 the south end of the beach joined the shores of Monomoy; earlier in the century the ocean surged over the beach at two or three points. One large breach resulted opposite Chatham Light in 1871 from the force of a storm; farther north near Tern Island the ocean opened a gap in the beach about a mile wide, forming two points facing each other, South Point and Nauset Beach Point. Currently, most of the beach stretches directly from Orleans toward the south end of Morris Island in Chatham, not far from where the brig *Owhyhee* foundered in 1826. The wreck of the *Sparrowhawk* in 1626 [now restored and on display at Pilgrim Hall, Plymouth, Massachusetts] is the earliest recorded loss of a ship on Nauset Beach. After the schooner *Calvin B. Orcutt* went aground, all hands lost, in 1897 the federal government constructed the Old Harbor Life Saving Station at the beach, now in Provincetown at the Seashore Park.

The Neck

The Neck bulges westward for two miles from Chatham Village. On three of its sides it has saltwater ponds [Oyster Pond, Mill Pond], saltwater rivers [Oyster Pond River, Mitchell River], and Stage Harbor on the south. Early settlers called it Great Neck for its sheer size; fishermen called it Stage Neck because of the many stages or platforms there for drying and salting cod and haddock. The Indian name is Saquanset, from *saquan* 'outlet' + *s* 'little' + *ut* 'at' = "at the little outlet" — a name for the end of the mouth of a river or pond rather than for the neck itself. The west end of the Neck is known as Skunks Neck; Stetson Cove on the north end is a part of Oyster Pond.

New Beach

So called because in the late 1930s the Commonwealth built a beach house on it and opened it to public bathing. This beach in Provincetown Harbor was once known as Hell Town in the days when fishermen who lived there were also beachcombers or "mooncussers." In the dark of night they would set out lights to mislead ships, throwing them off course, making them founder and expose their cargoes to the oncoming beachcombers.

New Boston

For a locality settled by Bostonians in northwestern Dennis, west of Route 6A. The New Boston River is close by.

Newcomb Hollow and Newcomb Hollow Beach

For the Newcombs of Wellfleet. During his walk up the lower Cape Thoreau stayed with John Newcomb, an oysterman. The hollow and beach are northeast of Wellfleet Village, and part of the Great Beach facing the Atlantic.

Newtown   ['nu,taʊn]

This neighborhood in Marstons Mills had its beginnings in the 1800s. It was at first a school district and then at the turn of the twentieth century became a community of its own.

Nickerson Neck

For the Nickerson family of Chatham. The neck hooks to the north of Crows Pond and ends at Eastward Point in Pleasant Bay. A spit of land, stretching into the bay and often flooded by high tides, connects Eastward Point to Fox Hill, a small island. During the 1800s the neck had shipyards that launched such schooners as the sixty-five-ton *Cape Cod*. Eastward Point once had saltworks.

Nickerson State Forest Park

For Roland G. Nickerson, a railroad executive whose widow deeded 1750 acres to the Commonwealth in 1934. Her bequest was a memorial to her husband and to her son, killed in World War I. The park includes Cliff, Little Cliff, and Grassy Nook Ponds and has clearings for overnight camping. Located in northeastern Brewster, it was the first Massachusetts park to fall under the supervision of the State Conservation Commission.

No Bottom Pond

It is said that *no bottom* is a name used for ponds that have an underground outlet to another waterway. No Bottom Pond on the Cape is in South Brewster, off Long Pond Road.

Nobska Point and Pond
['napskə]

The beach at the point is strewn with granite and other rocks. The form *nobska* is possibly related to Abnaki *panaooambskok* "at the fall of the rock." The point is on Vineyard Sound, east of Woods Hole. The pond, just west of the point, was also known as Dutchmans Pond in the 1600s, maybe because some sailors camped beside it. Nobska Point had a smallpox hospital in 1797, and a lighthouse in 1829 [rebuilt in 1876]. The Nobska horn warns sailors at sea in foggy weather, as far as twelve miles out.

Nobscusset   [,nab'skəsɪt]

Possibly related to Algonquian *wanashqu* 'at the end of' + *ompsk* 'rock' + *ut* 'at' = "at the end of the rock." Nobscusset is in northern Dennis between Hockanom and Brewster, and was the site of an Indian village. Nobscussset Point and Harbor — also called the Bite [a variant of bight] — are at the foot of Corporation Road in Dennis. Some large rocks are scattered along the shore.

North Bay

So called because it is north of Osterville and lies on the north side of Osterville Grand Island. It has several outlets: it runs into Cotuit Bay past Point Isabella, into West Bay past Little Island, and into Princes Cove past Baxters Neck. Along the shores near Osterville are Pine and St. Marys islands, both marshy, and Isham and Dam Pond, actually two salt-water arms of North Bay. During the second World War the Army trained soldiers at Camp Can-Do-It, at the head of North Bay, to run landing craft and to prepare for the invasion of the Pacific islands and Normandy. In the early days of Barnstable North Bay was known as Great Bay.

North Harwich

A village near the Brewster line. It was once known as Deerfield because of the plentiful deer in nearby woodlands.

Nye Neck

The brothers Ebenezer and Benjamin Nye, together with neighbors of North Falmouth, bought the neck from the town of Sandwich in 1704. The neck has also been known as Downers Point, for a local family who came to Falmouth in the 1800s. It forms the north shore of Wild Harbor.

Nye Pond

For the Nye family of Sandwich who from the 1600s on had carding and grist mills on the pond. In 1914 Helen Nye deeded her house, built in 1685, to the Commonwealth. Two years earlier the

Commonwealth had also acquired the Sandwich Trout Company, a hatchery on a brook running north from the pond. The State Hatchery produces about two hundred thousand fish a year, most of them brook trout, but also brown and rainbow fingerlings. The pond is in the east end of Sandwich near the Mid-Cape Highway.

O

Ockway Bay   [ˈakˌwe]

Possibly from Algonquian *ogguse* 'little, small.' The bay is an arm of Popponesset Bay, along the coast of Mashpee.

Old Drink Hole

Both *drink* and *hole* mean "a body of water — a bay, an inlet, a creek." The Old Drink Hole was near Gray Gables, Bourne.

Old Rose and Crown

A shoal southeast of Monomoy Point, Chatham, probably named by sailors for Rose and Crown Streets in Soho, London, an intersection described in 1720 as an "indifferent part of town." The shoal first appears on the maps of the Cape Cod coastline in 1717.

Old Run Swamp

This is a large swamp behind the Back River [also known as a brook or run] in the village of Bourne. In the 1850s Seth S. Maxim turned a part of the swamp into a cranberry bog. Seth's wife, Aunt Joan, was at first skeptical and told him, "Go to it, Seth, but if you ever make a dollar on your pesky cranberries, I'll spend every cent of it."

Old Ship Harbor

The harbor takes its name from a nearby dune on Nauset Beach, long known as Old Ship, that for years concealed the wreck of the *Sparrowhawk*, cast ashore in 1626 while en route to Virginia with English passengers. Storms in 1782 and 1863 uncovered the ship. The *Sparrowhawk* has since been restored and is on display at Pilgrim Hall in Plymouth. The harbor on Nauset Beach is on the east side of Pleasant Bay in Orleans.

Old Silver Beach

The summer colony at this beach is more recent than the one at Silver Beach. Soon after the town of Falmouth opened Old Silver Beach for bathing in the 1920s, the University Players — Margaret Sullivan, James Stewart, Henry Fonda — performed there for several years. In the early 1930s, before the theatre burned down, it had become a private gambling club. Old Silver Beach is on Buzzards Bay near Curley Boulevard.

Old Stone Dock

First built in 1807, the dock has two L-shaped sections where newly arrived ships once sold sperm oil and whalebone. Nowadays the center of the dock is known as the *kiddie puddle*, a wading pool for children at Surf Drive Beach near Falmouth Village.

Old Wharf Point

So called for a wharf built near the point in 1826 on Wellfleet Harbor between Indian Neck and Lieutenant Island. The wharf, since removed, served the schooners of Wellfleet that for many years were engaged in hauling mackerel. In 1876 the town had seventy-five schooners in the trade.

Opening Pond

The pond is near Forestdale and the Pocasset-Sandwich Roads in Bourne. Surrounded by thickets, it probably appeared as a clearing to the settlers who first named it.

Orleans

Three traditions account for the name of this town, incorporated in 1797. One is that the town's name honors the French city of Orleans. For it was to Orleans that Isaac Snow, a local resident taken prisoner by the British during the American Revolution, escaped and there found Lafayette who helped him return home. According to another view, Orleans honors Philippe, Duc d'Orleans, who during the French Revolution renounced his title and assumed the surname Égalité. In 1793 he was arrested during the Reign of Terror and lost his life on the guillotine. Others trace the town's name to the son of Phillipe, who visited New England in the 1790s, lived in Philadelphia, and returned to France, eventually becoming the citizen king, Louis Phillipe.

Osborn Pond

For Colonel John F. Osborne, a member of the 101st Engineers, Massachusetts National Guard, until his death in 1932. The pond is on the grounds of Otis Air Force Base, Bourne.

Osterville

This village is named for Oyster Island, just across North Bay, Barnstable. The early names were Oyster Island Village and Oysterville [a name still preferred by some], but Osterville was apparently the suggestion of school children. Benjamin F. Hallet, a local schoolmaster in the 1800s and also a district attorney in Franklin Pierce's administration, says that in February 1815 the school children met at an assembly to celebrate the end to the War of 1812 and to give their support for the name Osterville. During the 1700s the village was a settlement for the Lovell family and so was known as the Lovell neighborhood. The Algonquian name was Cotocheset, either from *quttuckshunksett* "at the turning place" or from *quttukqsheau* "it makes an angle of a boundary line." When the sachem Paupmumuck transferred to the town of Barnstable in 1648 all the lands from Mashpee to what is now Centerville, he reserved for himself and the members of his tribe a thirty-acre tract which he called Cotocheset and is now Osterville.

Osterville Grand Island

This is the official name that appears on maps. Local residents call the island Oyster Harbors, originally the name for a neighborhood of summer houses, with a hotel and country club built in 1925. Grand Island is another name in use since the later 1800s and still popular. The islands earliest name, Oyster Island, appeared on maps until 1900. The largest island on Cape Cod (300 acres), it is surrounded by the Sepuit River and by West, North, and Cotuit bays. Noisy Point, Tims Point, and Tims Cove are opposite Cotuit Bay, on the island's western shore. Little Island, a large marsh at the eastern end, divides North and West bays. It is said that Hannah Screecham wandered one day from her house in Osterville, past Little Island, to Noisy Point at the west end of Oyster Island. There she saw Captain Kidd and his men burying a chest filled with treasure. The pirates seized and slew her and tossed her body onto the chest. Ever since, Hannah's spirit has kept watch over the treasure, screeching from time to time through the winds blowing over Noisy Point. During the 1700s a dispute erupted between Indians who farmed land on the island and the proprietors of Barnstable. After several court trials the Indians won their claim, but had to sell their rights to their opponents to pay for lawyers' fees and the costs of litigation. In a petition to the General Court requesting permission to sell, the Indians said that they "are not advantaged one farthing for the Profitts of s[ai]d Island, and still remain in debt under difficult circumstances."

Otis Air Force Base

For Lieutenant Frank Jesse Otis, Jr., a flight surgeon and member of the Massachusetts National Guard, who died in 1937 in an airplane crash. The first runway opened to air traffic in 1942. The base is situated mostly in Sandwich and Bourne, less so in Falmouth and Mashpee.

Oyster Pond

Falmouth has two Oyster ponds, Chatham one. In Chatham the pond is a saltwater branch of Oyster Pond River, between Chatham Village and West Chatham, although geologists say that it was once an enclosed kettle hole. At low tide a bed of peat is visible, the remains from a prehistoric stand of hard maple and pine. Oyster Pond Beach, on the east shore, is for town bathers. In Falmouth the ponds are north of the Great Sippewisset Swamp and near the village of Quisset, a Quaker settlement in the later 1600s. None of these ponds has oysters.

P

Paine Hollow

For the Paines of Eastham and Wellfleet, descendants of John and Thomas Paine, Jr., who were "admitted" to the settlement in the late 1600s. It is said that at one time every family who lived in the hollow, between Paine Hollow Road and Cannon Hill, in South Wellfleet, was named Paine.

Paines Creek and Paines Creek Beach

For the burgeoning Paines of Wellfleet and Eastham, who spread westward toward the creek, actually the lower reaches of Stony Brook in West Brewster. The beach, open for public bathing, is on Cape Cod Bay, at the end of Paine Creek Road.

Palmer Pond

Probably for Samuel Palmer, the minister in 1730 of Falmouth's First Congregational Church. The pond is west of Spinnaker Avenue in Falmouth Village.

Pamet Harbor   ['pæmɪt]

A boat basin at the mouth of the Pamet River on Cape Cod Bay in Truro. After a century of unsuccessful effort the town finally had the harbor opened to boats in the 1920s by digging a new channel for the Pamet River, cutting into the nearby Jim Browns Creek, and filling in acres of marshland.

Pamet River

So called for a local tribe of Algonquians who sold the lands of Truro to proprietors in Eastham at the end of the seventeenth century. The name Pamet may come from *pummoh* 'the sea' + *ut* 'at' = "at the sea." The river extends almost from coast to coast, from Cape Cod Bay to the Atlantic. The construction of Wilder Dike at the midpoint of the river turned its eastern half into freshwater. The mouth of the river, once near Corn Hill, is now farther south and opens into a large, safe harbor just off Cape Cod Bay.

Pamet River Station

Established in 1872 by the United States Revenue Marine Service, the station stood overlooking the Atlantic not far from Ballston Beach, east of the Head of Pamet.

The Coast Guard abandoned the station in 1933 because of danger from encroaching tides.

Paradise Hollow

In South Truro and North Wellfleet. So called for its wild honeysuckle, old lilac bushes, tassel grass and pampas grass.

Parker Pond

For Captain James Parker, who had his house built at the pond at the turn of the nineteenth century. Some years later it was also known as Aunt Tempys Pond, for Temperance Crocker Parker, James's daughter-in-law. The pond is in Osterville.

Parkers River

Possibly for Benjamin Parker of Yarmouth, who received a share of the common lands in 1712. The river is not very long, and runs from Seine Pond to Nantucket Sound. Parkers Neck runs eastward from this river to the shores of Bass River. Parkers River Beach lies near South Shore Road in South Yarmouth.

Pasnecoy Lane [ˈpæsnə,kɔɪ]

This street in Davisville, Falmouth, preserves an old Indian name of the 1600s, Pasoutacoy, a neck of land just outside the village between two tidal bodies, Israel Cove and Bournes Pond. Pasoutacoy seems related to Abnaki *piscataqua*, from *peské* 'divided' + *tegooé* 'tidal river' = "divided tidal river."

Pattys Pond

Possibly for Patience Marston Bacon, whose husband Edward was sympathetic to the King at the outset of the Revolution. Patience died in 1764 at the age of forty. The pond is in Marstons Mills, east of the Santuit Newton Road.

Patuissett [ˌpæču'wɪsɪt]

A locality on a peninsula jutting out toward Bassett Island in Red Brook Harbor, Bourne. Patuissett is possibly related to Mohican *pootôae* 'jutting' + [*ompsk* 'rock'] + *s* 'little' + *ut* 'at' = "at the little jutting [rock?]."

Paw Wah Pond [ˈpɔ,wɔ]

Actually an inlet of Pleasant Bay, off Portanimicut Road in Orleans. Pompo the powwow [Paw Wah is an irregular spelling of the Algonquian word for conjurer] had much land in early Orleans. He apparently drowned in the pond; thereafter, fishermen would drop a quid of tobacco into the waters as an offering to him, and say, "Paw Waw, I give you tobac'. You give me some fish."

Peaked Cliff [pɪkɪt]

The cliff is more than 170 feet high and overlooks Cape Cod Bay, just south of the Plymouth line. In 1718 the town of Sandwich voted to build a fence six feet high and several miles long from Peaked Cliff to Buttermilk Bay to keep wolves off the Cape. But the vote came to nothing, after a town meeting member suggested that the fence would probably keep wolves in, not out.

Peaked Hill Bars [pikəd]

In the Atlantic off North Truro, the bars have been so treacherous for ships in heavy weather that they are known as "the graveyard of Cape Cod." The British frigate *Somerset*, engaged in the Battle of Bunker Hill, struck the bars three years later in 1778. Many crewmen drowned, but hundreds of soldiers survived and were made to march to Barnstable and to Boston, prisoners of the Truro militia. About a hundred years later the Italian bark *Monte Tabor* also went aground on the bars. So great was their distress that the Captain and a seaman slit their throats and the steward put a bullet through his head.

Peaked Hills   [pikəd]

The hills are a range of dunes, forty or more feet high, just off the Backside of the Cape, from Provincetown to High Head in North Truro.

Penquin Hole and Penquin Hole River   ['peŋkwin]

Penquin is possibly from *pohki* "it is clear, transparent" and describes a spring near the river where Indians once camped. Apparently white settlers named the hole and river north of Bennets Neck, Bourne, for the Indian spring.

Penzance   ['pen,zænts]

For Penzance Point in Cornwall — the Lands End of England. It means "saint's head" in Cornish. Another common name for the peninsula is Long Point. During the mid-1800s the Pacific Guano Company, which had its plant on the peninsula, imported guano from Howland Island, mixed it with menhaden, and produced fertilizer for farmers and a great stench for the nearby village of Woods Hole. In the twentieth century Penzance became a community of large estates. The peninsula borders Vineyard Sound and Buzzards Bay and was an island in prehistoric times.

Perch Pond

Beside this pond, it is said, King Philip and his Wampanoag braves held councils of war against the whites during the 1670s. The pond is a narrow inlet at the northwest corner of Great Pond, Falmouth.

Phinneys Bay   ['finiz]

Probably for Lot Phinney, a member of the Centerville School Committee in the 1800s. The bay is almost entirely surrounded by land, except for a small outlet into East Bay, off Barnstable.

Phinneys Harbor

For the Phinneys, who lived at the harbor at Buzzards Bay and Bourne from the 1700s. Perez H. Phinney, the village postmaster of Monument Beach, may have given the harbor its name. Until the 1930s and the dredging of the Cleveland Ledge and the Hog Island channels, ships would approach the east end of Cape Cod Canal through Phinneys Harbor.

Phinneys Lane

For Solomon Phinney, a tavern keeper at the south end of this road in Centerville. Phinney's Tavern welcomed militia men during the War of 1812, who would "file in and get a little of the 'oh, be joyful.' " The road runs from Centerville to the village of Barnstable.

The Pilgrim Heights Area

Extending in Truro from the Head of the Meadow Beach to Pilgrim Lake, the Pilgrim Heights Area of the Cape Cod National Seashore includes the sometimes active First or Pilgrim Spring [where the Pilgrims in 1620 found fresh water], Smalls Swamp, and the dunes about Pilgrim Lake, once a forested stretch of land.

Pilgrim Lake

In 1620, when this lake was a brackish harbor on Cape Cod Bay, the Pilgrims skirted its shores on their way to Corn Hill. More than two hundred years later, the Commonwealth built a roadway across the mouth of the harbor — it was called East Harbor — from Beach Point in North Truro to the Provincetown line. The lake is now freshwater and has a store of pickerel, perch and black bass.

Pilgrim Spring

Now a part of the Cape Cod National Seashore, the spring was the first that the Pilgrims found. Shebnah Rich has a verse in his history, *Truro-Cape Cod*, to honor the discovery of fresh water:

And coolly they sat on the
    Indian mound,
In that moment of history's dawn
    — the brink
Of a future we worshipped as
    past! hallowed ground,
And of the pure fluid they took
    their first drink.

Pin Oak Way

In the mid-1800s Robinson ["Booby"] C. Bodfish, a Falmouth speculator, planted two rows of fifty pin oaks along this street at Siders Pond. But Bodfish was unsuccessful in building summer houses near the trees and in developing Ocean Vista, a community he planned for summer people. He was more successful in helping Frederick Freeman, who wrote *The History of Cape Cod*, to raise funds for its publication. In turn, Freeman dedicated his chapter on Falmouth to Bodfish. In 1894, after Bodfish objected, the Falmouth newspaper withdrew its suggestion to rename Siders Pond for him.

Pinquickset Cove [pɪnˈkwɪksɪt]

Possibly related to Algonquian *punukquékontu* "on the bank of a river." The cove is a narrow stretch of salt water flowing between Fullers Marsh and Crocker Neck in Cotuit. The local name for the cove, Shoe String Bay, is due to its long, narrow channel.

Pitchers Way

For Joseph Pitcher, who in the 1700s lived near Fawcetts Pond, Hyannis. Pitcher's grandson Samuel concocted castoria, a patent medicine laxative. Pitchers Way goes south from West Main Street in Hyannis to Scudder Way.

Plains of Nauset

The plains were once fertile. They are a level stretch of ground that were also known as the Eastham Plateau or the Tablelands of Nauset. On the Atlantic coast, between Coast Guard Road and Nauset Light, they end abruptly atop cliffs seventy-five feet high, which have long been a landmark for mariners.

Plashes

Three Cape ponds are so identified: two called The Plashes in Dennisport, and Plashes Pond in West Yarmouth. The word *plash* has been defined as "a small collection of standing water; a puddle; a pool," but the West Yarmouth pond covers more than forty acres.

Pleasant Bay

So called since the 1700s, the bay is the largest of all on the ocean side of the lower Cape. The towns of Chatham, Orleans, Harwich, and Brewster all have frontage. It was earlier known as Monomoyick Bay.

Pleasant Lake

Not a lake, but a village in the northern part of Harwich, between Hinckleys and Long ponds. In earlier times when the village was first settled Hinckleys Pond was known as Pleasant Lake.

Pleasant Point

For a headland on Drummer Cove not far from South Wellfleet. East of the headland on Blackfish Creek is a locality of cottages, also called Pleasant Point.

Plowed Neck

The neck is surrounded, not by water, but by bogs and marshes in East Sandwich. For the settlers of the town in the 1600s a plowed neck was land firm enough for growing crops.

Pocasset and Pocasset Harbor [po'kæsɪt]

Pocasset is a common enough Algonquian name that means "the narrows open out." Several channels into Pocasset Harbor could easily fit a description of a waterway "opening out or widening." General Leonard Wood lived in the village of Pocasset before going off to medical school at Harvard. He was a physician to Grover Cleveland, a member of Theodore Roosevelt's Rough Riders in Cuba, the commander of a division in World War I, and a governor of the Philippines. The village and harbor are on Buzzards Bay, south of Bourne.

Pocasset River

So called for the Pocasset Iron Company, which like other factories had a mill at the river in the 1800s. To harness the power of the river the owners of these mills constructed dams and formed artificial ponds, now known as Mill and Shop ponds. The mouth of the river at Phinneys Harbor, Bourne, had sufficient anchorage to enable the shipping of bog iron from Martha's Vineyard and Wareham to the iron company. Barlows River was an early name of the stream, for an old family of Bourne and Sandwich.

Pochet and Little Pochet Islands ['počɪt]

Pochet is possibly from Algonquian *pâchau* 'the turning' + *ut* 'at' = "at the turning." The islands are at the east end of Little Pleasant Bay in Orleans, near the Atlantic. Little Pochet Island was once the site of Orleans Coast Guard Station. The bay turns northward from the island to Pochet Neck, the town landing.

Pocknett Neck

For the Pocknett family of Mashpee. The neck is at the north end of Great Neck on Ockway Bay.

Point Gammon

This headland at the southernmost tip of Great Island, West Yarmouth, overlooks treacherous currents in Nantucket Sound. The point had a lighthouse from 1815 until 1858, when the federal government installed a light on Bishop and Clerks. It is said that Gammon is a name taken from the game of backgammon. As the local writer Frothingham explained, "When you were gammoned you were lost, and many a ship went down off this headland."

Point Gilbert

For Bartholomew Gilbert, the co-captain of the *Concord*, who in 1602 sailed with Gosnold past this point off Chatham toward the Elizabeth Islands. The point has since been entirely eroded. Gilbert's father was Sir Humphrey Gilbert, who before he was drowned in 1583 sought to colonize Newfoundland.

Point of Rocks Beach and Road

A cluster of rocks offshore faces the beach in Brewster and gives it its name. The road leads from Route 6A to the beach.

Pollock Rip

So called for the darkly colored pollock of the North Atlantic, a fish related to the cod. The word *rip* is a term first used in the eighteenth century for turbulent waters caused by the action of currents and winds. The winds and currents of Pollock Rip forced the *Mayflower* to abandon its southerly course and to return to Cape Cod Bay. The Coast Guard dredged Pollock Rip Channel, east of Monomoy Island, in 1929 in order to provide ships ten fathoms of water. Pollock Rip Lightship began its service in the mid-1800s, but is no longer in use.

Pond Village

So called because of the pond in the village. In times past the village had a bayberry candle factory and a "freezer" for putting fish on ice. The Pilgrims camped beside the pond in 1620 and threw into it a large kettle they had taken from Corn Hill. The village is near Cape Cod Bay in North Truro.

Pond Villages

A name for several localities on the south shore of Falmouth: Mara Vista [east of Little Pond], Acapesket [east of Great Pond], Davisville [east of Green Pond], and Menauhant [east of Bournes Pond]. There is also a Pond Village in Barnstable [see Hinckley Pond].

Popple Bottom Road

Popple is a localism for the poplar tree. The road passes north of Spectacle and Lawrence ponds in the east end of Sandwich.

Popponesset Bay [ˌpapəˈnɛsɪt]

Possibly for the sachem Pop-pononett, who lived on the south shore of Mashpee in the 1600s. Or Popponesset may be related to Algonquian *popon* "winter" and *paponaumsû* "frost fish or tom cod." In the 1800s the oysters grown in the bay were known as Pell's Best, for Silas P. Pells, who had several beds. The five sons of the Indian giant Maushop, it is said, died at Popponesset Bay. Killed by the poisoned darts of their enemies, the sons lay dead among the pine trees of Popponesset Marsh. Maushop lifted their bodies and carried them to the waters of Succonesett. There he buried them at sea, and by covering them with huge mounds of sand formed a chain in Vineyard Sound, now part of the Elizabeth Islands.

Potenumacut [ˌpotəˈnəməkət]

This village of Nauset Indians [sixty-four in 1762] on Pleasant Bay near Harwich was, next to Mashpee, the largest native community on the Cape. Potenumacut is spelled in many different ways and is perhaps related to Algonquian *petuhqu'* 'round' + *ompsk* 'rock' + *ut* 'at' = "at the round rock."

Poverty Hollow

The poverty of the hollow, it is said, is from a lack of trees and vegetation. Within the hollow stands the Sacconesset Homestead, built of fieldstone and hewn oak, owned in 1678 by the Bowermans, a family of Quakers. Not far away is a place for a poor man's pipe dreams — Wishing Moon Hill. The hollow is near the Sacconesset Hills, not far from West Falmouth.

Powder Hole

Once an open harbor at the southeast corner of Monomoy Island, Powder Hole is now a salt pond. It may be named for the powder used by gunners to shoot ducks flying over the island toward Nantucket Sound. Some say that Powder Hole is from Powder Horn, a name that presumably described the shape of the harbor. Near Powder Hole are Big Station Pond, Station Pond Marsh, and Lighthouse Marsh, all close to the now burnt-out Monomoy Coast Guard Station [built in 1872] and Monomoy Light [built 1823].

Princes Cove

Probably for Prince Marston, who ran a fulling mill in the late 1700s and owned a brick house near the cove. The cove washes the west shore of Baxters Neck and the piles of Cotuit's landing.

The Province Lands Area

The northernmost part of the Cape Cod National Seashore, it includes Beech Forest, near the Great Pond in Provincetown [the forest had been set aside in 1670 by the Plymouth Colony for purposes of conservation]. This area of the National Seashore also includes Hatches Harbor, Herring Cove, and Race Point.

Provincetown

Separated from Truro and incorporated June 14, 1727, the town took its name from a provision in its charter that reserved title to all lands within it to the Province of Massachusetts. Not until 1893 did the General Court change the charter, reserving unoccupied areas [called "up back"] to the Commonwealth and granting townspeople deeds to the properties they held. Early records show that the Algonquians had two names for the Provincetown area: *meeshaum*, probably related to *mushauwomuk* 'where there is going-by-boat' [the Indian name for Boston]; and also *chequocket*, probably related to the Narragansett *chauquaquock* 'Englishman.' *Chauquaquock* in turn stems from *chohquog* 'knife'; *chequocket*, then, is "the place of the knife men." The Dutch called the area *Staten Hoek* 'place shaped like a hook.' John Smith's map of 1616 designates the area of Provincetown as Milford Haven, after the harbor in Pembrokeshire, Wales, from which Martin Pring sailed in 1603 on his voyage to Massachusetts Bay. In the 1800s many townsmen lived by whaling and fishing. In the twentieth century, P-town [the local nickname] has become a center for artists and summer theatre.

Provincetown Airport

Constructed by the Commonwealth in the 1930s. The runways now cover a part of Race Run, a sluggish saltwater creek that once reached as far as Oak Head. The airport is close to Race Point and the dike at Hatches Harbor.

Provincetown Harbor

Shaped like a half moon, the harbor opens onto Cape Cod Bay. Martin Pring weighed anchor in the harbor in 1603 and called it Whitsons Bay for John Whitson, his benefactor and the mayor of Bristol, England. The Pilgrims arrived in November 1620 and stayed long enough to explore parts of the lower Cape and to sign the Mayflower Compact. Before they set sail for Plymouth, Susanna Fuller White gave birth to a son Peregrine, but Dorothy May Bradford fell overboard and drowned. Thoreau says in his book *Cape Cod* that the harbor was called "Fuic [bownet?] Bay," a name suggesting a trap for catching eels. During the eighteenth and nineteenth centuries it was known as Cape Cod Harbor. Union Wharf, built by the Nickersons and Samuel Soper, was the first in Provincetown Harbor [1831] to provide a landing for fishing boats. Both the Commonwealth and the federal government have constructed dikes and breakwaters to prevent erosion in the harbor. But in 1885 House Point Island, at the west end, sank out of sight.

Q

Quahog Pond ['ko,hag]

A saltwater pond in the Great Sippewisset Swamp, Falmouth. Quahog is a shortened form of Narragansett *poquaûhock* "round clam."

Quaker Road

For the Quakers of Dennis who built a meetinghouse near the road that runs east toward Follins Pond. At the pond is Quaker Beach Road, and at Wrinkle Point in West Dennis is still another Quaker Road.

Quashnet River ['kwašnɛt]

Possibly for Quachatisset, one of the South Sea Indians who granted Richard Bourne a deed for Mashpee in 1660. It flows from Johns Pond to Waquoit Bay in South Mashpee.

Queen Annes Road

The road, first opened from Chatham to Yarmouth in 1678, antedates the reign of Queen Anne. It has been called the Old Monomoy Road [Monomoy was the early name of Chatham], Kings Road, Muddy Cove Way, and even Jury Way, for the jury or committee of men who laid it out. But in 1712, the year of Chatham's incorporation, the new town renamed its main road to honor the queen.

Quisset ['kwɪsɪt]

Quisset is a shortening of Wequamquissett, a neck sold to John Weeks in the 1600s by the descendants of the sachem Wequecoxett. In the 1800s yards at the neck built whalers, and saltworks shipped barrels of solar salt. The Quisset post office opened in 1897 and gave its name to the harbor and the village. Since the early 1900s the locality has had a number of estates on the harbor as well as a yacht club. Once, it is said, the Devil flew over Buzzards Bay and over the fields north of Woods Hole where the village is now. Overburdened by a load of rocks, he could not hold his apron strings together. Down came the rocks, strewing a large field outside Quisset.

Quisset Hill

A hill near Woods Hill, Falmouth, that was from 1800 to 1807 part of a telegraph system between Martha's Vineyard and Boston [see Telegraph Hill].

Quivet Creek

The creek serves as a boundary between Dennis and Brewster and was once called Bound Brook. The Algonquian name for the stream was Shuckquan, possibly from *sequanamaûquock* "spring [or early summer] fish."

R

Race Point

So called for the strong cross currents and rip tides at the point. It is near Hatches Harbor, just off the backside of the Cape in Provincetown. To assist ships caught in gales and heavy seas the federal government built a lighthouse at the point in 1817 and installed a lifesaving station in 1872.

Racing Beach

So called in the late 1800s because the villagers of Quisset would take their colts down to the beach, it is said, to break them to harness. Racing Beach became a Falmouth summer colony on Buzzards Bay after 1926.

Rafe Pond [ref]

For Jeremiah Ralph, who lived during the 1700s at the pond in East Brewster, southeast of Cliff Pond. *Rafe* is an old spelling, suggesting that Jeremiah's neighbors did not pronounce the *l* in his name.

Ragged Neck

So called in the 1600s because of its hilly terrain and dense growth. The neck is in West Chatham, between Bucks Creek and Oyster Pond River.

Ram Island

The Cape has had two Ram islands: one in Mystic Pond, Marstons Mills; the other, now washed away, at Chatham Harbor. Ram Island in Mystic Pond has the last stand of hemlock trees on Cape Cod. The Ram Island at Chatham was until 1851 [the year of Minot's Gale] a pasture for livestock. Champlain described the island in 1606 as a heavily wooded place, located in a "grand cul de sac." Its Algonquian name was Cothpinicut.

Raycroft Beach

For Louis B. Raycroft, who spent many of his summers near Old Wharf Road and Sea Street in Dennisport. The beach is just off Raycroft Parkway.

Red Brook Pond

This pond is in South Pocasset, Bourne, just off Red Brook Harbor. Like other waterways called Red Brook and Red River [they are in Mashpee and on the Chatham-Harwich line], the pond takes its name from the reddish clay of the beds and the color of the water. In the 1800s Red Brook Pond was known as Handys Pond, for Captain William Handy, Jr., who fought in the Revolution, skippered ships on the high seas, and owned a shipyard near his house on Buzzards Bay.

Red Lily Pond

For the pink lilies that once grew at the north end. It was also known as Lily and Centerville ponds, and lies north of a causeway on the south side of Barnstable, close to Centerville.

Red Maple Swamp

The swamp is a part of the Cape Cod National Seashore in Eastham. The Fort Hill Trail crosses the swamp and is accessible either from the hill just to the north or from Hemenway Landing on Nauset Marsh.

Red Top Hill

So called because of the reddish sands on the hill. In 1927 Harry M. Aldrich bought one of the four granite towers of the dismantled Fitchburg Terminal in Boston and had it removed to the hill in Truro, not far from Highland Light. The tower was a landmark of Boston in the 1850s, because Jenny Lind sang from it to thousands of Bostonians who had bought tickets for an oversubscribed concert — it was known as the Jenny Lind Tower.

Rendezvous Creek

So called, it is said, because the first settlers in Barnstable gathered near it when they arrived from Scituate. The creek runs north into Barnstable Harbor, not far west of the town fairgrounds. To help drain the marshes close to the creek the town built a dike at its mouth in the harbor and installed a clapper valve to keep salt water out.

Robbins Pond

For the Robbins family of Harwich, descendants of James and Roger Robbins, who had land near the pond in the early 1700s. Another Robbins, Eleazer, helped incorporate Harwich's South Precinct in 1746. The pond is in North Harwich, above Route 6 and east of Depot Street. Near the Harwich-Dennis line is White Pond, once known as Aunt Lizzie Robbins Pond. Farther north in Brewster on Cape Cod Bay are Robbins Hill Landing and Beach.

Rock Harbor and Rock Harbor Creek

So called for the rocks at the entrance to the village and creek on Cape Cod Bay on the Eastham-Orleans line. The creek has anchorage for small craft and fishing boats, with a tide that rises and falls eight feet. During the War of 1812, when the village was a busy port, the British tried to blockade American shipping there.

Rocky Point

The point curves around the north side of the entrance to Back River in Phinneys Harbor, Bourne. Rocks, both big and little, extend from one side of the point to the other; its beaches have patches of stone and gravel. At the center of the point is Fishermens Range, a large rock split apart. When the tide is unusually high, it pours in, covering beaches and rocks. Before the construction of a causeway to nearby Hog and Mashnee islands the point was treacherous for ships sailing up Buzzards Bay. Once the sloop *Victoria*, sailing toward the point from Woods Hole, started to toss in a strong wind. The Captain and his mate could not agree where to put in, either at Back River or farther north at Agawam Point. Near the mouth of Back River they both grabbed the tiller and between them drove the sloop onto Rocky Point.

Round Swamp

On Jefferson Road in the United States Military Reservation in Bourne, the swamp was once a haunt for Uncle Bill Freeman, who in the 1800s would roam the woods nearby just to be "let alone" and to spend his time chiseling rocks and carving sticks. It was said that Uncle Bill was a rejected lover. Not far to the northeast of the swamp are the Marked or Sal N. Pry Rocks. One rock was flat, the other an oval nearly fifty-four feet around, chiseled over with markings and the initials S.L.P. and C.S.P.N. But no one ever knew who or what was meant.

Ryder Beach

For the Ryders who owned a fishery in South Truro. The beach faces Cape Cod Bay and is open to bathers. Before 1920, when it was largely inaccessible, it was known as South Truro Beach.

Ryders Cove

For the Ryder family, who first came to Chatham during the eighteenth century. The cove lies just north of the Orleans Road [Route 28] in Chathamport and flows into Bassing Harbor. In

1795 it was called Redens Cove, also Eldridges Cove [for William Eldridge, an early settler]. William Nickerson, the first settler at the cove, knew it as the Alewife or the Herring River.

S

Sacconesset Hills [sækə'nɛsɪt]

Sacconesset is related to Narragansett *suckauanaûsuck* "black shells" or "black shellfish" from *súcki* 'black' + *anâwsuck* 'shells.' The houses and roads throughout the hills and the stone walls that run along their ridges suggest to some the atmosphere of Dorsetshire. The hills rise from Buzzards Bay, north of Little Sippewisset Lake in Falmouth.

Sachemas Neck ['seč̌əməs]

For Sachemas, a Saquatucket Indian of the 1600s, but a name no longer in use. The neck is in West Brewster between Stony Brook and Freemans Pond.

Sacrament Rock

The Reverend Joseph Hull and his congregation of seventeen families, it is said, gathered together at the rock during the summer of 1639 to hold communion. Later in the year Mr. John Lothrop may have also conducted a service for his congregation from Scituate. In the early 1800s the rock was blown up with a strong charge of powder. The town salvaged the fragments and shards for the foundation of a new jail in Barnstable Village. In 1916 the Barnstable Congregational

Church had a geologist reassemble the rock from its fragments and then gathered about it to celebrate the three hundredth anniversary of John Lothrop's ministry in England, in the days before he and his parishioners had to flee persecution. Nowadays a plaque commemorating the early site of the rock is to be found on Route 6A, four hundred yards west of Hinckley Pond.

Saddle and Pillion Rocks

These two rocks bear bronze tablets to commemorate Edmund and Elizabeth Freeman, buried together in 1682. Edmund Freeman, the first magistrate on the Cape, survived his wife by six years. The rocks resemble a saddle and pillion: Edmund placed the large, round pillion on his wife's grave in 1676; a son placed the saddle on his. They are on Tupper Road, near the intersection with Route 130 in Sandwich.

Sagamore

This village in Bourne is south of the Cape Cod Canal on Route 130. It was known as West Sandwich before the incorporation of Bourne in 1884; still earlier it was called Scusset. The village was a resort in the 1690s for fishermen, who would stay at Tom Swift's, one of the first inns on the Cape. In the early 1800s Benjamin Burgess had the brigs *Cordelia* and *Sarah Williams* and the schooner *Cardine* built at the village. In 1854 Hannah Rebecca Burgess sailed with her husband Captain William Howes Burgess aboard the clipper *Challenge* to the Pacific. En route the Captain died, but Hannah, who had taught herself navigation, was able to guide the ship to Valparaiso. Hannah then boarded the *Harriet Irving*, returned to Sagamore, and remained in the village for the rest of her life. The village had other interests than the sea. During the 1800s the Keiths of Sagamore built carriages, stagecoaches, and prairie schooners. Later they built freight cars for the Old Colony and other railroads. Sagamore is the Algonquian word for "chief."

Sagamore Highlands

A locality in Bourne, largely developed since World War II, near Cape Cod Bay and the highlands near Peaked Cliff on the Plymouth line.

Sagamore Hill

There are two Sagamore hills close to the Cape Cod Canal. One hill is north of the canal near Scusset Beach, Sandwich. The second, also called Powwow Hill, is now mostly a remnant, because much of it became part of the traffic circle at the south approach to the Bourne Bridge. This second Sagamore Hill once held a storehouse of Indian relics, including a tomahawk and carvings in bone and wood. It is said that in early days this second hill was a rendezvous for English settlers and Indian sagamores. Although *sagamore* and *powwow* are Algonquian words, English settlers gave the hills their names.

Salt Pond

The Cape has two Salt ponds, one in Eastham, the other in Falmouth. The pond in Eastham, churned out by a glacial ice-block, is an inlet of Salt Pond Bay. Nearby is the Salt Pond Visitor Center for the Cape Cod National Seashore. The pond in Falmouth, east of the village, was also, until the turn of the twentieth century, a sea inlet. But the construction of Surf Beach Drive along Vineyard Sound has all but enclosed it. Among the first to live at the pond was Isaac Robinson, who came to Falmouth in the 1660s after being expelled from the Barnstable church for failing to support orthodoxy. The Pilgrim magistrates had wanted him to persuade Quakers to convert, but as one historian says, "The reverse occurred, he turned to their faith."

Salten Point

Now a small community on Barnstable Harbor, the point in the 1800s was a place for salt-making. The word *saltern* [local speech drops the *r*] refers to the sheds that housed the tubs for boiling and evaporating salt. A few years after the start of salt-making the War of 1812 broke out, and the local militia armed the point with cannon in order to defend the town from British marauders.

Salt Works Road

So called for the saltworks of East Dennis, constructed in the late 1700s by Captain John Sears. Using windmills, Sears pumped sea water into large wooden pans; the water then evaporated and left bushels of solar salt for barreling. Edward Kendall traveled through the Cape in the early 1800s and reported that Dennis led all the other towns in salt-making. But in 1888, after salt mines had opened in New York, the last of the Cape's saltworks closed.

Sampson Island

For Sampson, who exchanged his rights to the whales stranded on the beaches of Wellfleet for the island on the east side of Little Pleasant Bay in Orleans. The island was also known as Potonumecot, and as Squonicut, from the Algonquian *m'squamaug* 'salmon' + *ut* 'at' = "at the place for taking salmon."

Sampsons Island

For Josiah Sampson, the owner of a grist mill, who died so heavily in debt that his son Josiah had to auction off the island in 1831. It is said that the auction earned him a single dollar. Later Josiah was able to buy back much of the land he had lost. The island is south of Grand Osterville Island, at the west end of Dead Neck, and belongs to the Audubon Society.

Sand Pond

A descriptive name for the bed of the pond, just north of the Great Western Road in North Harwich. It was once called Berrys Pond, for John Berry, an early resident.

Sandwich

The town is named for Sandwich in Kent, the home for some years of John Humphrey, who in the 1630s served as the Assistant Governor of the Massachusetts Bay Colony. In 1637 Humphrey sponsored the move of sixty families from Saugus [north of Boston] to their new settlement on the Cape. For Thoreau, who rode through the town in a dismal rain two hundred years later, the streets and houses offered a dismal prospect. Thoreau's view of the town was that it left him with the taste of "but half a Sandwich at most, and that must have fallen on the buttered side some time." The Algonquian name for Sandwich was Shawme and has the same meaning as Shawmut [the name of Boston] "he goes by boat." The villages of Sandwich include East Sandwich, Scorton Neck, Farmersville, Forestdale, and Wakeby. Sandwich faces Cape Cod Bay to the south of Plymouth.

Sandwich Harbor

In the early 1800s Timothy Dwight wrote that in travels to Sandwich he saw about thirty ships in the harbor "employed in the coasting business, especially, in carrying wood to Boston." Mill, Dock, and Old Harbor creeks converge at the harbor and then flow past two parallel breakwaters, designed to check heavy tides and great shifts of sand.

Sandy Neck

Trailing eastward for seven miles from Scorton Neck in Sandwich and the Great Marshes of Barnstable, the dunes of Sandy Neck protect Barnstable Harbor from the rollers of Cape Cod Bay. Timothy Dwight describes Sandy Neck Beach in his travels as "long, lofty, wild and fantastical . . . , thrown into a thousand grotesque forms by the united force of wind and waves." The townspeople of Barnstable have from early times tried to safeguard the dunes of the neck, to keep them from eroding and drifting into Barnstable Harbor. In the 1700s the town tried to

keep farmers from feeding their horses and cattle on the meadows near the beach. Likewise, offshore whalers had to limit the supply of wood they could take directly from the neck for firing their boilers and rendering oil from blubber. After the wreck of the *Almira* on the shores of Dennis the federal government installed Sandy Neck Lighthouse on the east end in 1836. During the Second World War the Coast Guard trained dogs for military service at Lovell's Sandy Neck Camp, and quartered soldiers and trainers at Blueberry Patch. At the west end of the neck is also Bodfish Park, a public beach donated by John Bodfish in honor of his father Jonathan. Granny Squant, a one-eyed witch, was the earliest resident of the Neck according to legend.

Santuit Pond   [sæn'tuit]

Close to the boundaries of Barnstable and Sandwich, this large pond is the source of the Santuit River that flows into Popponesset Bay. Several cranberry bogs border the pond, especially at the south end near the headwaters of the Santuit River. Richard Bourne first began to minister to the Indians on the shores of the pond in 1660. At the outset of his ministry, it is said, Bourne argued with a powwow. The powwow soon lost his temper, chanted a bog rhyme, and mired Bourne's feet in quicksand. For fifteen days they tried to outwit each other, Bourne helped by a white dove which fed him "cherries" to relieve his thirst and hunger. Unable to cast a spell upon the bird [only one of its cherries dropped in the bog], the powwow fell exhausted to the ground. Freed at last, Bourne saw that the "cherry" in the bog had grown and spread. It was the first cranberry to thrive on Cape Cod.

Santuit River

The river flows from Santuit Pond through the village of Santuit to Popponesset Bay. Until the mid-1800s both the river and the village were known as Cotuit. An Indian legend ascribes the origins of the Santuit River to Mishque, the great red fish. Mishque had grown ancient and wished to retire from the heavy seas of Nantucket Sound to Cape Cod Bay. But to swim all the way around Race Point and past its currents demanded more strength than Mishque had. So while he fed offshore near Mashpee he thought of what to do. A Wampanoag girl saw him and guessed his thoughts: "Old Mishque! Go to the quiet waters and rest. Or are you like some braves in the tribe who have never known they are old?" "Oh, I am old enough," Mishque said. "If I could, I'd swim to the quiet waters."

The girl laughed and said, "Come to me, old fish," and beckoned him ashore.

Old Mishque came up the beach; the girl mounted his back. He struggled and twisted and felt his strength wane. Ahead of him he saw a pool and dived in. The girl was still on his back. They were never seen again, but in his wake Old Mishque left the gully that soon became the Santuit River.

Saquatucket Harbor

[ˌsækwəˈtəkɪt]

Probably from *sauki* 'outlet' + *tuk* 'tidal river' + *ut* 'at' = "at the outlet of a tidal river." The harbor, just east of Wychmere Harbor in Harwich Port, is for pleasure craft.

Sarahs Swamp

For Sarah, who lived near the swamp in the 1700s and was a daughter of the Indian deacon Elisha Nauhaught. The swamp is in Yarmouth Port, on the north side of Long Pond.

Savage Point

For John Savage, a settler in the early 1700s, who owned this wooded peninsula on the Pamet River in Truro.

Scargo Hill

The hill borders on Scargo Lake and is the highest [160 feet] in the mid-Cape region. A stone tower atop the hill, erected in 1902, commemorates Thomas Tobey, who settled in Dennis in 1678. The Tobey family donated the tower to the town in 1929.

Scargo Lake

It is said that this lake in Dennis Village, just off Route 6A, is the creation of Maushop, who dug a hole deep and broad enough for its fifty-three acres, and then while he rested lit a pipe that brought on dark clouds and rain enough for all the brown and rainbow trout. Others speak of Princess Scargo, the daughter of a sachem who had the "royal touch." She once had a gift of fingerlings that swam inside a pumpkin. Fearful that they would die, she had the squaws of her tribe dig a large hole and the braves dance in prayer to the gods of rain. Then she took the pumpkin filled with fish and placed it at the center of the hole. Suddenly rain fell so hard that it filled the hole and drowned the Princess.

But the lake remains well-stocked with fish. Along the shore of the lake is Princess Beach, open to the public. This is one of the few bodies of water on the Cape to be called a lake.

Scattertee

Possibly an Indian name for the neck jutting eastward into the harbor at North Chatham. The point of the neck is known as Ministers Point or Allen Point, perhaps for Allen Nickerson, who owned a saltworks nearby in the 1800s. Some say that Bartholomew Gosnold anchored off the point in 1602 on his way to the Elizabeth Islands.

Schoolhouse Pond

The pond is not far from the Old Hyannis Port School on Scudder Avenue. It was also known as Bottomless Pond, because of its muddy bottom.

Schooner Bar

Until the 1850s there were three or four fathoms of water between the bar and Monomoy Island, Chatham — a safe place to anchor. By 1872 there were no more than two feet of water, the effects of storms and shifting sands. The anchorage was also known as Stewarts Bend. Joseph Stewart had a tavern in the 1700s near the bar. Stewarts Knoll and Stewarts Channel on Monomoy Island are also named for him.

Scorton Creek

This large creek flows through the Great Marshes into Barnstable Harbor. At its mouth are three small islands — Wicks, Fish, and Jackson islands. In early days the farmers called the stream Great Creek. Scorton is possibly related to Algonquian *scauton* or *scata'cook* "the place where the stream branches."

Scorton Hill

The hill, in West Barnstable and not far from Sandwich, was the birthplace of John "Mad Jack" Percival, the skipper of the *U.S.S. Constitution* when she sailed around the world in the 1840s. When just fourteen, it is said, young Percival quarreled with his parents and ran away from home, stopping long enough at a high rock on the hill to gaze toward Provincetown and then toward Boston. The pull westward was stronger, and Percival went to Boston, signed up on a ship, and sailed the seas.

Scorton Neck

The neck is firm ground, surrounded by marshes, by the beaches of Sandy Neck, and by Scorton Creek at the east end of Sandwich.

Scrabbletown

This is a nickname for Chatham and for the beachcombers who lived at the lower end of the town and supported themselves on the loot they took from shipwrecks. Rudyard Kipling has some Gloucester fishermen say in *Captains Courageous*, "Ye scrabbletowners, ye Chatham wreckers! Git oout with your brick in your stockin!"

Scraggy Neck

So called for the thickets that once covered much of this neck on the south side of Red Brook Harbor, near Cataumet in Bourne. During the 1700s the First Parish of Sandwich owned the neck — it was then called Ministers Neck — and from the sale of wood and the rental of pasture supported their preachers. The Algonquian name for the neck was Pocasset, "where the narrows open out."

Scudder Lane

For Nelson and Daniel Scudder, who owned a wharf at the end of the lane at Calves Pasture Point, near Barnstable Village. Even before the Scudders, in the 1700s John Gorham brought cod and haddock from the Grand Banks to the wharf and traded the fish for West Indian rum and molasses. Scudder Lane passes east of Hinckley Pond and was first called Calf Pasture Lane.

Scudders Bay

For Ebenezer Scudder, who lived near the bay in the 1700s, or for his son Thomas, who ran a local market until he moved to Maine. The bay is near Centerville River and Harbor.

Scusset Beach   ['skəsɪt]

Scusset is a shortening of Moonoonuscusset, possibly related to Narragansett *munnawhatteaûg* "the menhaden used for fertilizer." A place for bathers and fishermen, the beach is directly north of Cape Cod Canal Bay in Sandwich. In early days Indians had a settlement near the beach, and the Pilgrims congregated not far away.

Seapit River   ['sipɪt]

Possibly for Sepet, who lived with his father Quachatasset near the early Falmouth settlements. The river is a saltwater channel northwest of Washburn Island between Eel Pond and Waquoit Bay.

Searsville and Searsville Road

An early name for East Dennis. The road is farther south in Dennisport. Both are named for early members of the Sears family.

Sesuit Harbor

The harbor in East Dennis has limited accommodations for sailing craft. But in the 1800s it was large enough for the Shiverick family to build sailing vessels. In the first decades Asa Shiverick launched schooners and brigs. In 1848 his three sons enlarged the yard and designed eight clipper ships, two of them of more than a thousand tons. The shipyard closed in the 1860s, but a commemorative tablet, dedicated in 1924, still overlooks the harbor. At the end of the harbor is Sesuit Creek, and to the west is Sesuit Neck. Sesuit is sometimes shortened to Suet, as in Thoreau's note that he had passed through "the village of Suet, in Dennis, on Suet and Quivet Necks."

Seymour Pond

For John Seymour, a tanner of the late 1700s, who lived near the pond, which is half in Harwich, half in Brewster. It was also known as Bangs Pond, for John D. Bangs, the town clerk of Harwich in the early 1800s.

Shank Painter Pond

A long, narrow pond that lies east of Herring Cove toward Telegraph Hill in Provincetown. The origin of the name is unknown, although a shank-painter is a rope or chain that ties the shank of a catted anchor securely to a ship, the flukes resting on the rail. If Cape Cod looks like a ship about to set sail [the lower Cape the prow, the mid and upper Cape the hull], then Shank Painter Pond might suggest to a fanciful eye the anchor secured by a chain. In his book *Cape Cod* Thoreau reports that he went walking to Shank Painter Swamp.

Shanks Pond

This is an imaginary place. According to Joseph Robinson and Maltiah Gifford, neighbors during the 1800s in the Great Sippewisset Swamp in Falmouth, a large family of Indians named

Shanks lived in wigwams beside a salt pond. One of the Shanks, an especially tall man, would string clam shells all about his wigwam and let them turn brown from the smoke of his fires. From time to time he would stagger home from a tavern on the shores of Buzzards Bay. Another Shanks tried unsuccessfully to grow hay in the swamp. He once bought a scythe, heated the blade, and plunged it into the pond, only to pull it out warped and useless. The last of the Shanks was Teb, who farmed fifty acres long after the others had sold out and left.

The Shaving Hill Bog

So called because of the shavings brought from a nearby barrel shop to a road in the bog to help keep it passable during the muddy season. The bog is on Pinquickset Cove in Cotuit.

Shawme-Crowell State Forest

['šɔm 'krol]

The Commonwealth acquired the lands for the forest, west of Sandwich Village, in the 1920s and established a nursery for young pine and spruce. During the Second World War the federal government bought five thousand acres of the forest for use as an artillery range. The forest has had two severe fires, one in 1923, the other in 1965. Shawme is the Indian name for Sandwich. Lincoln Crowell was a state forester on the Cape until his death in 1938.

Shawme Pond and Upper Shawme Lake

The pond is directly north of the Upper Lake, and ten feet lower. The settlers first dammed the pond in 1665; then in 1811 the town formed the Upper Lake from marshland. The dam provided power for a number of mills, including Thomas Dexter's grist mill, built before 1640 and restored in 1961. The Hoxie House, the oldest saltbox on the Cape [dated 1637], overlooks Shawme Pond. Next to it on a hill once stood the Sandwich Academy, a college preparatory school from 1804 until 1882 [the first in Barnstable County]. Thereafter, until 1960 it was known as the Lake House. Nearby is the Thornton Burgess Museum. The Heritage Plantation, close to the pond, has nature trails, a restored mill of 1800, and various exhibits, including antique firearms and restored automobiles. The two ponds are at the south end of Sandwich Village. In the 1800s they were called the Upper Mill Pond and the Lower Mill Pond.

Sheepfold Hill

A hill in Conrad Aiken's poem "Mayflower." Aiken describes the pinkwinks, a local word for frogs, "crying from the bog's edge to lost Sheepfold Hill." He lived with his wife Mary on a farm in Brewster, and in his poem also mentions Quivett Creek, Stony Brook, and Payne Creek.

Shirttail Point

They say that boys would go swimming without their shirttails [skinny-dipping?] at this point, located south of Wellfleet Village on the harbor. In early days mackerel fishermen would beach their boats at the point and deliver their catches to nearby fish houses.

Shiverick Pond

For Samuel Shiverick, the first minister of the Congregational Church in Falmouth. The pond is close to the church on the village green.

Shiverick Road

For the Shivericks of Sesuit Harbor, East Dennis, shipbuilders of the 1800s.

Shoot Flying Hill

The highest on Cape Cod, the hill was a station in early days for hunters of geese and ducks flying to Barnstable Harbor or Nantucket Sound. The Mid-Cape highway now crosses the hill, close to the junction with Route 132 in Barnstable. From the 1700s on the hill had a fire tower to enable guards to send alarms by semaphore up and down the Cape and across the bay to the mainland. Wequaquet Lake lies at the foot of the hill.

Short Wharf Creek

A tidal creek in Yarmouth Port. It was also called Simpkins Creek for the Simpkins family, residents in town since the early 1800s, who trace themselves back to Nicholas Simpkins, an early settler [1639] who left after five years.

Shovelful Shoal

So called, possibly, because this shoal south off Monomoy Point sits under no more than a "shovelful" of water. In 1902 the barge *Wadena* ran aground on the rocks and sandbars of the shoal. Captain Seth Ellis and seven men from the lifesaving station on Monomoy tried to rescue the bargemen on the *Wadena*, but as the lifeboat headed back toward land, the sea began to spill over its sides. The rescued bargemen, already afraid, could not sit still in the boat and caused it to capsize. Spotting the lifeboat's distress, Captain Elmer Mayo rowed a dory out to the men in the water, but all were lost except Captain Ellis. The Mack Monument near Chatham Lighthouse commemorates the wreck and the attempted rescue. When the schooner *Nancy M. Foster* ran aground on Shovelful Shoal, it soon collapsed under heavy seas and splitting seams. The crew abandoned ship and swam toward shore on planks, hatch covers, and hen coops. When one crewman neared the shore, he saw some men staring at him.

"What town is this?" he hollered.

"Chatham," he heard.

"Goodbye," he said, and turned back to sea on his plank.

Siders Pond [ˈsɪdərz]

For Consider Hatch, who lived in Falmouth Village not far from the pond. Consider's ancestors, according to tradition, arrived in Falmouth from Barnstable in 1660 together with other Quakers, and settled beside the pond next to a swamp of flags. Sarah Hatch gave birth the very first night of settlement. She named her son Moses because, she said, "He was born among the flags." Another account delays the birth of Moses until 1662, when he was born on a bed of bulrushes in a hut topped by a whale boat. Summer people often say "Ciders" instead of "Sidders" Pond. A common name in the 1800s was Fresh Pond. The outlet from the pond to Vineyard Sound is Fresh River.

Signal Hill

The hill is just west of Bournedale and north of the Cape Cod Canal.

It has also been known as Telegraph Hill and Hio Hill. Jonathan Grout used it in the early 1800s to send signals from Martha's Vineyard to Boston [see Telegraph Hill, Falmouth]. It is said that Indians, long before Grout's time, also sent signals from the South Sea [Vineyard Sound] to this hill near Cape Cod Bay.

The name Hio Hill stems from a conversation that Mr. Gibbs, who lived near the hill, had with Cape Codders bound west. They passed Gibbs one morning while he was clearing his swamp, and called out to him from Conestoga wagons, "Come on, come on — all going to Ohio, to Ohio." Gibbs looked up and called back, "Huh-Hio be damned. Huh — to Hio. Guess I've got all I can do in this here swamp, let alone go to Hio." Gibbs's swamp was known as Hio Swamp and a pond close by was Hio Pond — its clay was good for daubing.

Silver Beach

The developers of this district on Wild Harbor in North Falmouth named it for the silvery sand on the beach. Before 1897 it was commonly known as the Ox Pasture.

Silver Spring Brook

So called for the white sand at the bottom of the spring. Thoreau said that Silver Springs in South Wellfleet, near Cape Cod Bay, was "an extensive bare plain tract." It is now in the Audubon Wildlife Sanctuary. Silver Spring Beach is farther south in Eastham, off Steele Road.

Simmons Pond

For the Simmons family of Hyannis, some of them shipmasters in the 1800s. Lemuel B. Simmons took his wife and daughter with him on a cruise around the world; he was also the first "no-rum" skipper out of Boston. A generation later, in 1847, Jehial Simmons brought food to Ireland when the crops failed. In the 1800s the pond had a grist mill and also a dam, useful for making and cutting slabs of ice.

Sipsons Island

For the sachem John Sipson and his brother Tom [or Little Tom], who in 1713 sold flats and sedge ground to Samuel Mayo and Joshua Hopkins of Eastham. The island was also known as Esnews, Little Toms, and Chequesset. It is in Pleasant Bay, south of Hog Island, and is now in Orleans.

Skaket Beach   ['skækɪt]

Skaket is a short form of Namskaket "at the fishing place." The beach is on Cape Cod Bay, northeast of Namskaket Creek in Orleans.

Skinequit Pond   ['skɪnə,kwɪt]

For John Skinequit, an Indian who lived at the pond near Uncle Venies Road in South Harwich. In the past the whole region bordering the pond was called Skinequit.

Skunknet Woods   ['skəŋk,nɛt]

Skunknet is probably related to Algonquian *ouschankamaug* "a fishing place for eels." There is a brook in the woods that empties into Scudders Bay. In the 1800s the woods contained large earthen pits and burners for turning logs into charcoal. The charcoal helped in the smelting of bog iron in the foundries of Barnstable.

Sladesville

For C. Arnold Slade, an artist who lived in this locality in Truro in the 1920s. The locality is near the Pamet River.

Sliding Rock

A natural slide for children near Deep Pond in Beebe Woods, Falmouth. The rock is a huge boulder, fifty feet high.

Smalls Hill

For Francis Small, who owned it in the later 1700s. It rises 140 feet and is south of Ballston Beach in Truro, on the Atlantic coast.

Smalltown

This village is named for the Small family, residents in the east end of Falmouth since the early 1800s. Once it was known as Calico Town, because the women in the village, it is said, wore calico dresses.

Theophilus F. Smith Road

An access road from Route 134 to the Dennis town dump. Theophilus was at one time the dump's custodian.

Snake Pond

The snakes of Cape Cod include the northern water snake, the northern black racer, the garter snake and the puff adder, none of them poisonous. The pond is north of Otis Air Force Base in Sandwich.

Ed Snow Pond

Ed Snow was an active member of the town meeting in the early 1700s. The pond, in West Brewster, was also known as Smiths Pond in the 1800s.

Snows Creek

Probably for Samuel Snow, a Barnstable selectman of the 1850s. The creek flows from salt marshes into Lewis Bay. At the head of the creek were the first yards in Hyannis to build ships.

Sols Pond

For Solomon Robinson, who had some land at the pond in Falmouth Village in the 1800s and was a descendant of an early settler, Isaac Robinson.

South Village Beach

In early days South Village was a fishing hamlet near the beach on Nantucket Sound, West Dennis. Four streets north of the beach still recall the village: South Village Road, Lane, Circle, and Drive. In the 1800s it was also known as Battletown. According to Anthony Gage, who in the late 1800s lived on Lower County Road [or Battletown Road], "Men used to raise sons to send 'em down here to fight." Battletown ran between Weir Creek and Swan River.

Spectacle Pond

A descriptive name for several Cape ponds that look like eyeglasses. There are two in Falmouth, one in the Wellfleet section of the Cape Cod National Seashore, and another in Sandwich.

Spencer Baird Road

For Professor Spencer Baird, a secretary of the Smithsonian Institution in the nineteenth century and the member of the U.S. Fish Commission responsible for selecting the village of Woods Hole as suitable for a marine research station. The road is in the village.

Spring Hill

So called for the many springs on the sides and summit of the hill. The abundance of water prompted early settlers to build their houses on its slopes and to erect a grist mill on nearby Spring Hill Creek. These early houses had sturdy walls of white oak, thick enough to serve as a fort. The Quakers lived on Spring Hill and held their first meeting of Friends in 1657 at the house of William Allen, the first such meeting in New England. The Old Quaker Meetinghouse, at the creek, was rebuilt three times after 1672. The hill is east of Sandwich Village.

Spruce Pond

The trees on this pond are not spruce but a variety of American hemlock. At one time the word "spruce" applied to three kinds of tree in New England: the bog spruce, the pine, and the hemlock. The pond has an outlet into Bridge Creek, west of Interchange 6 on the Mid-Cape Highway. It is in Barnstable.

Squaw Hollow

This hollow near the intersection of the Pocasset-Sandwich and Forestdale Roads in Bourne has the shape of a large heel. It is said that the Devil left his mark at the spot while on his way to Nantucket. Not far from the hollow is a stretch of rocky ledges and rugged boulders. The Devil dropped these rocks on the fields when his apron strings broke.

Squaw Island

Probably for an Indian woman who lived on the island in the 1600s. A causeway connects the island to Hyannis Port over a channel now filled in. In 1907 W. Y. Humphreys, a Mississippi Congressman, built "Indian Rock," the first house on the island.

Squeteague Harbor [skwə'tig]

The harbor is north of Amrita Island at Cataumet, Bourne. The squeteague or weakfish is common to the waters of Buzzards Bay. The Narragansetts made glue from the fish and named it *peskwiteag* "they give glue."

Squopenik ['skwɔpənɪk]

A peninsula in Truro, between the Little Pamet and the Pamet River. According to tradition the name means "Squaw-broke-her-neck" and refers to an accident of the distant past. What its Algonquian origin is remains unknown.

Stage Harbor

So called for the docks and drying racks or stages in the harbor where fishermen used to prepare cod and haddock for market. The harbor lies near Morris Island, Harding Beach, and the Neck in Chatham. Sieur de Poutrincourt, the sailing master for Samuel de Champlain, named the harbor Port Fortuné, an ironic contrast to the fate his crew had on the

Neck when they encountered local Indians. De Poutrincourt fomented a clash between his crew and the Indians that resulted in the death of ten men. The French had to set sail at once and so lost a chance to trade and to establish a settlement. Port Fortuné or Cape Fortuné appeared on maps of the seventeenth century. Admiral Block rendered it in Dutch as the Ungluckige Haven.

Station Avenue

This street, which once served the South Yarmouth Station of the Old Colony Railroad, runs northward to Union Street. Passenger service on the railway, halted in 1964, may be resumed. Freight trains still make stops as far east as South Dennis.

Steamboat Wharf

Built in 1879 at the east end of Stage Harbor, the wharf never did serve steamboat packets. Instead, it was a dock for sailing packets that ran between Chatham and New Bedford from 1879 to 1896.

Stillwater Pond

This is a name of the late 1800s that replaced the earlier Pasture Pond. Pasture Pond was once a watering hole on the Nickerson Farm, near Chathamport. Stillwater Pond suggests a place of ease and restfulness. The pond is just north of Lovers Lake.

Stone Horse Shoal

Possibly so called because a *stone horse* was an old phrase for a stallion presumably strong enough to kick in the sides of a ship. In past days an old wreck near the shoal was a favorite spot for fishermen to catch pollack and cod. Captain John L. Veeder of Woods Hole once helped to break up a ship wrecked on the shoal. When he and his men rolled the ship over,

they uncovered a large mound of "dark sand" filled with bones. Although the captain did not look closely at the bones, he believed that they were the skeletons of horses. Stone Horse Shoal is in Nantucket Sound, south of Monomoy Point, Chatham.

Stony Brook

The brook flows northward from Walkers Pond, through Upper and Lower mill ponds, to Cape Cod Bay. Local residents call it West Brewster's Herring Run, because alewives swim upstream to spawn in the spring and then return with their young to the bay in the fall. In the past the brook has powered four mills on its banks, and it still turns the wheel of one restored mill on Stony Brook Road. The Indian name for Stony Brook was Sauquatucket, from *sauki* 'outlet' + *tuck* 'tidal river' + *ut* 'at' = "at the outlet of a tidal river." Other names have been Setucket River, Mill Brook, and Winslows Brook [named for the Winslow brothers, who in 1814 began to work a fulling mill]. Its lower reaches are called Paines Creek.

Strawberry Lane

Strawberries grow well in the sandy soil of the Cape. The lane is near the Yarmouth Port post office. Adjacent are botanical trails in a fifty-three acre tract. Within the tract is Millers Pond, a kettlehole. The Bangs Hallet house, now occupied by the Historical Society of Old Yarmouth, stands atop the curiously named Shapely Bottom, a low hill.

Strouts Creek

Also called Stouts Creek, it once ran inland from the southeast corner of Provincetown Harbor. Toward the close of the eighteenth century the creek was buried by sand. The Strouts apparently lived in Truro and Provincetown before the Revolution.

Succonessett Point [ˌsækəˈnɛsɪt]

Possibly from Algonquian *sequan* "early summer" and *sâkwaninik* "in the spring." Seconsett Island, on the east side of Waquoit Bay, may stem from the same Algonquian forms. It is said that the giant Maushop once grew fearful of a canoe in the waters off Succonessett Point. When the canoe drifted closer to shore, Maushop saw two white skins on it, draped over poles. Frightened by what he saw, he sacrificed his wife Quaunt by dashing her against the rocks at the point and then fled south. He never returned, and some say that the power of the canoe brought on his death. The point is on Nantucket Sound, south of Maushop Village in Mashpee.

Summer Street

Sandwich, Dennisport, West Yarmouth, Yarmouth Port, Nantucket, Edgartown, and Vineyard Haven all have Summer streets. Summer Street in Yarmouth Port was once called Hawes Lane, after a local resident Edmund Hawes [d. 1693], who was for many years a deputy to the General Court at Plymouth. This street was also known as Cow Lane, because farmers would drive their livestock along this road to the eastern shore of Dennis Pond in order to water them. The name Summer Street first appeared on a map of 1880, a time when summer people were just beginning to spend their holidays on the Cape. Street names began to proliferate in New England after the Civil War, and many towns copied Boston, not only with Summer Street, but State, Pleasant, Winter, and Spring streets as well. The Summer Street in Yarmouth Port runs southwestward toward Hyannis.

Sunken Meadow Beach

So called because of the low salt marshes near the beach on Cape Cod Bay in North Eastham. The beach lies at the end of South Sunken Meadow Road.

Sunset Hill

This hill in Hyannis Port took its name in the late 1800s from Sunshine Crest, a house built by the Falvey-Prendergast families. Farther up the hill, at the summit, stands St. Andrews by-the-Sea [built 1911], which overlooks Centerville Harbor and Nantucket Sound.

Swan Pond

Swans are rare on Cape Cod. Whistling swans apparently graced the Cape during the springs and falls of colonial times, but were very rare by 1850. More likely, *swan* is from the Algonquian *sowan* "south." The pond lies in Dennisport, off Depot Road, and is the source of Swan Pond River. It was known as Jamies Pond, pronounced [jæmiz], for a local resident, Uncle James Chase. Another Swan Pond, also called Seine Pond, lies in South Yarmouth.

Swifts Hill

Probably for Elijah Swift, who was a smuggler during the War of 1812 and later was the first to build whalers, the *Sarah Herrick* among them. In 1821 Swift founded the Falmouth National Bank, the first on the Cape. He also planted the elms about Falmouth Village Green. The hill is near Sippewisset on Buzzards Bay.

T

Talbot Creek

In 1963 Dr. and Mrs. Fritz B. Talbot donated their land near Scorton Creek at the west end of Sandy Neck to the Sandwich Conservation Commission. The point is a sanctuary for several varieties of marsh grass and pine trees and for stands of fir and beech.

Tavern Field

So called for a tavern built by Samuel Perry along the Old County Road in the village of Monument [now Bourne]. His grandson Seth pulled it down in the late 1700s, presumably because of diminishing business.

Taylor Pond

Probably for Samuel Taylor, who came to South Chatham in the 1700s. In the 1600s it was known as Little Oyster Pond. The Algonquians called the pond Machpoxet, from *mache* 'unpleasant' + *paug* 'pond' + *s* 'little' + *ut* 'at' = "at the small, unpleasant pond." This saltwater pond empties into Nantucket Sound through a cove once known as Tomlins Cove.

Taylors Point

The campus of the Massachusetts Maritime Academy is at the Point in the village of Buzzards Bay, Bourne. The Academy came to the Point in 1948 and since then has had three training ships, all named the *Bay State*. Charles Henry Taylor, the editor of the *Boston Globe* in the late 1800s, owned land at that Point. He was also a brigadier general in the state militia.

Teaticket   ['ti,tɪkɪt]

A locality of Falmouth on Perch and Great ponds that is known locally as the "garden of heaven." Teaticket is related to Natick *keht* 'great' + *tuk* 'river' + *ut* 'at' = "at the great river." Teaticket was an active Revolutionary village which sent militia men to Falmouth, marching to the tune of Stephen Swift's fife, to drive British marines back to their ships and to their base in Tarpaulin Cove. But no one in the village ever sold tickets for tea.

Telegraph Hill

From 1800 to 1807 signalmen on the hill helped to relay messages by semaphore to Boston merchants on the arrival of ships at Martha's Vineyard. Jonathan Grout, a lawyer who designed the system, employed signalmen on fourteen hills from September through May and guaranteed quick delivery of messages over the distance of ninety miles. In the later 1800s the hill was also

known as Falmouth Hill and Observatory Hill. Franklin King of Boston, a dealer in paints, chemicals and dyes, built an observatory on its summit. The hill, in West Falmouth, now supports a fire tower.

Tern Island

So called since the 1930s for the thousands of terns that fly to the island in summer to breed, from as far away as the Falklands in the South Atlantic. In the 1800s Tern Island was known as Little Beach on Chatham Harbor. It thereafter became an island as a result of storms and erosion.

Thacher Channel

This channel as well as Great Thatch and Little Thatch [islands once called Great and Little Thacher] are probably named for John Thacher, who in 1792 had the first weekly mail service between Barnstable and Boston. The channel and the islands are near the middle of Barnstable Harbor.

Thumpertown

A thumper was a religious revivalist, who would come down hard on strong points of faith. In the early 1800s Methodists would return in summer to Thumpertown and to nearby Millennium Grove on the Bay side of Eastham for revivalist meetings. In his book on the *Notions of the Americans* [1828], James Fenimore Cooper spoke of the downright emphases of "Thumpers, and Dunkers, and other enthusiasts."

Toby Island

For the Tobey family of Sandwich and Bourne. In the late 1800s Elisha Tobey had beds of oysters in the coves of the island, just off the coast of Monument Beach in Phinneys Harbor. Before the island came wholly into private

hands, townspeople in the 1800s would return each fall to gather hazelnuts. Burgess Island was an early name, probably for Thomas Burgess, a settler in 1637. The island was also known in the 1600s as Cocopatante, probably the name of an Indian who lived on it. The shape of Toby Island is highly irregular and resembles a crane suspended in flight.

Toms Neck

Probably for Great Tom, an Indian sued for defamation in Plymouth Court by William Nickerson, the first English settler in Chatham. The neck is southeast of Chatham Village and north of Morris Island.

Tonset ['tansɪt]

Possibly a shortening of Algonquian *keht* 'great' + *ompsk* 'rock' + *ut* 'at' = "at the great rock." It is now a community in northern Orleans, close to Nauset Harbor.

Town Beach

This is a public beach at Sandwich Village on Cape Cod Bay. Before the construction of a boardwalk in 1835 townspeople would wade out during low tide in search of lobsters. The east end of the beach also had large deposits of clay suitable for making brick. Kilns installed on the beach during the War of 1812 kept a British frigate farther off shore, because the Captain took them for a fort. After 1860 local Sandwich brick became too expensive to make, and so the kilns shut down.

Town Cove

A large cove in the heart of Orleans, also known as Orleans Cove. The head of the cove is opposite Orleans Village; the mouth of the cove opens into Nauset Harbor.

Town Neck

The neck is on Cape Cod Bay, northeast of Sandwich Village. In the 1600s it was a calf pasture, and in the 1700s had kilns for baking brick. From the 1690s until 1930 the neck was land held in common, the last of such properties in Massachusetts. Thereafter it became a community of small lots. Early on it was also called Shawme Neck.

Trotting Park Road

For a racetrack off the road in West Dennis, popular in town during the late 1800s. The road runs south from Main Street to Nantucket Sound. At the intersection of Main Street and the road is "Jericho," a house built in 1801 by Captain Theophilus Baker, later owned by Elizabeth Reynard, who wrote *The Narrow Land*, and Dr. Virginia Gildersleeve, president of Barnard College. They gave the house to the town of Dennis in 1962, and it is now a museum of local history. The Dennis Historical Society says that "Jericho" was so called because its walls were about to "tumble down" before Miss Reynard and Dr. Gildersleeve had them restored.

Truro

Incorporated in 1709, the town took its name, at the suggestion of Thomas Paine, Jr. [one of the Pamet Proprietors who bought up the land from the Indians] from Truro in Cornwall. Earlier names for Truro were Pamet [the name of the Indians living there] and Dangerfield. A party of Pilgrims under Captain Miles Standish surveyed the territory of Truro on November 15, 1620 OS — their "First Discovery" — and stopped at places later called Back Beach, Stouts Creek, East Harbor, East Harbor Creek, High Head, Pamet River, and Pond Village. Truro, in Cornish, means "the place of the hill."

Turpentine Road

The road was built for local residents of Sandwich, who tapped pine trees and shipped most of the sap to Boston for making turpentine and pitch. It is also the boundary between Sandwich and Bourne, beginning at the Pocasset-Sandwich Road and running south to Barberry Hill Road in Hatchville.

U

Uncle Barneys Road

For Barnabas Baker, who in the 1800s had a saltworks at the end of this road which runs along the east bank of Bass River, in West Dennis.

Up-along and Down-along

These are local terms in Provincetown to identify the town's principal streets, Commercial and Bradford. Many residents call Commercial Street "Front Street"; the common name for Bradford Street is "Back Street." To go as far as Gull Hill, to the northeast, is to go "way-up-along." "Up-along" and "down-along" have been in use since the early 1800s.

Upper Cape

The part of the Cape that stretches from the elbow at Chatham and Orleans to the Canal in Bourne. The lower Cape runs northward to Provincetown.

Vineyard Sound

In 1602 Bartholomew Gosnold was one of the first English sea captains to explore the Sound from Falmouth on the east to Martha's Vineyard on the south, and the Elizabeth Islands to the west. For some time the eastern stretches of the Sound and the other waters of the Atlantic along the coast of Cape Cod were known as the South Sea.

Wakeby Pond   ['wɪgbɪ]

The pond drains past Conaumet Neck into Mashpee Pond. Wakeby is probably from the Algonquian *wikopi*, a name for the inner bark of the basswood tree, which Indians used for making ropes and mats. The pond was a favorite of President Grover Cleveland and of his friends, Richard Watson Gilder and Joseph Jefferson. Together they owned three islands on the pond — Cometoit, Getoffit, and Stayonit — named by them in imitation of such places as Cotuit and Santuit.

Waquoit   [wa'kwɔɪt]

Families came from Barnstable in the 1700s to settle in this village on Waquoit Bay in the east end of Falmouth. Daniel Webster enjoyed it for its fishing. Princeton professors bought summer houses at the village after the turn of the twentieth century. Waquoit is

probably from Algonquian *uk-quaé* 'point or head' + *ut* 'at' = "at the head of the bay."

Waquoit Bay

A breakwater guards the entrance to the bay, which is a gunkhole suitable for anchoring small boats. The bay is at the border of Mashpee and Falmouth on Vineyard Sound.

Walkers Pond

The Cape has two Walkers ponds, one in Harwich, one in Brewster. The pond in Harwich, south of Long Pond, is probably named for Jeremiah Walker, who built a windmill on its shores in the late 1700s. The pond in West Brewster is south of Upper mill pond.

Washburn Island

For Albert Henry Washburn, minister to Austria and Professor of Political Science and International Law at Dartmouth in the 1920s. Washburn and his family had a house on the island, west of Waquoit Bay, Falmouth. During World War II the Army Corps of Engineers built a bridge from what was known as Tent City [now Seacoast Shores] to Washburn Island, and installed gunnery mounts there.

Watch Hill

Marcellus Eldridge's name for his house and other property near Chatham Harbor. Eldridge, a brewer in Portsmouth, New Hampshire, built his house in the late 1800s. The coach house and two brick gates are still standing.

Webbs Island

This island is the Atlantis of Cape Cod. It is said that it was once northeast of Monomoy Point and that it sank beneath the tides of the Atlantic at the close of the seventeenth century. The *Massachusetts Magazine* of 1790 described the remains of the island as a large rock rising from the bottom of the sea.

Weeset ['wisɪt]

A community in northeastern Orleans. The name is probably Algonquian in origin; it may mean a "slippery or shiny place."

Weir Village

So called for the weirs once set out across streams near the village. The weirs were either small dams or fence-traps for fish. The village was in northeastern Yarmouth, south of Route 6A. Weirmill Brook, not far off, is the head of Bass River, connected to a chain of ponds.

Wellfleet

Incorporated in 1763 from the North Precinct of Eastham, the town was first called Poole, for a seaport in Dorsetshire that was also a stronghold of the Parliamentary armies in the English Civil War. But the townspeople preferred the name Wellfleet because, some say, it recalls the "whale fleet" of men who earned their livelihood from sperm oil and whalebone. A more likely account is that the oystermen of Wellfleet chose the name of the town in remembrance of the Wallfleet oyster beds of England. From 1830 on, for about forty years, Wellfleet had the best oysters in New England, but they suddenly stopped growing. The uncertainties of earning a livelihood in Wellfleet possibly prompted such local names as Dogtown and Skunks Misery [a swamp too dismal, it is said, for even a skunk].

Wellfleet Bay Wildlife Sanctuary

A tract of 650 acres in South Wellfleet, also known as the Audubon Wildlife Sanctuary.

Visitors to the sanctuary have spotted more than 250 species of birds along its two trails to the bay and to Gull Pond. The sanctuary was first called the Austin Ornithological Research Station for Dr. Oliver L. Austin, Sr. and his son, ornithologists who studied the birds on their tract, banded many of them, and wrote several works. The Massachusetts Audubon Society bought the sanctuary in 1958.

Wellfleet by the Sea

This village is on the Atlantic shore, north of LeCount Hollow.

Wellfleet Harbor

This is the second largest harbor on Cape Cod Bay. It has a town marina of 210 slips and has a wide anchorage at its head, ten feet deep. Samuel de Champlain named the harbor St. Suzanne de Cap Blanc, and the Pilgrims, several years later, called it Grampus Bay, because of the grampuses or blackfish beached there. In his history *Of Plimoth Plantation*, William Bradford recalls an Indian "cutting up a great fish like a grampus."

Wequaquet Lake

In 1891, to help sponsor a regatta on this, the largest pond on Cape Cod, Howard Marston, a restaurant owner, named it Wequaquet Lake. Marston chose Wequaquet partly because it was the old name of Centerville, the village south of the pond. Earlier in the century the pond had the names Great Pond, Iyanoughs Pond, and Nine Mile Pond. Iyanough was the sachem who befriended the Pilgrims in the 1620s, only to find himself betrayed and pursued to his death by Miles Standish and his men. Why the pond was known as Nine Mile Pond is uncertain. One possibility is that Barnstable is nine miles long, from corner to corner [Cotuit to Cummaquid, West Barnstable to Hyannis]. Another possibility is that the circumference of the lake, by a rough and ready measurement, came to about nine miles. The earliest name was Coopers Pond, for Deacon John Cooper, who owned large tracts on its shores in the 1600s. Wequaquet stems from the Algonquian *wehqu-auk* "end of the land."

West Barnstable

A village in the northwest corner of the town. The early name for the village was Great Marshes, for the marshlands near the local pastures. In the 1700s the village name was West Parish, for the meetinghouse recently constructed. In 1976 West Barnstable was called the Village of Flags, because Old Glory, which had first flown over the Capitol in Washington, draped the flagpole in front of the West Parish Church, accompanied by other flags. Indians lived at West Barnstable until the late 1700s. There were nineteen wigwams in the village in 1767, and Knopper Spring is named for the last member of the old Indian community.

West Bay

So called because it is west of Osterville. The bay has access to North Bay and also to Nantucket Sound [through a cut across Dead Neck]. Eel River flows southeastward from the bay along the shores of Wianno Village. The Crosby family of Osterville opened a shipyard, long known as Crosbytown, on West Bay in the early 1800s. After some years and some changes in design, Horace and Worthington Crosby built a fast, safe, and seaworthy boat with a square stern, a wide beam, and a single mast near the bow. It is said that the Crosbys had the help of their mother Tirza, a spiritualist who would fall into a trance and consult her dead husband, Andrew. In 1850 the Crosby boat *Little Eva* overcame the doubts of skeptics, proved easy to handle, and was nicknamed a catboat, because fishermen would say on seeing her turn or come about that she was "quick as a cat, b'gosh." Crosbytown is near the bridge from Osterville to Little Island.

West Brewster

A village on Stony Brook near the Lower mill pond. It was once an Indian village, probably known as Setucket, just as Stony Brook was once called the Sauquatucket River. Some say that Setucket was actually at Brewster Village, not West Brewster.

West Falmouth

West Falmouth Village and Harbor border Buzzards Bay, about three miles north of Woods Hole. The federal government opened a post office at the village in 1827. The Quakers came to West Falmouth in 1668 and before long established a Friends Meeting.

White Crest Beach

Surfers come to this beach of white caps and rolling breakers, south of Cahoon Hollow Beach, on the backside of Wellfleet.

White Pond

So called since the 1600s because of the way the light strikes the water. The pond is just east of Blue Pond and Black Pond in West Chatham. To the west is a pond once called Ockpeset by the Indians, possibly from *ukque* 'end' + *ape* 'water' + *s* 'little' + *ut* 'at' = "at the end of the little waterway." Another White Pond straddles the Dennis-Harwich line [see Robbins Pond].

Whites Brook

For Jonathan White [b. 1658], son of Peregrine White, the first Pilgrim child born in New England. Jonathan lived near the brook, a tributary of Chase Garden Creek, near Center Street in Yarmouth.

Wianno   [wɪ'jano]

This community, developed after the Civil War, was named for Yanno, a sachem who lived near the South Sea in the 1600s. In the early 1900s Wianno and nearby Osterville and Centerville were known as the "boiled shirt" section of the Cape, probably because many residents were wealthy. In early days, before the development of Wianno, the land was called Hither Neck and Dead Neck.

Wickertree Road

Wickertree is a local name for a willow tree. The road is in Silver Beach, North Falmouth. An early settler, Benjamin Nye, purchased a hundred acres in 1655 in North Falmouth, known as Wickertree Field, for his sons John and Ebenezer.

Wilbur Preserve

For Dr. George B. Wilbur who in the 1970s left the wooded area where he lived on Bass River to the town of Dennis. The preserve is in the village of South Dennis, at Wilbur Cove.

Wilder Dike

Built in the early 1900s and probably named for Josiah Wilder, a storekeeper and postmaster, the dike divides the Pamet River at the center of Truro. The river west of the dike toward Cape Cod Bay is still saltwater; upstream toward the Head of Pamet it is fresh.

Wild Harbor

This harbor on Buzzards Bay at the village of Silver Beach takes its name from the southwest winds that blow up rough seas and make anchorage dangerous. The Indians called it Cataumet, related to Narragansett *kitthan* 'the sea' + *ut* 'at' = "at the sea."

Wild Hunter Road

Named for the clipper *Wild Hunter*, launched in 1855 at the Shiverick yard in East Dennis.

The *Wild Hunter* made it to California and China, and to the guano ports of the Howland Islands in the southeastern Pacific. The Cape has two Wild Hunter roads, one in Dennis, the other in Yarmouth.

William H. Covell Memorial Beach

So called since 1973 for William Covell, a teacher in Barnstable who for many years was a manager at Craigville Beach. From 1955 to 1962 Mr. Covell was the Chairman of Antiques for the Hyannis Historical Society. The beach is at the east end of Craigville Beach. It had long been known as Jacks Beach.

Wings Island

For John Wing, the first of the settlers to come to Old Harwich in the 1600s. The island has thirty-three acres, surrounded by a salt-marsh and a beach on Cape Cod Bay. The Cape Cod Museum of Natural History, the owner of the island, has a marked trail for visitors.

Wings Neck

So called for the Wings, an early Sandwich family. In 1848 the federal government erected Wings Neck Light on the order of Stephen Pleasanton, the Fifth Auditor of the Treasury and the manager of the United States Lighthouse Service from 1820 until 1852. At the tip of the neck, the light provided a century of service. In the 1880s a number of families bought the lands of the neck to construct summer houses. The Algonquian name for the neck was Wenaumet, possibly from *wónkinnumunát* "to bend," an expression that suggests the "bending" contour of the land at Buzzards Bay.

Wings Pond

Presbery Wing brought his family from Sandwich and settled beside this pond in North Falmouth, near Old Silver Beach and Route 28.

Winslows Pond

For the Winslows of Brewster and their forebear Kenelm Winslow, a settler of the later 1600s. The pond, also called Upper Mill Pond, feeds Stony Brook in West Brewster.

Witch Pond

It is said that Sarah Screecham [or Screecher] built a house by the pond, close to the forest. She hated hunters and warned them off her land. No matter how often they tried to shoot deer or a great, black mare near her house, they always missed. One day at dusk Sarah tried to warn off a young man, but he stayed put. Darkness fell and Sarah disappeared, when suddenly a young doe leaped through the nearby brush. Loading his rifle with a silver bullet, the young man took aim, fired, and hit the doe in the breast. The doe leaped again and sped off. Through the marshes and woods near the pond the young man followed the spoor of the doe. Dawn

came. Empty-handed, the young man returned to Sarah's house. Beside the hearth he found her dead, the silver bullet in her breast. The pond is on Great Neck, northeast of Maushop Village in Mashpee.

Wolf Trap Neck

So called because in the 1600s the villagers of Sandwich trapped some wolves on the neck. In the 1800s the neck had factories that produced cotton, tacks, and braids. In the 1920s the Ford Company had a factory for timer parts there. It is a narrow strip of land at the upper end of Shawme Pond.

Wood End

Named for a stand of trees that once grew on it. According to *Mourt's Relation* the Pilgrims who anchored not far from Wood End in Provincetown Harbor noted that the shore "was compassed about to the very Sea with Okes, Pines, Juniper, Sassafrass, and other sweet wood." But Thoreau says in *Cape Cod* that "we must make some allowance for the greenness of the Pilgrims in these matters, which caused them to see green." He preferred the account of John Smith, who described the Cape as a "headland of high hills of sand, overgrown with shrubby pines, hurts [i.e. whorts or whortleberries], and such trash . . . ." Located on the same stretch of beach as Long Point, Wood End is now barren land, with only the light erected in 1872.

Woods Hole

A village at the southwest corner of Falmouth, between Vineyard Sound and Buzzards Bay. Bartholomew Gosnold came ashore in 1602, it is said, during his voyage from Falmouth, England, to the Elizabeth Islands. The first settlers arrived in the 1670s and divided land in sixty-acre lots northward toward Quissett, and eastward toward the Coonamessett River. Before the 1740s Benjamin Hatch was sailing a sloop named *Woods Hole*, but who or what *Woods* means no one knows. In the early 1800s villagers had already forgotten that the word *hole* can mean "a small bay, cove, or narrow waterway" and so began to call the community Woodville. Fifty years after the Woods Hole post office opened in 1826 Joseph S. Fay won a decision in federal court to change the name of the village. According to Fay's petition, the correct name should be Woods Holl, because in the distant past Norsemen had "passed along Cape Cod through Vineyard Sound to Narragansett Bay," stopped at the site of the village and called the surrounding hills "holls." The court restored the name Woods Hole, however, in 1899. The village built whaling ships in the first half of the nineteenth century. In the last half [1885] the United States Fish and Wildlife Service opened its Bureau of Commercial Fisheries on Great Harbor — now known as the Northeast Fisheries Center. The Marine Biological Laboratory began its research activities in 1888. And in 1930 the Woods Hole Oceanographic Institute began studies of the sea and of underwater life.

Woods Hole Passage

This channel between Buzzards Bay and Vineyard Haven is difficult to navigate. It has strong tidal currents and countervailing winds. It is, for one Cape Cod sailor, Julius Wilensky, a passage "as rough as a pistol." Channel buoys mark two lanes through the numerous reefs and rocks: one is called the Strait, the other Broadway.

Wreck Cove

This early name in Chatham appears in a request to the General Court for the town's incorporation. Chatham was "a Place of Relief to Many Ship wracked Vessels & Englishmen Cast ashore in Storms upon the Beech of Sandy Point or Rack Cove . . . ." The Cove was a harbor on the east side of Monomoy Island, but has long since washed away. In 1729 the *George and Ann*, some say, came to anchor in the cove after a four-month voyage from Dublin. Under the command of Captain Rymer, the ship had sailed westward and remained on course even after an epidemic erupted that killed at least a hundred passengers. The ship also ran into bad weather and suffered from short rations. But nothing could persuade the Captain to turn back. Finally the ship sailed into Nantucket Sound. Catching sight of a Boston packet, the passengers rebelled and placed the ship under the control of Captain Lothrop, who was bound for Martha's Vineyard. Lothrop took the distressed ship in tow and commanded it to follow in the wake of his packet. Arriving at Wreck Cove, he ordered the distressed passengers to disembark and to seek help from Joseph Stewart, who kept a tavern nearby. They had Captain Rymer arrested and after his trial for neglect of life and cruelty, he returned to Dublin in irons, sentenced to hang.

Wrinkle Point

Wrinkle is an old local word for the periwinkle. The point is on the east bank of Bass River in West Dennis and is also a name for a fairly new community.

Wychmere Harbor ['wɪč,mɪr]

A man-made harbor of the late 1800s, earlier known as Salt or Oyster Pond. A racetrack once ringed the pond, before developers dredged it and had a channel cut for small craft and yachts. They built summer cottages and a hotel on its shores. The earliest name of the pond was Annosara-kumitt, of Algonquian origin, but the developers renamed it Wychmere Harbor. Wychmere is no doubt a combination of *wych* 'salt spring' or 'brine pit' + *mere* 'pool, pond' = "salt pond." The harbor lies just off Harwich Port.

Y

Yarmouth ['jar,muθ]

The town is probably named for Yarmouth in Norfolk, England, although it was not the home of the early settlers. Some suggest that the Pilgrims embarked for Leyden, Holland, from Yarmouth, and others think that the local alewives on Cape Cod reminded the early settlers of English bloaters. Settled in 1639, Yarmouth straddles the mid-Cape, but lost a good part of its eastern lands at the incorporation of Dennis. In early days the northwestern section of Yarmouth was called Matacheese, the northeastern Hockanom, and the lands along Lewis Bay were known as the South Sea.

Yarmouth Port

A village that once depended heavily on fishing and shipping. It is in northwestern Yarmouth and retains in such names as Wharf Lane and Short Wharf Creek remembrances of past trade.

Yarmouth Station

A locality in Yarmouth near Dennis Pond, so called because of its railway station.

Elizabeth Islands

B

Blaney Pond ['blɛnɪ]

The pond is west of Tarpaulin Cove on Naushon Island. In the late 1600s Anthony Blaney was a tenant farmer for Wait Winthrop, who inherited the island from his father John Winthrop, the first governor of the Massachusetts Bay Colony.

Bowdoin Road ['bodɪn]

For James Bowdoin, a merchant of Boston, who bought Naushon Island from the heirs of Wait Still Winthrop in 1717. The road begins at South Bluff and passes northeast of Tarpaulin Cove to Main Road. During the Bowdoins' ownership of the island, one of them was Governor of Massachusetts [1785-1787] and others founded Bowdoin College.

Burma Road

The soldiers stationed on Nashawena during World War II built a road from the dock at Canapitsit Channel to their barracks. The men trucking in the cargo from the ships gave the road its name as a salute to the exploits of General Vinegar Joe Stilwell's men.

Buzzards Bay

The bay is named for the bald buzzard, also called an osprey or fishhawk. In the 1700s it was also known as Fishhawk Bay. The Algonquians called the bay Poughkeeste, "where the waters open out." Early settlers at Sandwich called it Manomet or Monument Bay, names derived from nearby settlements of Indians. De Laet in *Beschrijvinghevan West-Indien* records it as Baai van Nassau, in honor of William the Silent of the house of Nassau, who led the Dutch rebellion against the Spaniards. Those who sailed with Bartholomew Gosnold aboard the *Concord* named the bay Gosnolds Hope — *hope* is an old word for a body of water such as a sound.

C

Canapitsit Channel
['kænɪ,pitsɪt] or [,kænɪ'pitsɪt]

Canapitsit is possibly from Algonquian *quin* 'long' + *ape* 'water' + *s* 'little' + *ut* 'at' = "at the [relatively] long water." The passage, between Cuttyhunk and Nashawena islands, is about fifty yards wide.

Copicut Neck ['kopəkət]

Probably from Algonquian *kob-pog* 'closed-in place' + *ut* 'at' = "at the haven." The neck hooks around the north end of Cuttyhunk Pond and so helps to make a harbor protected from open seas, sufficiently sheltered for the ferry from New Bedford.

Cuttyhunk Island and Village
[,kəti'həŋk] or ['kəti,həŋk]

This is the only village in the Elizabeth Islands. The number of year-round families is few; most earn their livelihood from fishing or by letting rooms to tourists. Gosnold described the island in 1602 as forested with "high timbered oaks . . . , cedars straight and tall, beech, elm, holly, walnut trees in abundance, hazelnut trees, cherry trees, sassafrass trees — fruit trees." By 1850 not a tree remained on the island. On Gosnold Island, in the pond at the west end of Cuttyhunk, the members of the Cuttyhunk Club and the Old Dartmouth Historical Society erected a tower in 1903, a monument dedicated to Bartholomew Gosnold. The dedication credits Gosnold with constructing the first English house on the island. Cuttyhunk is related to Mohegan *poquetan'noc* "land opened or broken up," lands that had been prepared for planting. Gosnold himself named Cuttyhunk Elizabeths Isle. In the later seventeenth century Cuttyhunk was known as Sanford Island, for Peleg Sanford, the owner of much of the land.

E

Elizabeth Islands

A group of sixteen islands, incorporated as Gosnold in 1863, dividing Vineyard Sound and Buzzards Bay westward from Woods Hole. Cuttyhunk, the westernmost of the islands, was first named Elizabeths Isle by Bartholomew Gosnold in 1602, either to honor the Queen of England or because of his fondness for his sister. In 1702 Elizabeths Island was the name for Naushon, the largest in the group. Early on, however, the Elizabeth Isles or Islands included the entire chain, and Thomas Mayhew, Governor of Martha's Vineyard, had the right in 1641 to have them settled. The islands probably are the residue of a long peninsula, cut through and splintered by the force of a retreating glacier and by floods. Strewn with glacial rocks and boulders, their shores are naturally resistant to further erosion.

F

The French Watering Place

A pond southwest of Tarpaulin Cove lighthouse on Naushon Island. At the turn of the eighteenth century French marauders would slip from their ships near the coast of the island and then steal cattle and sheep from tenant farmers. They probably filled their casks with water at the pond.

G

Goats Neck

The neck is at the east end of Naushon Island. Wait Still Winthrop, who owned the island at the turn of the eighteenth century, probably imported his "guinea" goats from the Azores and had them pastured on the neck.

Gosnold

For Bartholomew Gosnold, who sailed west from Falmouth, Cornwall, in 1602 aboard the *Concord* and explored the southeast shores and islands of Massachusetts. Petitioners in 1863 requested that this town of sixteen islands have the name Monohanset, but the General Court preferred Gosnold. Although Thomas Mayhew, Governor of Martha's Vineyard, secured the rights to the islands in 1641, the first settlers did not arrive until the 1670s. Nowadays only one island, Cuttyhunk, has year-round residents.

The Graveyard

For the south shores of Pasque and Nashawena Islands, close to Quicks Hole. The tides from Vineyard Sound and Buzzards Bay have been so unpredictable that in earlier days sudden changes in their force and direction would throw ships up against the shores and rocks near Fox Point [on Nashawena] and South Rock [on Pasque].

H

Hadley Harbor

Possibly for John Hadley, an Englishman whose quadrant, invented in 1731, greatly improved the art of navigation. In 1807 James Freeman described the "harbour, called the Hadleys, . . . [as] good anchorage for vessels drawing not more than twelve feet of water." It lies between Uncatena and Nonamesset Islands.

I

Inner Harbor

Between Goats Neck, at the east end of Naushon, and Bull Island, just off Uncatena. In the late 1600s it was known as Mr. Weeks Harbor for John Weeks, a tenant farmer of Wait Still Winthrop.

J

Jobs Neck

For Job Antiko, an Indian who in the 1600s had title to Nonamesset and other small islands nearby. The neck is at the southeast corner of Naushon Island.

L

Lackeys Bay

The bay is at the east end of Naushon Island. William Lackey served six months on Naushon Island during the Revolution. He was a mariner and probably ran supplies between the island and Falmouth.

M

Marys Lake

The lake is at the east end of Naushon Island, not far from the mansion built by the Bowdoins. Mary and James Temple Bowdoin lived in the mansion in the early 1800s, and there she had a son. The lake is a kettle hole, eighteen feet deep.

Middle Pond

The pond is at the center of Nashawena Island. It was once called Wash Pond, because the shepherds would drive their flocks to the water for a bath before shearing their wool. There is also a Wash Pond at the west end of Cuttyhunk.

Monohansett Island

[ˌmɔnəˈhænsɪt] or [ˌmonoˈhænsɪt]

The island is just east of Naushon Island in Lackeys Bay. Monohansett is from Algonquian *munnohhan* 'island' + *s* 'little' + *ut* 'at the' = "at the little island."

Monsod Bay

Monsod is a blend of the name Mount Sod, for a hill described in 1815 by Thomas L. Winthrop as high, "intersected with veins of stone," and planted on a stone base at the southwest shore of Nonamesset Island.

Mount Cary

This hill, near Memory Road at the center of Naushon Island, is 120 feet high. It is named for Edward M. Cary, the husband of Alice Forbes, whose family owns the island.

N

Nashawena [ˌnæšəˈwinə]

Located between Pasque and Cuttyhunk islands at the west end of Gosnold, Nashawena is probably related to Algonquian *nashin* "it lies between." The two largest ponds on the island are Middle and Quicks Hole ponds. During the 1700s and 1800s the Slocums of Dartmouth, Massachusetts, owned Nashawena and called it Slocum Island.

Naushon Island
[ˈnɔˌšɔn] or [ˌnɔˈšɔn]

Naushon is [like Nashawena] related to the Algonquian *nashin* "it is between" and was apparently the Indian name for all the Elizabeth Islands, which divide Buzzards Bay from Vineyard Sound. In the 1700s Naushon became the name for the largest island in the chain, not far west of Woods Hole. In the 1600s and early 1700s this island had also been known as Elizabeths Island, Tarpaulin Cove Island, Katymuck, and Winthrops Island [for Wait Still Winthrop, its owner from 1682 to 1717]. The name Katymuck is also Algonquian, from *keht* 'great' + *amaug* 'fishing place' = "great fishing place." Naushon Island was the name preferred by the Bowdoin family, who owned it from 1730 until 1843. John W. Forbes, a China merchant, bought the island thereafter, and it is now part of his family's Naushon Trust. The island also contains the last example in New England of a stable, self-perpetuating forest of oak and beech trees. Oliver Wendell Holmes called the island a "splendid domain"; Henry Thoreau praised its "noble primitive wood." John Winthrop said that before the arrival of the English the Indians kept a white whale in Westend Pond.

Nonamesset Island [ˌnɔnəˈmɛsɪt]

This island in Gosnold is closest to Woods Hole. John Winthrop related the following story about the island in 1702: "The Devil was making a stone bridge over from the main to Nanemesit Island, and while he was rowling the stones and placing them underwater, a crab catched him by the fingers, with which he snatched up his hand and flung it towards Nantucket, and the crabs breed there ever since."

P

Pasque [pæsk]

This island lies between Naushon on the east and Nashawena on the west. Pasque is a shortened form of Paskitchannesset, possibly from Algonquian *peské* 'divided' + *tchuan* 'current' + *s* 'little' + *ut* 'at' = "at the little, divided current." The Tucker family of New Bedford owned the island from the 1700s until 1866 — it was known then as Tuckers Island — but afterward sold it to John Crosby Brown and his friends, who formed the Pasque Island Club. This club of fishermen continued active until the 1920s, before selling the island some years later to the Naushon Trust. The natural growth of trees on Pasque was blunted very early from cutting over and from sheep grazing, but in the 1950s pine trees began to reappear.

Penikese Island

['pɛnə,kis]   or   [,pɛnə'kis]

North of Cuttyhunk and Nasha-wena islands in Buzzards Bay, Penikese may be a commemorative name for Penachson, who fled to the island together with his uncle Tatoson in 1676, after the uprising of their leader Metacomet [King Philip] against the English in Massachusetts failed. Gosnold called the island Hills Hap [to honor a seaman's luck?], "an islet in compass half a mile, full of cedars." Nearly two hundred years later John Anderson, a merchant from New York, gave the island and $50,000 to Louis Agassiz, a professor of zoology at Harvard, to found a school and laboratory of natural history, one of the first in the United States. The John Anderson School of Natural History opened on July 18, 1873, to fifty students, but closed within two years, after Professor Agassiz's death. From 1905 to 1921 the island was a center, under the direction of Dr. Frank Parker, for the treatment of leprosy. Three years later the Massachusetts Department of Fisheries and Game made it a sanctuary for birds. And in 1973 Penikese Island School initiated a program of vocational training for adolescent boys recommended by the Massachusetts Department of Youth Services.

Q

Quicks Hole

A channel almost a mile wide between Pasque and Nashawena islands. The hole may be named for William Quick, a seaman who moved from Charlestown to Newport in 1638, or else for Captain Cornelius Quick, who sailed the waters of the Elizabeth Islands in the late seventeenth century and traded with Captain Kidd.

Quicks Hole Pond

The pond is at the east end of Nashawena Island. During World War II the air force used it as a bombing area.

R

Rams Head

This cliff on the northwest coast of Naushon Island is about 140 feet high. It contains a mixture of rock and gravel that sparkles in the sun, but observers differ on whether it actually resembles a ram's profile.

Rattlesnake Neck

Wait Still Winthrop said in 1702 of this neck at the northeast corner of Naushon Island that "an Indian powwow — meeting with some affront from the Indians that inhabited Naushon Island out of revenge got the Devil to throw over a Rattlesnake which increased much and soon after a squaw was bit by one."

Robinsons Hole

For the Robinsons who lived at the west end of Naushon Island in the 1600s. The current in the hole rushes over rocks and boulders so rapidly that it can easily endanger small craft.

S

Saddleback

This hill with the profile of a saddle lies just west of Middle Road on Nashawena.

Sow and Pigs Reef

A large ledge bordered by smaller rocks, the reef was once an island at the west end of Cuttyhunk in Buzzards Bay. The last whaler to leave New Bedford, the *Wanderer*, struck the reef during a squall in 1924 and foundered. Some say that in the early 1900s mooncussers would lure passing vessels on to Sow and Pigs by displacing beacon lights at the west end of Cuttyhunk.

ment built a light tower at the cove, but it was too late for any sustained, practical use, because railroads were rapidly increasing their capacity to carry freight through coastal New England.

Timmy Point

At the north end of Uncatena Island. Timmy is not the name of an inhabitant, but stems from a play on the pronunciation of Uncatena. In the early 1800s the common pronunciation was *Onkey Tonkey*, a happy rhyme that was meaningless. But in keeping with the practice, at least on the Cape, of naming places after one's uncle, the point began to be called [on the model of *Onkey Tonkey*] Uncle Timmy. Some years later the *uncle* was dropped.

T

Tarpaulin Cove formerly [tarˈpɒlɪn] now [tarˈpɒlɪn] or [ˈtɑrpəlɪn]

So called by sailors in the 1600s because they would anchor there to repair the keels of their ships by tarring them [a process of "tarpawling"]; or else the cove honors a tarpaulin captain, who had risen through the ranks to assume command of his ship. On the south side of Naushon Island, the cove was in early days a battle station. Captain Samuel Pease of the sloop *Mary* lost his life in the 1690s near the cove in battle against Thomas Pound and his ship *Pirate*. The British navy stationed ships at the cove during the Revolution and the War of 1812. During the later 1800s the cove was a port of trade. Coasters bearing coal and cement, lumber and lime, would dock at the cove, take on supplies from the Tarpaulin Cove Farm, and wait for a favorable change of tide. In 1892 the federal govern-

U

Uncatena Island [ˌəŋkəˈtinə]

Uncatena is probably related to Natick *ongkoue* "beyond [the water]," an appropriate name because the island faces Naushon directly across Northwest Gutter. In the 1800s the gutter was still shallow enough for cattle to cross from Naushon to the pastures of Uncatena.

V

Vekatimest Islands [ˈvɛkəˈtɪməst]

The islands or stepping stones between Naushon and Nonamesset. They were once known as Ram Islands [for their pastures of sheep] and as Buck Islands. Eleazar Buck was a pirate on the sloop *Mary*, served under the pirate Thomas Pound, and had the aid of Wait Still Winthrop, a judge of Massachusetts who tried him in court but spared him from the gallows. Vekatimest [also Uckatimest] may stem from Algonquian *ahquedne* 'island' + *s* 'little' + *ut* 'at' = "at the little island."

W

Weepecket Islands [ˌwiˈpɛkɪt]

These little islands north of Naushon are named for Webacowett, an Indian who once owned land in the Elizabeth Islands.

Martha's Vineyard

A

Abel Hill

For Abel Wauwompuhque, whose uncle the Sachem Mittark was the first preacher at the Gay Head Church in the 1600s. The hill is not in Gay Head but north of Chilmark Pond. There are two burial grounds on the hill, one for Indians, the other for whites. The oldest tombstone is dated 1712.

Abels Spring

For Abel Wauwompuhque, the brother of Sachem Mittark, both of them preachers to the Gay Head Indians in the late 1600s. A gravestone at the spring is said to be Abel's memorial. And it is also said that cattle watering at the spring, not far from Gay Head Lighthouse, feel a presence beyond the power of human sensibility that makes them leap and bellow.

Allen Point

For the Allens of Chilmark, who were tradesmen, selectmen, and carpenters. The point is on Chilmark Pond.

B

Barnhouse Beach

Near the Wequobsque Cliffs in Chilmark, this beach on the Atlantic is named for a structure owned by Roger Allen, to which in the 1930s and 1940s men [including Boardman Robinson, Roger Baldwin, and Max Eastman] would come, before crossing a marsh for a day of swimming.

Bass Creek

The creek takes its name, it is said, from the large numbers of sea bass that were frozen in its icy waters during the winter of 1778. In that cold winter the fish fed many hungry families on the Vineyard. They had suffered from General Grey and his British marines' raid and from the loss of ten thousand sheep and three hundred head of cattle. For some time the creek had been the harbor for the ferry from Falmouth or the "Continent," as local people said, but in the early 1800s storms and tides obstructed its channel with so much sand that the town of Tisbury had the docks moved elsewhere. Several years later all traces of the creek disappeared after the construction of Water Street and Howard Avenue between Vineyard Haven Harbor and Lagoon Pond.

Bassetts Hill

For the Bassetts of Chilmark, who donated lands near the hill on Middle Road for a town cemetery. In 1792 Benjamin Bassett wrote a book of anthropology, *Fabulous Traditions and Customs of the Indians of Martha's Vineyard*. Chilmark's first town hall, built on the hill in 1844, came to be known as Woodpecker Hall, because of the holes drilled by the birds in its beams.

Beach Road

The road runs along a barrier beach between Vineyard Haven Harbor and Lagoon Pond. In the early 1900s an electric trolley ran between Oak Bluffs and Vineyard Haven, and carpenters and caulkers worked in the boatyards on the beach. The Martha's Vineyard Hospital, opened in 1929, stands at the foot of the road in Oak Bluffs. Quinniaaumuck was the Algonquian name of a waterway through the barrier beach, from *quinni* 'long' + *amaug* 'fishing place' = "long fishing place." The barrier beach itself had the name *Quinniumuh*, possibly from *quinni* 'long' + *munnoh* 'island' = "long island," although the distinction between an island and a barrier beach among Indians is not clear.

Beetle Swamp

For the Beetles, an old Vineyard family. The swamp is just opposite Jernegan Pond. At the edge of the swamp is Sweetened Water Pond, probably so called to contrast it with the usually brackish water of salt marshes.

Beetlebung Corner

Beetlebung is a local word for the tupelo, a hardwood tree that is used to make beetles or mallets and also bungs for casks. In the early 1700s Chilmark Village planted tupelos, also called *beetlebound* and *beetlewood*, to mark a property line. The corner in the village is the juncture of three roads — South, Middle, and Menemsha Cross roads.

Black Brook

The brook flows through marshland from South Road, Gay Head, to Squibnocket Pond. Its dark red, almost black, waters are especially tasty, it is said, for horses. Gay Headers speak of a wild horse, hard-breathing, that roams up and down along the brook.

Black Point Pond

So called because black grass, a winter feed for cattle, grew in the marshes at the pond, west of Tisbury Great Pond on the Atlantic. The Algonquians called the land near the pond Meshpootacha, possibly from *massa* 'big' + *pe* 'water' + *auk* 'land' + *ut* 'at' = "at the land on the great cove."

Black Pond

The dark water in the pond is the inflow of brooks from peat bogs. It was also called Witch Pond, because its dark color was supposedly the work of the Devil's agents. Indians said, however, that Michabo kept his white whale in the pond when it hibernated. The pond is west of Squibnocket, not far from South Road, Gay Head.

Blackwater Brook

So called because the water in this brook east of James Pond, West Tisbury, has a source in a peat bog. Not far north of the brook, in the days after the Revolution, Islanders found bog iron. The mining of the iron began soon after, and in 1814 it was used for producing cannon balls for the *U.S.S. Constitution*. The Indians called the brook Wechpoquaset, possibly from *wequa* 'the end' + *paug* 'pond' + *s* 'little' + *ut* 'at' = "at the end of the little pond."

Bluefish Point

The point is on the southwest shore of Katama Bay in Edgartown. Bluefish, plentiful in the waters off the point, feed voraciously on schools of alewives.

Bold Water Point

For the strong current near the point on Poketapaces Neck, on the west shore of Edgartown Great Pond.

Boston Hill

So called because on clear days, it is said, an old Chilmark skipper, his spyglass to his eye, would sit atop the hill [105 feet high] and scan the coasts almost to Boston. It was also known as Chair Hill, for the skipper's chair, and also as Rumpus Ridge, because there were once hard feelings among neighbors. North of the hill and east of Chilmark Village, Thomas Hart Benton had a summer studio, where he painted portraits of local townsmen.

Brandy Brow

So called, it is said, because a taverner in the village of West Tisbury once had his dram shop on top of the brow near Parsonage Pond. Others say that during Grey's Raid in the days of the Revolution, some villagers hid a barrel of brandy in the walls of a saltbox on the brow. Most people

on the island, however, drank rum. In the 1600s there was also a Brandy Brow on the Merrimack River in Amesbury.

Brush Pond

A pond in the village of Eastville, Oak Bluffs, it has an outlet into Lagoon Pond. Its Algonquian name was Uncawamuck, probably from *wonki* 'crooked' + *amaug* 'fishing place' = "crooked fishing place." The outlet into Lagoon Pond was Assunutaaket, from *assun* 'stony' + *tuk* 'estuary' + *ut* 'at' = "at the stony estuary."

C

Cape Higgon formerly [kə'pɪgən] now [kep] ['hɪgən]

Maybe from Algonquian *kobpog* "place shut in, haven, cove." Early in this century Cape Higgon, on Vineyard Sound near Paint Mill Brook, Chilmark, was a community of farmers and fishermen. The farmers raised sheep and dairy herds; the fishermen set traps for cod and lobsters.

Cape Poge formerly [ka'pog] now [kep] [pog]

This is a long, sickle-shaped neck at the east end of Chappaquiddick Island. After map makers of the 1600s first transcribed Algonquian *capoak* as Cape Ack or Cape Wack, the new spellings took hold and turned into such names as Cape Poge Bay, Cape Poge Elbow, and Cape Poge Gut. Capoak is probably related to *kobpog* "haven, cove," a name suitable to a number of harbors on Cape Poge Bay. Cape Poge Elbow is a beach barrier between the bay and Nantucket Sound. Cape Poge Gut is a narrow channel between the Elbow and North Neck on Chappaquiddick Island. Some day the growing deposits of sediment may close the channel and turn Cape Poge Bay into a large pond. Before the hurricane of 1722 closed a breach from the Atlantic Ocean into Poucha Pond, Cape Poge was actually an island. At the northeast point of Cape Poge in 1801 the federal government constructed a lighthouse, since rebuilt several times. In 1959, the Trustees of Reservations set aside 391 acres as a wildlife preserve on Cape Poge. Another Algonquian name for the lands of Cape Poge was Natuck, probably from *naiag* 'point of land' + *tuk* 'tidal estuary' + *ut* 'at' = "at the point on the tidal estuary." In the 1700s Cape Poge was also called Great Neck.

Cedar Tree Neck

In West Tisbury on Vineyard Sound, near Daggetts Pond. In the 1700s Mayhew Norton built his house atop a bluff near the neck. In the 1800s the Daggetts grew cranberries in a bog at the neck, and a telegraph cable ran from the neck to the Elizabeth Islands. The hurricane of 1938 destroyed the bog, but in the 1960s the neck became a wildlife sanctuary of the Sheriffs Meadow Foundation. Indians called the neck Squemmechchue, possibly related to *m'shqui* 'red' + *amaug* 'fishing place' + *ut* 'at' = "fishing place for salmon." Cedar Tree is presumably for a stand of cedars.

Chappaquiddick Island

[ˌčæpəˈkwɪdɪk]

From Algonquian *chappa* 'separated' + *aquidne* 'island' + *ut* 'at' = "at the separated island." In 1715 the Province of Massachusetts reserved the control of the island to about one hundred Indians, but by the end of the 1800s

only seven descendants remained. Meanwhile English settlers brought their cattle from Edgartown to the island. They often paid very little for pasturage and drove the Indians off to poorer terrain. The local name for the island is Chappy.

Chappaquonsett [ˌčæpəˈkwɔnsɪt]

A creek between Lake Tashmoo and Vineyard Sound in Tisbury. During the 1930s the town of Tisbury had the creek's channel straightened to enable boats to have safer access to the lake. But the straightened channel increased the flow of salt water and diminished the runs of herring that had in earlier years spawned in the lake's fresh water. The Chickemmoo gristmill, built by Thomas Smith, Jr. in 1734, stood on the creek for a hundred and fifty years, turning out sacks of flour for local farmers.

Cheepies Cornfield

For Cheepie the Evil One, a troublemaker who disappeared forever on a dark night after a powwow on a hill near his field. The cornfield was close to the Gay Head Cliffs and Lighthouse.

Chickemmoo [ˈčɪkəˌmʊ]

Although this name probably stems from Algonquian *chick'amaug* "a fishing place with a weir," English settlers in the 1600s applied it to all the land between Lake Tashmoo and Lamberts Cove. The Mayhews acquired Chickemmoo in 1671. Soon after, it became a part of Chilmark and in 1736 a part of Tisbury. The division of Tisbury in 1892 also divided Chickemmoo, and the western half became a part of West Tisbury.

Chilmark

In the early years of English settlement the lands of Chilmark were the property of Thomas Mayhew, the Vineyard's governor. For the first nine years of his charter [1671-80], Mayhew called his land Tisbury Manor in honor of his English birthplace. But in 1680 he began to call his manor Chilmark to distinguish it from neighboring Tisbury. [In England, too, Chilmark and Tisbury are bordering villages.] Soon after 1694 Chilmark was no longer a manor but became a town in the Province of Massachusetts. The Indian praying village near the Mayhews was Nashowa-kummuck, from *nashowa* 'halfway' + *kommuck* 'house' = "halfway house," maybe a stockade or schoolhouse. Chilmark borders West Tisbury and Gay Head.

Chilmark Pond

As thin as a lizard, the pond lies between the South Road and the Atlantic. The width of the pond has continually contracted in the past three hundred years, because the barrier beach on its south side has had to retreat before the rolling assault of breakers. Several times a year the town of Chilmark opens the barrier to the sea and thereby retains sufficient salinity in the pond for the needs of shellfish.

Christiantown

A village for praying Indians, laid out in 1659 with the consent of the sachem Kitteanumin, on a mile-square grant south of Indian Hill in West Tisbury. The Algonquian name for the village was Manettouwatootan, from *manitou* 'God' + *wetu* 'house' + *otun* 'village' = "village of God's house." Kitteanumin's uncle, John Papamick, had a field of his own — Papamicks Field — in a large tract known as Mackkonnetchasqua, probably related to Narragansett *mickúckaskeete* 'meadow.' In 1698 eighty-two Indians lived in the village. In 1903 there were three. The Indians worshipped in a chapel but also outdoors on the Dancing Field, where they prayed to the sun and moon for the good of their crops and for good riddance to illness and enemies.

Clevelandtown

For an old family of Edgartown, residents on the south side of the village since the late 1600s.

Coopers Landing

For the Coopers of Gay Head and for James Cooper, who in the late 1920s still retained a few words and phrases of his native Algonquian language. The landing, not far from the Gay Head Coast Guard Station, was busy a century ago when fishermen docked their boats in preparation for their departure for Nomans Land. Near the landing stood Baptism Rock, where until recently the local church held rites of immersion.

Crackatuxet Cove [ˌkræke'təksɪt]

Crackatuxet is possibly related to Pequod *cachauxet*, "a small, edible fish, known as the chogset or blue perch"; *cachauxet* comes itself from *chohchohkeset* "marked with spots, striped." The cove is actually enclosed, separated from the southeast shores of Edgartown Great Pond by a strip of beach. In the 1600s a number of waterways connected Edgartown Great Pond to Mattakeeset Bay, but severe storms and the erosive power of the sea have left none of them but the cove.

Cranberry Lands

For the wild cranberries that grow in the bogs of northeastern

Gay Head. In years past Gay Head would celebrate its own harvest festival — Cranberry Day. Each year a town officer would choose a day appropriate for picking the berries and for holding a festival. But profits declined and so did Cranberry Day.

Crocker Pond

In the 1700s Richard W. Crocker had a farm and mill at the pond, formed by a dam in Mill Brook, which flows through North Tisbury Village. In the 1600s Josiah the Sachem had, in the same locality, a meadow known as Wampache, probably from *wampaskeht* "meadow." The land near the brook was called Nittowouhtohquay, related in part to Algonquian *wetawauk*, from *wetu* 'wigwam' + *auk* 'place' = "place of wigwams."

Crystal Lake

A name frequently used by speculators with a view for profitable ventures. Before the 1870s the lake was known as Ice House Pond, for a large storage barn on its shores. The lake was an arm of Vineyard Haven Harbor at the northwest corner of East Chop, until a growing sandbar enclosed it altogether.

D

Daggetts Pond ['dægɪts]

For Obed Daggett, who in the 1800s owned a farm bordering a small pond near Vineyard Sound in West Tisbury. The Algonquian name for the pond was Nepisse from *nippi* 'water' + *s* 'little' + *ut* 'at' = "at the little water."

Davis Pond

For Malatiah Davis, a Colonel in the Vineyard militia, who served as a selectman in Tisbury after the Revolution. The pond lies behind a dam on the Tiasquam River just off Music Street in the village of West Tisbury.

Deep Bottom and Deep Bottom Cove

The cove reaches northeastward in Tisbury Great Pond; the bottom runs farther north into Martha's Vineyard State Forest. In the 1600s the Indians of Tisbury had settlements on the cove.

Devils Bed and Pillows

A cluster of four glacial boulders near the Middle Road east of Chilmark Village. In the past the largest boulder lay like a bed beneath the other three, two of them pillows, the third flat as a bolster. But now the two pillows and the bolster have slid off onto the ground. The rocks are also called Maushops Bed.

Devils Bridge

It is said that the Indian giant Michabo [a devil to the English] once cast some huge boulders during a fit of rage into Vineyard Sound at the base of Gay Head Cliffs. When he set out to cross the sound to Cuttyhunk he bore a great many rocks in his apron to help make a bridge. But as he stepped barefoot into the water a crab bit his toe and so enraged him that he threw down all the rocks. Since then many ships have broken up on Michabo's reef. In January 1884 the steamer *City of Columbus*, under way from Boston to Savannah, foundered on the reef at night and lost 121 passengers and crew.

Devils Den

So called because Michabo the Indian giant [called a devil by the English] kept a fire going in the den's hollow. He would fetch logs and drag in game for his wife to cook for them and their children. Others say that the den is actually a dormant volcano that spews flames and ashes from time to time. But geologists explain that the den is a hollow carved by centuries of waves from the loose stone and clay at the edge of Gay Head Cliffs. [See also Wequobsque Cliffs].

Devils Hollow

Near Cedar Tree Neck and Vineyard Sound. In the 1800s islanders would follow a path through a dark thicket to this hollow, where they would hold evening services. It is said that the glow of a kerosene lamp kept the islanders from going astray and that on nights for prayer meetings the devil stayed away. The path to the hollow, four miles over rough ground, is no longer in use.

Dividend Point

On Sengekontacket Pond, southeast of Majors Cove and Felix Neck. The word *dividend* appears in old deeds to designate a parcel of land granted to a proprietor. The point itself was part of the property long held in common by the Smith, Norton, Beetle, and Weeks families.

Dodger Hole

Just west of Majors Cove on Sengekontacket Pond, the hole is a glacial kettle once filled with loggerhead turtles. It is a small pond, named possibly for the skill needed by boys and hunters to elude the snapping jaws of the turtles.

Dogfish Bar

Schools of dogfish feed on herring along the coast of Menemsha Bight. The bar, opposite Lobsterville, is a shield for fishermen's boats against the strong seas.

Drinking Water and Washing Water Ponds

Small, twin ponds, named possibly by shepherds who would have their flocks washed at one pond and watered at the other. The ponds are north of Seths Pond on Lamberts Cove Road, West Tisbury.

Dukes County

Dukes County, established by the Provincial Assembly of New York in 1683, included Nantucket, Martha's Vineyard, the Elizabeth Islands, and Nomans Land. The same Assembly also made Brooklyn Kings County and much of Long Island Queens County. But when Dukes County aligned itself with Massachusetts in 1695, the General Court agreed to a separate county for Nantucket, and united the other islands as Dukes County. The County was named for James, Duke of York.

E

East Chop

An old meaning for *chop* is a "division of land." A Paston letter of the fifteenth century speaks of "a choppe of xx pownd of lond." Some say that *chop* is the name for the side of a vise; others think it comes from *mutton chop*. In 1646 when Governor Thomas Mayhew described the land as the "Easternmost chop of Homses

Hole," he apparently included the entire neck from Vineyard Haven Harbor to Farm Pond. But nowadays the Chop is the name only for the headland at the north end of Oak Bluff. During the Revolution, when the British General Grey had his troops carry off sheep, cattle, arms, and money, it was said that he had left behind the two Chops [East and West] only because he could not take them with him.

Eastville

So called because of its location on the east side of Vineyard Haven Harbor. In earlier times it had the nickname, the Barbary Coast, because many of its villagers were fishermen, sailors, skippers, and shipwreckers. It was also known as the East Side.

Edgartown

Southeast on the Vineyard, Edgartown is the county seat. It is the oldest settlement in Dukes County [1641] and was for some time called Great Harbor. In 1671 Thomas Mayhew had it incorporated as Edgartown by the Province of New York and had himself appointed governor of the island. The town was named for Edgar, the Duke of York's four-year-old son, who died in childhood. During the 1800s many whaling captains lived in Edgartown, yet the nickname for the residents as a whole was the "Old Town Turkies." The word "turkey" is a localism for herring, so called by the workers at the nearby Mattakeeset Creek Fishing Company, who found their catches as profitable as a flock of game fowl.

Edgartown Great Pond

In the south end of town, separated from the Atlantic by a barrier beach. In times of storm it is occasionally flooded by sea water breaking through the barrier beach. In the 1800s it was known as Great Herring Pond, and local fishermen hauled in catches of nearly 700,000 herring. The Algonquians called the cove at the head of the pond Wintucket, from *winne* 'good' + *tuck* 'tidal river' + *ut* 'at' = "at the good, tidal river."

Edgartown Harbor

The harbor extends from Edgartown Village to Cape Poge Elbow, north of Chappaquiddick Beach. In the 1800s it was known as Old Town Harbor; in the 1600s it was Great or Martha's Vineyard Harbor. Edgartown Lighthouse, built in the 1830s, faces the inner harbor at Ned Point.

Eel Pond

Now an open bay north of Edgartown Village. In the 1700s it was known as Daniels Pond or Gurnet Pond. In an account of Dukes County in 1807 James Freeman says that the silver eel is not slimy but fat, is caught in late fall, and tastes as good as the common eel. Eel Pond used to yield fifteen barrels of eels a night.

F

Farm Pond

At the east side of Farm Neck, Oak Bluffs. Once an arm of Nantucket Sound, it is now a brackish pond, divided from the sea by a sandbar but open through sluices to alewives that spawn in the spring. For a time in the late 1800s Methodists at Wesleyan Grove called the pond Lake Tiberias in remembrance of the Holy Land. In the 1600s the pond was known as Muddy Cove.

Fayal ['faɪəl]

A community in Oak Bluffs near the Sacred Heart Church, named for the westernmost island of the Azores. The first Portuguese to live in Fayal were whaling families.

Felix Neck

Felix was the last Indian in the 1700s to live at the neck on the west shore of Sengekontacket Pond in Edgartown. It is said that he once accused an Indian girl of stealing and as retribution had her sold into slavery. The neck has two hundred acres and is now a sanctuary for wildlife under the care of the Felix Neck Wildlife Trust.

Ferry Boat Island

So called because Isaac Chase, the first ferryman between the Vineyard and Falmouth, anchored his boat at the island, where he had built a landing stage at the turn of the eighteenth century. The island is at the northwest corner of Lagoon Pond.

Ferryboat Creek

So called because in the 1800s the ferryboat from Falmouth docked at this creek at the south end of Vineyard Haven Harbor. The creek was deep enough to enable seagoing ships to sail through and come to anchor in Lagoon Pond.

Fisher Pond

For Daniel Fisher, M.D., who in the 1800s invested in whalers, candle factories, and mills. The pond is on the Mill Brook just west of North Tisbury, and still washes against the remains of a mill dam, a wall of cut stone. The pond is more recently known as Woods Pond, for a family of Californians who own property nearby.

Fisher Road

Dr. Daniel Fisher had this road built from North Tisbury Village to Edgartown as a convenience for his teamster wagons bearing ground flour from his mills at Fisher and Crocker ponds to a bakery at the wharf on Edgartown Harbor. The ovens of the bakery supplied whalers with hardtack. Fisher grew his own grain on the Vineyard.

Fish Hook

West of Cedar Tree Neck, West Tisbury. George Hough, who owned the land in the late 1800s, dubbed it Fish Hook in a moment of delight. He had almost given up fishing one day for lack of a hook when a friend, rummaging through a box, pulled one out. Since 1967 it has been a sanctuary

for wildlife and adjoins the Alexander Reed Bird Refuge, deeded in the 1960s to the Vineyard by Lucy Reed, who donated $10,000 to establish it. Alexander S. Reed was a close relative who went out on a boat one day and never came back.

Fresh Pond

This kettle pond west of Majors Cove in Oak Bluffs is called *fresh* to contrast its water with the brackishness of Sengekontacket Pond. The Algonquians called the pond Quatupog, probably from *ukquáe* 'end' + *paug* 'pond' = "point at the end of a pond." In the 1800s it was also known as Nortons Pond for an old Vineyard family. Daniel Webster occasionally camped at the pond.

Fulling Mill Brook

On this brook was a fulling mill where oil spots and smudges were removed from cloth. Near the brook, too, tanners of the 1700s cured hides for shoes and saddles. Nowadays the brook is one of the best trout streams on the Vineyard, flowing southward under Middle Road into Chilmark Pond. It is also known as Beldens Pond for a local family.

G

Gay Head

The town farthest west on the island, incorporated in 1870. The name Gay Head is quite old [in use before 1662] and describes the town's majestic cliffs of gaily colored sands and clays. Some say that when in 1602 Bartholomew Gosnold came upon Gay Head, he called it Dover Cliffs for the seaport back home in England. The Indians living at Gay Head long

ago spoke of their land as Aquiniuh, probably related to *qunnukque* 'high' + *auke* 'land' = "high land." There is a legend that the god Michabo lived at the cliffs with his wife Squantum — she had square eyes covered over by hair — and their twelve daughters. Squantum died, it is said, when she leaped from the highest of the cliffs and disappeared into the Atlantic.

Gay Head Cliffs and Neck

At the west end of Gay Head and of Vineyard Sound. The federal government built the lighthouse on the neck in 1798 and then installed a lifesaving station [now at Menemsha] about sixty years later. Rising 150 feet above the sea, the cliffs are the highest on both the Atlantic and Pacific coasts. The clays that form the cliffs are a mixture of reds and yellows, whites and browns.

Gravel Island

Next to Brush Island in the northwest corner of Sengekontacket Pond. The Algonquians called these islands Quanames, from *quinn* 'long' + *amaug* 'fishing place' = "long fishing place." *Qunnamaug*, according to Roger Williams, means "lamprey." The name "gravel" describes the condition of the soil on the island.

Gravelly Hill

At the east end of Gay Head near the South Road. It is next to Fatty Pasture, so called because of its plentiful feed for cattle . Years ago two sisters living at the hill saw a pair of black oxen trudging toward them, their heads swaying from side to side. The sisters took fright and ran off, although no one else has ever seen a black ox in Gay Head.

Green Hollow

It is said that John Pease, William Vincent, Nicholas Norton, Malachi Browning, and Thomas Trapp all came to the Vineyard in 1632, about ten years before the Mayhews, who are known as the first settlers. The five men dug out caves at Green Hollow, supposedly south of Edgartown, and spent their first winter living on fish and fowl, helped by the Indians. In the spring they went to Plymouth and returned a year later with wives to settle on the Vineyard for good. But as Charles E. Banks says in his history, Vincent was only five and Trapp had not yet been born.

H

Harts Harbor or Harthaven

For the Hart family, who built summer cottages at the harbor in the late 1800s. The harbor is a narrow channel southeast of Farm Pond, cut off by a sandbar from Nantucket Sound.

Herring Creek

The creek helps to divide Gay Head from Chilmark. Laborers deepened it in the 1840s to enable the herring of Menemsha Pond to spawn in Squibnocket.

The Highland Wharf

About the turn of the twentieth century the Highland Wharf on Nantucket Sound in Oak Bluffs was a stopping point for ferries from New Bedford and Woods Hole. Behind the wharf was the Martha's Vineyard Summer Institute, opened in 1875 as the first summer school in the United States for college students. Two of the instructors at the school were Edmund S. Burgess, a botanist, and Amelia Watson, who did the watercolors for Thoreau's *Cape Cod*. The Institute lost students and had to close in the early 1900s, after many colleges throughout the nation began to offer summer courses for credit. In the mid-1800s the wharf was known as Baptist Landing, because of the temple nearby that was used for summer meetings.

Hilliards Cove

In the 1800s Captain Hilliard Mayhew had a house overlooking this cove at the head of Squibnocket Pond near the road from Chilmark to Gay Head. Mayhew was a whaling captain who is said to have single-handedly quelled a mutiny aboard his ship. Taken captive by the cannibals of an island, he freed himself by running down to the beach and dragging a boat behind him. Captain Mayhew commanded the *Lexington* in 1854, but maybe the story of mutiny aboard his ship stems from Melville's account in *Moby Dick* of the madman Gabriel aboard the *Jeroboam*. The name of the captain, made helpless by Gabriel and the ship's crew, was also Mayhew.

Hines Point

For the Hines family, who first came to the point near the northwest corner of Lagoon Pond in the 1870s. The Hineses themselves called their property Cedar

Neck in the hope of selling parcels to off-Islanders. Earlier the point had been known as Little Neck. During the War of 1812 and the British blockade of the Vineyard, Captain David Smith was sailing back from New York with provisions when he found himself pursued by two barges of British marines. Smith slipped through Bass Creek and into the shallows of Lagoon Pond near Little Neck. The British barges were too big to follow, but the marines went ashore on the neck and fired at Smith from the beach. The sand gave them poor footing and so Smith was able to escape. The Algonquians called the neck Uquiessa from *wequa* 'end, point' + *s* 'little' + *ut* 'at' = "at the little point."

Holmes Hole Neck

An old name for the land between Lake Tashmoo and Vineyard Haven Harbor, including the village of Vineyard Haven. The Indian name for the large neck was Nobnocket, possibly from *nuppe* 'pool or pond' + *auk* 'land' + *ut* 'at' = "land at the pond." John Holmes was probably a blacksmith and early settler. [See Vineyard Haven]

Homers Pond

No one knows who Homer was, but some say that the pond's name stems from Pasquanammin, who in the 1600s planted maize next to the pond on Scrubby Neck. The shortening is supposedly due to a gradual change from the original Pasquanammin to Nashamons in the 1700s, and finally to Homers. The pond is on the Atlantic, east of Tisbury Great Pond.

Husselton Head and Hollow
['hɔzltən]

For Francis Usselton, a squatter in the 1600s at the hollow on the west shore of Vineyard Haven Harbor. Governor Thomas Mayhew brought suit against him and had him expelled from the Vineyard in 1667. During the Revolution a Tory sympathizer by the name of Dagget lived just north of Husselton Head and entertained British sailors. One night a group appeared with a Falmouth pilot they had seized and threatened with death unless he would take them past the shoals to Cape Cod. But before the evening was over the prisoner's friends, armed with muskets, surrounded the house and freed him. During the 1800s the hollow had a wharf, a shipyard, and a candle factory.

I

Indian Hill

Once the setting of Indian dances and rites in Christiantown, the hill, now privately owned, is in a locality of West Tisbury no longer directly accessible. Another Indian Hill lies farther west, so called because of the native graves found on it.

J

James Pond

For James, Duke of York, the holder of the royal patent to New York in the late 1600s and the proprietor of Martha's Vineyard until 1671. It has also been called Great James Pond and Pond Royall. Its Algonquian name was Onkokemmy, probably from *ongkoúe* 'beyond' + *amaug* 'fishing place' = "beyond the fishing place." There were good catches of herring at the mouth of the pond on Lamberts Cove, West Tisbury.

Jerneganville and Jernegan Pond   [ˈjərnəgənvɪl]

For the Jernegans, who came to the Vineyard at the turn of the eighteenth century. In the mid-1700s William Jernegan was representative to the General Court in Boston. In the 1800s some Jernegans were captains aboard whalers. Nathaniel Jernegan, a sea captain, opened an unsuccessful shoe factory in Edgartown. The village nearby is west of Vineyard Haven Road. The pond is opposite Beetle Swamp on West Tisbury Road.

Jobs Neck and Jobs Neck Cove

Possibly for Jawb Washarum, who with Elizabeth Nataquam agreed in 1696 to grant Thomas Daggett and Matthew Mayhew of Edgartown "all the wrecks and whales which may be cast on shore, reserving one tenth part to King William, our Liege Lord and Sovereign, reserving to themselves of each whale stranded one flock (fluke) or part of the tayle and one fin to be severed and one yard square of blubber." The neck and cove are at the west end of Edgartown Great Pond. The Indians called the locality Sopotaming.

John Oliver Point

For John Oliver Norton, called by his crews the "hardest ticket" among the whaling captains. He sailed the seas with his wife Charity and brought his ships home laden with whale oil. After he retired to the point on Cape Poge Bay, he took summer visitors out fishing in his sloop *Minnie*.

K

Kanomika Neck   [kəˈnamɪkə]

A long stretch of land at the north end of Edgartown Great Pond.

Kanomika is related to Algonquian *quinn* 'long' + *amaug* 'fishing place' = "long fishing place."

Katama Bay and Point   [kəˈtemə]

Katama is probably from Algonquian *kehte* 'great' + *amaug* 'fishing place' = "great fishing place." The bay flows between the west shore of Chappaquiddick and Edgartown. The point faces the bay near the south shore of the town. The quahogs in the bay are locally called "hard-shell Baptists." Katama, it is said, was a beautiful maiden and Mattakeeset a handsome chief. Their love for each other angered hostile warriors. And so, to escape their enemies, they swam out to sea and died in the waves.

The Kings Highway

This road from West Tisbury to Gay Head was set out along the south shore before the Revolution. It went over Abel Hill and along Wequobsque Cliffs to Stonewall Beach and Nashaquitsa. It remained the principal road to Gay Head until the extension of South Road over Hariphs Creek in the mid-1800s.

The Kings Land

A triangular cut of land laid out before the Revolution at the intersection of County Road and Takemmy Trail in West Tisbury. On one side of the triangle was a courthouse, on the other side a whipping post, stocks, and a jail. During General Grey's raid on the Vineyard in 1777 the Islanders concealed gunpowder at the courthouse. It is said that a young woman sat on the keg, hiding it with her skirts, and knitted while the British mariners searched. The setting at the Kings Land may have suggested to Nathaniel Hawthorne, when he stayed at the Vineyard, the opening scene of *The Scarlet Letter*.

L

Lagoon Bridge

In the 1870s the bridge was built on the north shore of Lagoon Pond, close to Quays Neck, where schooners would dock. One day the *Splendid* came into port after a voyage to the South Pacific. There were three captains aboard, two of them masters of ships lost en route from Java to the Moluccas. Each of them had secured from the holds of their foundered vessels a cache of gold coins that they agreed to share with the captain of the *Splendid*. In port at Quays Neck, the three captains decided to bury their money near Lagoon Bridge. Soon after, the *Splendid* sailed. The two rescued captains dug up the gold and hired Clifford Dunham to row them to Falmouth. They reached shore in the dark and began once more to bury their horde. But townsmen awakened by their noise soon seized them and put their gold in Falmouth Bank. Some days later it disappeared for good. Even Clifford Dunham lost the bucket of coins he earned for rowing. The two captains — Pitman and Brown — stood trial for theft in Salem Court, and were convicted.

Lagoon Pond

First called a *lagoon* in 1743, the pond is, as the word suggests, separated by a beach barrier from Vineyard Haven Harbor. In the 1800s a number of saltworks lined the shores of the pond. In the 1950s the Commonwealth installed a hatchery for lobsters. The Algonquians called the pond Waketquay, from *waqua* 'head' + *tukq* 'tidal estuary' + *ut* 'at' = "at the head of the tidal water." A rip-rapped channel still links the pond to Vineyard Haven Harbor.

Lake Tashmoo [ˈtæš,mu]

Some say the pond in north central Tisbury is named for Nicholas Tissimoo, who lived on its shores. It is more likely that the name stems from a spring at the head of the lake, called by the Indians Kehtashimet, from *keht* 'great' + *ashim* 'spring' + *ut* 'at' = "at the great spring." The spring flows into the lake and in the late 1800s became the source of supply for the Vineyard Haven water system. An old legend tells of two men who sailed into Lake Tashmoo through the creek at its mouth and buried a large bundle at a great rock near the shore. Islanders did not believe the men's story that they had dug a grave for a pox victim, and instead suspected that they had actually buried gold. So one night some time later three Islanders took lanterns and shovels and uncovered the grave. After an hour or two they unearthed a skull, and a short time later one of them thought he had struck the treasure chest itself. Digging all the harder, one of them suddenly sank into the ground up to his armpits amid a din of strange noises. His two companions rescued him, then quickly filled the hole. But not long after, the rescued man fell ill with a fatal disease.

Lamberts Cove

For Jonathan Lambert, a deaf-mute and a carpenter, who lived near the cove at James Pond in the early 1700s. During the War of 1812 a packet sloop captured by a British privateer went aground during a night squall. The next morning the British discovered that the beached sloop had already lost its mast to American defenders and so sailed off without their prize. The cove was a safe anchorage for sailing vessels; it was once known as Onkemmy Bay.

Lily Pond

The water lilies in this pond between Zacks Cliffs and Squibnocket Pond, Gayhead, have white blossoms. It was also known as Hebrons Pond for Hebron Wamsley, who lived nearby in the 1800s. Aunt Esther Howwoswee, a neighbor of Wamsley's, worked as a midwife throughout the Vineyard and was called the Indian doctress.

Little Pond

On Fisher Road in Martha's Vineyard State Forest. The pond is a hundred twenty feet above sea level, has no outlet, and is never dry. Some say that during a wet summer the pond loses two more feet of water than during a dry one.

Lobsterville

So called because lobstermen spent summers at the village, preparing traps to set on the mussel beds farther east in Vineyard Sound. The best beds where lobsters feed are Lucas Shoal (near Cape Higgon) and Middle Ground (off West Chop). Soon after the first days of the village in 1878, the Gayhead Clay Company shipped loads of kaolin for several years to kilns along the eastern seaboard. In the early 1900s the lobstermen began to take their boats to Menemsha, because it had safer anchorage. The coming of summer houses, however, has restored Lobsterville.

Lookout Hill

So called because in the 1700s spotters on the hill would scan the south coast of the Vineyard for signs of whales. At a signal six crewmen would push off in a whaleboat from the beach below the hill at Squibnocket Bight, their gear in readiness.

M

Majors Cove

For Peter Norton (1718-1792), who was the Major of the Dukes County Regiment in the 1760s and a tory High Sheriff at the outset of the Revolution. He was also one of the richest, fattest men on the Vineyard. Indians lived at the Cove, on the east side of Sengekontacket Pond, until the beginning of the 1800s.

Makonikey Head [məˈkanɪki]

The spellings of this Indian name in the 1700s were Nowconaca or Conaconaket, possibly from *nukkon* 'old' + *auk* 'land' + *ut* 'at' = "at the old land," although *nukkon* is seldom part of an Algonquian place name. In the 1800s the head had kilns for making yellow bricks and terra cotta. At the turn of the twentieth century a summer hotel on the head failed after a few years. Makonikey Head is at the end of Lamberts Cove on Vineyard Sound.

Manters Hill

For Jonathan Manter, a large landholder of the 1700s, whose daughter Parnell and her friends Maria Allen and Peggy Daggett, it is said, blew up a liberty pole at the foot of the hill, now the intersection of Main Street and Colonial Lane in Vineyard Haven. Soon after the villagers had erected the pole as a pledge of support for the American Revolution, the British ship *Unicorn* docked in the harbor in search of a spar to replace its disabled mast. The only suitable replacement on the island was the liberty pole. But before the British sailors could remove the pole, Parnell and her friends set to work. They took augers, pierced the pole all about, crammed the holes with gunpowder, and lit a fuse. Soon after, the pole shattered into a spray of wood chips and splinters. The Liberty Pole Museum in Vineyard Haven commemorates the girls' defiance. Another name for Manters Hill was Mill Hill, so called because in 1807 Lothrop Merry built on it the only windmill in the village.

Martha's Vineyard

The name first appears in John Brereton's description of the Gosnold voyage (1602) as Marthaes Vineyard. In 1610 William Strachey mentions it in his *Travaille into Virginia*, and a map of the same year shows Martha's Vineyard as the name for Nomans Land. Some say that the Vineyard is named for the vines that covered the island when explorers first landed. Martha, it is said, was the name of Gosnold's daughter or perhaps his mother-in-law Martha Goulding, who contributed funds for the voyage. Apocryphal accounts, all off-island, say that Martha is a mistake for Martin, and that Gosnold actually named the island Martins Vineyard for John Martin, a captain of a ship in Gosnold's expedition. Martins Vineyard appears as late as 1688 on a Dutch map. Still another view is that the name Martin supplanted Martha for a time, because Gosnold originally named the island for the Catholic Saint Martha, hateful to the Puritans. The Dutch first called the island Texel for two Frisian Islands off the coast of the Netherlands. Champlain referred to it as La Soupconeuse, because he wasn't at all sure that it was an island — he had his suspicions. John Smith called it the Isle of Capawack, probably from Algonquian *kuppaug* "enclosed place, harbor." The Algonquians apparently spoke of it as *noe* 'middle' + *pe* 'water' = "middle of the waters." At the beginning of the sixteenth century Verrazano may have called the island Luisa. It is most often called *the Vineyard* or simply *the Island*.

Martha's Vineyard State Forest

This forest, mostly pine, includes more than 4500 acres at the center of the island and a neck of land on Edgartown Great Pond. The first acquisition by the Commonwealth (1908) established a sanctuary for the heath hen. The bulk of the forest became state property in the 1920s. Unfortunately, the effort to preserve the heath hen failed. A brush fire in 1916 destroyed most of the nests, and unchecked hunting by sportsmen and stray cats wiped the birds out by 1932.

Mashacket Cove and Neck
[məˈšækɪt]

Mashacket is possibly a shortened form of Algonquian Mashakomu-ket, from *masha* 'great' + *komuk* 'house' + *ut* 'at' = "at the great house," a palisaded enclosure of the Indians. The neck, a part of the Martha's Vineyard State Forest, and the cove are at the north end of Edgartown Great Pond.

Mashshachaquack
[ˌmæšəˈčaˌkwæk]

This is a little stream in a swampy area north of Long Point on the west end of Chappaquiddick. Mashshachaquack may be related to Narragansett *muskēchogē* "place where rushes grow." [??]

Mattakeeset Herring Brook
[ˌmætəˈkisɪt]

Mattakeeset is possibly from Algonquian *matche* 'bad, unpleasant' + *auk* 'land' + *s* 'little' + *ut* 'at' = "at the little, bad (unsafe?) land." The land is on the shores of Mattakeeset Bay, from which fishermen in the 1720s had a channel dug to Edgartown Great Pond to create an artificial brook. The new brook probably went through Ameshoak Creek, a natural stream into the bay. Ameshoak is related to Narragansett *aumsûog* "herring." After the completion of the channel alewives could swim directly into the pond to spawn.

Menada Creek [məˈnadə]

Menada is possibly related to Natick *menadchu* "[there to] the left hand [of the path.]" Local fishermen at the creek at the south end of Sengekontacket Pond used to catch bushels of blue crabs or blue claw crabs, as they were called. It is also known as Trapps Creek, for an early sheriff.

Menemsha [məˈnɛmšə]

This is the Indian name for a village and for three bodies of water: a pond, an inlet [once a creek] and a bight. In the 1600s Menamshounk, an old spelling of Menemsha, was the name of the creek, possibly from Algonquian *manunushaw nippe* "still water." In 1904 the Commonwealth had the creek dredged and jetties built at the nearby village to provide safe anchorage for small craft. The jetties also prevent currents from clogging the pond, farther south, with sand. The pond itself has deposits of brick red clay along its shoreline that local kilns once baked into terra cotta. Northeast of the village near Vineyard Sound are the Menemsha Hills, a sanctuary for wildlife deeded by the Harrises of Chilmark to the Trustees of Reservations. Menemsha Bight is an arm of Vineyard Sound that swoops along the north shore from Chilmark, past Menemsha Inlet, to Gay Head. The mouth of Menemsha Inlet bore the Algonquian name Wawattick, possibly from *wohway* 'winding about' + *tuk* 'tidal estuary' = "a winding estuary."

Middle Road

This secondary road, built in the 1840s, runs from Chilmark Village to Baxters Corner in the village of West Tisbury. It is the middle road between the Vineyard's North and South roads.

Mill Brook

Many mills have lined the shores of this brook, the largest on the Vineyard, which runs from Chilmark to Tisbury Great Pond. One mill, an old satinet factory, has become in recent years the headquarters of the Martha's Vineyard Garden Club, a group concerned with conservation.

Mill Hill

So called for a windmill constructed on it in the 1680s by its first owner, Thomas Jones. It was also known as Jones Hill until his widow lost their property and died a pauper. Edgartown had a water tower constructed on the hill in 1906. Near the hill in the 1700s ran Mob Street, a boarding house of sailors on one corner, a house of drifters on another. The sailors and drifters would carouse and revel up and down the street all night long. Mill Hill is south of Clevelandtown and west of Herring Creek [or Airport] Road.

Mills Brook

Also known as Miles Brook, it runs from a pond in the Edgartown Golf Course to Eel Pond. The Indians called the marshland near the brook Aquampache, possibly from Algonquian *ukquae* 'point, end' + *paug* 'pond' = "end of the pond." Another stretch of land within the same area was known as Matuhhukqus-

see, probably related to *matuh'tuck* 'place without wood' + *s* 'little' + *ut* 'at' = "at the little, treeless land." In the 1600s the land between the brook and Weeks Neck on Edgartown Beach was the planting field for eighteen proprietors.

Mink Meadows and Mink Meadow Pond

The meadows and pond are near West Chop in the north part of Tisbury. Very early in Vineyard history mink was valuable in the island's fur trade. In 1685 Matthew Mayhew promised to pay Colonel Thomas Dongan two mink skins a year "forever" for the "land called Nashawaqueedse," a neck in Chilmark. So extensive was the trapping of mink that by 1865 it had become extinct on the island. More than seventy-five years later, breeders reintroduced it briefly, but without success.

Money Hill

So called, it is said, because rescuers or shipwrecked sailors once buried treasure, still unrecovered, on the slopes of this hill at Squibnocket Beach on the Atlantic. In 1800 the Commonwealth established a lifesaving station at the hill.

Mount Aldworth Road

So called because Charles H. Brown, a local landowner in the late 1800s, said that the explorer Martin Pring sailed, not into Provincetown Harbor, but into Vineyard Haven Harbor and named the hill overlooking his anchored ship for his benefactor Thomas Aldworth of Bristol, England. The hill is near the Edgartown Road.

Music Street

In the mid-1800s the families on this street in West Tisbury village had seven daughters, and each played a piano. Captain George A. Smith, a whaling captain, bought a piano for his daughter, and then six neighbors followed suit. Others in the village, however, called the street Cowturd Lane.

N

Nabs Corner

Nab was the nickname of Abigail Dunham, who in the 1700s lived alone in her wigwam on South Road at the juncture of Chilmark and West Tisbury. In the 1800s Lucy P. Adams and her sister Sarah, both about four feet high, grew up at the corner and toured the country as singers in General Tom Thumb's Company.

Nashamoies Neck [ˌnæšəˈmɔɪz]

Nashamoies is possibly from Algonquian *nashuae* 'in the middle' + *mayash* 'ways' = "in the middle of the ways." The neck is at the north end of Edgartown Great Pond. In the 1600s Nashamoies was also the name of an Indian

praying town, a community of Christian converts. Another name for the locality was Shokamocket, from *k'che* 'great' + *komuk* 'house or lodge' + *ut* 'at' = "at the great house [of a sachem.]"

Nashaquitsa Pond, Village and Cliffs [ˈkwitsə] or [ˌnæšəˈkwitsə]

Nashaquitsa most likely stems from Algonquian *nashawe* 'midway' + *aquidne* 'island' + *es* 'little' + *ut* 'at' = "at the little, midway island." In Nashaquitsa Pond, near Hariphs Creek and the South Road, a three-cornered island lies midway between the east and west shores. At the west end of the pond, near Nashaquitsa Village, is Clam Point Cove, where fishermen go eeling in the summer and scalloping in the winter. The cliffs are across South Road, overlooking Squibnocket Bight. Local villagers at this west end of Chilmark generally call the pond Quitsa.

Ned Point

Probably for Captain Edward W. Carpender, an inspector of lighthouses for the Department of the Treasury in the mid-1800s. In his report of 1839 on the lighthouse at the point, Captain Carpender called the lamps too bright, the breakwater too weak, and the worms in the walls destructive. The point is at the south end of Little Beach on Harbor Pond at Edgartown Village.

Nimpanickhickanuh

[nɪmˈpænɪkˌhɪˈkænu]

The residence of Experience Mayhew in Chilmark, who was a minister to the Indians and in the 1700s wrote *Indian Converts* and *Indian Narratives*, books of biography and folklore. Mayhew says that the name of his residence means "the place of thunder clefts," because during a thunderstorm the Indians had seen a tree struck and split apart.

Nomans Land

There are at least three accounts for the name Noman: 1] it is a mispronunciation of Norman, the Viking leader who came to New England centuries ago; 2] it comes from the fact that no man ever owned the island outright — off by itself; and 3] it is short for Tequenoman, a powwow who lived on the island in the 1600s. The Dutch named the island Hendrik Christiaensens Eylant or Ile de Hendrick for an early explorer. In the 1600s it was also known as the Isle of Man and Dock Island. The Indians called it Cappoaquidnet, from *chappa* 'separated' + *aquidn*- 'island' + *ut* 'at' = "at the separated island." The island is now a barren target area for Navy bombers, about four miles southwest of Squibnocket Point in Chilmark. When Bartholomew Gosnold first anchored at the island in 1602, it was dense with shrubs and vines, fruit trees and evergreens. But thereafter farmers cleared land for their cattle and sheep, and fishermen built shacks and wood fires. During the 1800s the island had two fishing villages, Crow Town and Jimmy Town, on its north side. Not far from the villages was Stony Point, five acres of clean stone used by the fishermen to cure codfish. It is said that buried treasure still remains untouched on Nomans Land.

North Neck

The neck extends northeastward toward John Oliver Point on Cape Poge Bay, Chappaquiddick. The Indians called the neck Menechew, possibly related to Natick *menadchu* "[there to] the left hand [of the way.]"

North Tisbury

Postmasters of the mid-1800s gave this village at the juncture of North and Vineyard Haven Roads its name. Earlier on it was known as Middletown, an old name in West Tisbury, so called by the first settlers who plowed land and pastured sheep at the center of the Vineyard. In the 1700s, when the local name for Edgartown was Old Town, North Tisbury was also known as Newton.

Norton Point

For the Nortons of Edgartown, a family of preachers, farmers, and whalers, whose forebear Nicholas came in the mid-1600s and was known as a sharp trader. The point is a long spit, tapering almost three miles eastward from Mattakeeset Bay to Wasque Outlet at Chappaquiddick. There is another Norton Point east of Makonikey Head, on Vineyard Sound.

O

Oak Bluffs

Both a town and a village at the north end of the island. The village on Nantucket Sound [built on what had been Great Pasture] takes its name from a summer colony of the mid-1800s. The town assumed its present name in 1907, twenty-eight years after it was incorporated. Earlier it was known as Cottage City because of the temporary summer quarters built throughout the town in such communities as Vineyard Highlands, Forest Hill, and Oak Grove, and also at Wesleyan Grove where the Methodists had annual camp meetings. The town gradually found the name Cottage City unsatisfactory, because *cottage* sounded drab and *city* overblown. The sharp, angular town boundaries on Oak Bluffs's west side marked the limits in the 1600s of the territory of Ponit, a sachem of Nobscusset.

Oak Bluffs Airport

On County Road, about half a mile south of Wing Road in Oak Bluffs. In the 1600s the land was known as Tom Tylers Field. Tyler had come to the Vineyard after his father, the Sagamore Maskanomet, had sold the lands bordering Ipswich Bay to Governor John Winthrop. Fifty years later, on Tylers Creek, which ran from the field into Sengekontacket Pond, Simeon Butler had a tannery.

Oak Bluffs Harbor

The harbor opens into Nantucket Sound north of Oak Bluffs Village. In the early 1800s, before the town had a channel cut through a beach barrier to the sound, the harbor was known as Squash Meadow Pond. Later in the century, about 1870, the Wesleyan Camp Meeting decided to construct a road across the pond to make access to its tabernacle easier. The west side of the divided pond was called Sunset Pond, a name it still has. Before the opening of the harbor the east

side was known as Lake Anthony, possibly for Abraham Anthony, an officer of the camp meeting. The Methodists said that crossing the road to the tabernacle reminded them of the Israelites "crossing the Jordan." The harbor is now a basin, mostly for yachts and small craft.

Occooch Pond [ɔ'kuč]

For John Occooch, who lived much of his hundred years at the pond and was a descendant of an old Indian family in Gay Head. The pond is a half mile south of Gay Head Village.

Ocean Heights

A fairly recent community in Edgartown. It is not on the ocean but on Sengekontacket Pond. Until the beginning of this century the locality was known as Weeks Neck, for an early settler, William Weeks.

Ohhomeek [o'humik]

Probably from Algonquian *oohoomau* 'owl' + *auk* 'place' = "owl place." It was a marshland southeast of Farm Pond, pronounced in the 1700s as "hummock."

Oklahoma

Probably so called by Wallace Barnes, the developer of this summer community west of Lagoon Pond, as a playful expansion of *Ahoma*, the name for the springs on the east side. From 1872 until 1907 [the year of a destructive fire], Professor Bristol offered musical instruction for the community, and Katherine Cornell, while a little girl, performed in some stage performances. It was earlier known as Chunks Hill, a name pulled from the middle syllables of the Algonquian Manehchahankkanah.

Old House Pond

Southeast of James Pond in West Tisbury, the pond takes its name from an ice house that once stood on its banks. The pond's Indian name was Nanaquayak, listed in 1699 as a point on the bounds of Christiantown.

P

Paint Mill Brook

For a mill of the 1800s that produced pigments for paint from ground ocher. Also known as Howlands Brook, for a local family, it runs into Vineyard Sound east of Cape Higgon, Chilmark.

Parsonage Pond

In 1762 the parishioners of West Tisbury Village built the parsonage at the pond for their newly ordained minister, George Damon. The pond is near the intersection of South Road and the Edgartown-West Tisbury Road.

Pauls Point

For Old Paul, an Indian who lived in Christiantown in the mid-1600s. At the west end of Lamberts Cove on Vineyard Sound, the point was once rich in blackberries.

Peaked Hill [pikəd]

During the Second World War the peak of this hill in Chilmark, north of Middle Road, was flattened by the federal government in order to install a radar station. Lowered from 311 to 298 feet, the hill also lost the glacial rocks that had strewn its summit. In the 1970s a visitor to the Vineyard bought the hill as an investment soon after he climbed to the top and looked south to the Atlantic and north to the Sound.

Pease Point Way

A street close to the harbor in Edgartown Village. Some say that before the Mayhews arrived on the Vineyard in 1641-42, John Pease and a few voyagers from England made the first landing. They docked close to what is now Pease Point Way and met a group of Indians who held up a pine bough as a sign of peace. In return John Pease laid a red coat on the ground and offered it as a gift to the sachem. The sachem took the coat and directed Pease and the others to the runs of herring at the creek between Edgartown Great Pond and Mattakeeset Bay. The Peases remained a large family in Edgartown.

Pechakers Creek
[pə'čakər] or ['čakəz]

Pechaker is from Algonquian *pâchau* 'turning' + *auk* 'place' = "turning place," an accurate name for the creek's curving banks between Menemsha and Nashaquitsa ponds. The local name, Chawkus Creek, is a shortening of Pechakers.

Pecoye [pə'kɔɪ]

From Algonquian *pohque* 'open' + *auk* 'land' = "open land." Pecoye is a small neck, mostly marsh and beach, opposite Brush and Gravel islands in Sengekontacket Pond. In the 1600s Thomas Mayhew, Jr. preached to the Indians at Pulpit Rock, a large boulder on Pecoye.

Pilot Hill

So called for the pilots of Tisbury, who guided ships through Vineyard Sound to Cape Cod. In the years after the Revolution it was known as Red Coat Hill, supposedly for the tattered belongings left behind by British soldiers after Grey's Raid. The hill is on Lamberts Cove Road, west of Lake Tashmoo.

Place by the Wayside

Near the intersection of Airport Road and the Takemmy Trail in Edgartown. In 1657 Thomas Mayhew, Jr. preached to hundreds of Indian parishioners at the wayside before sailing for England to settle family affairs [he was to look after the inheritance left to his brother-in-law] and to report to the Commissioners of the United Colonies on his work as a missionary. But his ship was lost at sea. After his death Indians passing the place of his sermon would cast stones on a heap that before long became a cairn.

Pohoganot Road [pɔˈhɔgənət]

Pohoganot is probably from Algonquian *pauqu'un* 'clear, open' + *auk* 'land' = "open land." Farmers and fishermen used to live along this road that runs southwestward from Martha's Vineyard State Forest to Oyster Pond on the bounds of Edgartown.

Poketapaces Neck [pəˈkɛtəˌpesəz]

For John Poketapace, an Indian sachem of the 1600s, who apparently sold land without the authority of his tribe to Thomas Layton and Peter Tallman, early settlers of Edgartown. The neck is on the west side of Edgartown Great Pond.

Poucha Pond [ˈpočə]

Poucha is possibly from Algonquian *poochóag* "corner." The pond at the southeast corner of Chappaquiddick was also known as Wassaechtaack, probably from *awwasse* 'on the farther side' + *auke* 'land' = "place beyond or on the farther side." In the 1600s this salt water pond was some distance from the Indian settlements on Chappaquiddick.

Powwow Hill

This hill in West Chilmark, between Menemsha and Squibnocket ponds, stands above a former village of Indians, who apparently held powwows, danced, and feasted on its slopes.

Prospect Hill

The highest hill [308 feet] on Martha's Vineyard. In the 1700s Crèvecoeur says in his *Letters From An American Farmer* that he stopped at an iron mine near the hill just beyond the North Road, Chilmark and learned that the forge for smelting the ore was in Taunton. During the War of 1812 Simon Mayhew spotted an English brig in Menemsha Bight and, summoning his neighbors, marched them up Prospect Hill and across its summit all day long. Their efforts succeeded in making the British believe that the steady movement of troops was a sign of a large American force and so they sailed away. Deposits of the bluish gray Gardiners clay near the hill supplied the needs of potters for a time.

Q

Quampache Bottom [kwamˈpæčə]

Quampache is possibly from Algonquian *ukquaé* 'point, end' +

paug 'pond' = "end of the pond." The bottom is directly east of Martha's Vineyard Airport. At the south edge of the bottom is Oyster Pond, open to the ocean and rich in shellfish.

Quansoo   ['kwansu]

A marshy, sandy neck between Black Point and Tisbury Great Pond, Chilmark. Experience Mayhew, a missionary to the Indians and a speaker of their language, lived on the neck in the early 1700s. An early spelling of Quansoo is Quannaimes, possibly from Algonquian *qunnamaugsuck* 'lampreys.'

R

Roaring Brook

In the 1850s this brook in Chilmark supplied power to a gristmill, a brick mill, and a china clay mill, on its way to Vineyard Sound. But the cordwood also needed by these mills became too expensive, and in the 1870s they closed down.

Roque Avenue   [rok]

Roque is a shortening of *roquet* and means "the striking of a ball against that of an opponent's." In the late 1800s this avenue in Oak Bluffs Village had clay courts [long since gone] for Vineyarders who were the first to play the game of roque, a form of croquet.

Round Pond

At Squibnocket Ridge, in the southwest corner of Chilmark. Near the pond was a peat bog large enough to supply the people of the town with fuel from the 1700s until 1850. In the early 1800s men digging in the bog unearthed so many human bones that they refused ever to dig in that place again.

S

Sampson Hill

Near the center of Chappaquiddick. A semaphore erected atop the hill in 1845 sent messages to Nantucket and to Boston concerning whalers. Years later a Marine Church held services near the hill for the island's Indians. Sampson may have been a local Chappaquiddick Indian.

Sarson Island

For Richard Sarson, who married Jane Mayhew seven years after her first husband Thomas died on his way to England. For some time in the later 1600s Sarson was a governor's assistant and judge. The island is near Dividend Point in Sengekontacket Pond.

Scotchmans Bridge Lane

In the late 1600s Robert Cathcart, a Scotch emigrant, had a bridge built over Mill Brook, West Tisbury Village, near his tavern. Nearby the West Tisbury race course once held meetings for trotters during the county fair.

Scrubby Neck

So called for the stunted oaks, birch, and pine trees on this neck between Homers and Watcha ponds in West Tisbury. The Indians had several names for particular sections of the neck: Mussoowonkwhonk, Peanaskenamset, and Wechekemmipihquiah. Wechekemmipihquiah seems related to Natick *weatchiminneahtek* "field of corn."

Seconnet   [sə'kanɪt]

A mythical reef near Devils Bridge at Gay Head, said to be the remains of Michabo's wife. Once in a fit of anger Michabo threw his wife over the cliffs of Gay Head into the offshore waters. There she remained many years, a threat to Indian canoes sailing nearby, relentless in her demand for cargo from them. As she became older she grew stonier and was at last petrified. When the English arrived they hacked off her arms and her head and left her torso rooted like a reef beneath the waves.

Sengekontacket Pond
[,sɛnjəkən'tækɪt]

Sengekontacket is probably related to Abnaki *sanghede'aki* 'land at the mouth' + *ut* 'at' = "at the land at the mouth." The barrier on the east side of the pond between Edgartown and Oak Bluffs has always had openings directly into Nantucket Sound. Nowadays a bar five hundred feet long is kept open for the sake of shellfish in the protected waters. Brants, ducks, and geese were once plentiful on this long, narrow pond. Anthiers Pond is a popular alternate to the tongue-twisting Sengekontacket. Anthier is a blend of Aunt Tiah [short for Bethiah], the daughter of Governor Thomas Mayhew. When Bethiah was about to marry, her father gave her bridegroom Thomas Henlock the south end of Sengekontacket and the surrounding land. Bethiah came to be called Aunt Tiah during the years when she helped to raise the children of her brother Thomas, Jr., who died en route to England.

Seths Pond

For Uncle Seth Luce, who in the 1800s lived at the pond, south of James Pond in West Tisbury. It was earlier known as Half-Moon Pond, was once well-stocked with eels, and is still good for ice skating.

Seven Gates Farm

In the late 1800s Professor Nathaniel S. Shaler, a Harvard geologist, bought several adjacent farms north of Mill Brook in Chilmark and West Tisbury. To reach his house, he had to pass through seven gates connecting the farms he bought. The property now belongs to a consortium of families.

Shear Pen Pond

A saltwater pond in the northeast end of Cape Poge Bay, next to Little Neck. In earlier years it was also known as Sheep Shear Pond. Shepherds would wash their flocks in the pond before shearing them.

Sheriffs Meadow and Pond

Close to Eel Pond at the north end of Edgartown Village. Isaiah D. Pease, a former sheriff of Edgartown, owned land near the pond in the earlier 1800s. Elizabeth and Henry Beetle Hough of Sheriffs Lane bought the pond in the 1950s and turned it into a wildlife sanctuary.

Shotnigher Hill

So called because hunters climbed the hill to draw closer to ducks and geese flying overhead to Menemsha and Squibnocket ponds. It is also known as Shot and Arrow Hill. Its Algonquian name was Mashatan, from *massa* 'great' + *aden* 'hill' = "great hill." The hill is near Herring Creek and South Road, Gay Head.

Skissi Hill   [skɪsɪ]

Skissi is possibly related to Narragansett *askáski* "it is green." The Indians of Gay Head once held green corn festivals on the hill as well as powwows and, in the 1800s, they greeted returning whalers with a ceremonial smoking of the peace pipe. The hill was also an Indian burial ground. In more recent years Max Eastman, poet and critic, built his house at the top of the hill [140 feet high] and so had a view of Vineyard Sound, Menemsha Pond, and the Atlantic. Near the hill is East Pasture, one of the commons for Gay Head's cattle.

South Beach

In Edgartown at the Atlantic Ocean. The beach is part of a long thin barrier, stretching from Jobs Neck on the west to the east end of Nortons Point, more than six miles. The barrier has in recent decades suffered considerably from the erosive force of the ocean. In the 1700s a narrow basin ran the distance between the barrier and the plains of Martha's Vineyard from Tisbury Great Pond to Edgartown.

South Road

In the 1700s the road was known as the Mill Path, and ran from Edgartown up-island to the mill streams in West Tisbury and Chilmark. It was the Vineyard's first highway, laid out over Indian trails.

Squash Meadow

A shoal in Nantucket Sound east of Oak Bluffs Harbor. In early days Squash Meadow was the name of the land bordering the harbor, but after the arrival of the Methodist Camp Meeting and the summer communities, the name moved eastward, first on the water as Squash Meadow Pond, and then under, as a shoal.

Squibnocket Beach, Bight, Point, Pond, Ridge   [skwɪb'nakɪt]

Squibnocket is possibly related to Algonquian *m'squi* 'red' + *penugqué* 'bank' + *ut* 'at' = "at the red bank [of a river]." As late as 1780 Squibnocket Pond had a channel wide enough for boats to sail into the Atlantic, but the shifting sands of the beach have since clogged it. Squibnocket Beach, the property of the Cape Cod Cranberry Company, is open to the town of Chilmark for picnics and bathing. At the east end of the beach, on Squibnocket Point, a group of sportsmen, known as the New York Club, returned each summer during the 1890s and early 1900s to fish for striped bass. From Squibnocket Point, too, it is said, a low, narrow isthmus once ran four miles through shallows in the Atlantic to Nomans Land. But one day, while Michabo the Indian giant was watching his children play on the isthmus, he cut notches into it. Soon the sea flooded the isthmus and had nearly pulled Michabo's children under; he then fetched them out of the waves and turned them into killer whales. Directly north of the beach is Squibnocket Ridge and half a mile farther north is Squibnocket Pond, the largest freshwater pond on the Vineyard. In recent years swans have been returning to the pond. All the coastal areas which are called Squibnocket, from the bight to the east end of the beach, are in Chilmark. The western half of Squibnocket Pond is in Gay Head.

Starbuck Neck

For Nathaniel Starbuck, a Quaker and resident of Edgartown in the late 1600s. Starbuck Neck lies opposite the Harbor Pond and Edgartown Lighthouse.

Stonewall Beach and Pond

So called because of the cluster of glacial rock strewn on the beach and near the pond to the east of Wequobsque Cliffs, Chilmark.

Sugar Loaf Hill

So called because at the summit of the hill is a keystone, shaped like a sugar loaf, draped by a circlet of boulders. The hill is east of Chilmark Village near Middle Road.

Swan Neck and Swan Neck Point

The neck is not named for swans but for the Algonquian *sowan* 'south' + *auk* 'land' = "south land or country." It is on the west side of Edgartown Great Pond.

Sylvia Beach

For Joseph A. Sylvia, the Vineyard's representative to the General Court [1936-1966]. Commonly known as State Beach, it is on Nantucket Sound, from Edgartown to Oak Bluffs.

T

Tea Lane

In Chilmark, between North and Middle roads. Before the Revolu-

tion Captain Robert Hillman smuggled some tea onto Martha's Vineyard. He hid the tea so well in his Aunt Eunice's barn that despite a search, none of it could be found. It is said that for some time afterward Eunice, who was an invalid, took great comfort in her nephew's gift.

Thumb Cove

So called because the neck on its west shores looks like a thumb. The cove is in Tisbury Great Pond.

Tiasquam River   [ˌtaɪˈæskwam]

Tiasquam is possibly related to Narragansett *toyusk* "at the bridge or the wading place." The source of the river is east of Tea Lane, Chilmark; it flows south of West Tisbury Village and empties into Town Cove on Tisbury Great Pond. It was once called New Mill River for the mill built on it in the days of Thomas Look, the first to acquire water rights in the 1600s.

Tisbury and West Tisbury

Once the largest town on Martha's Vineyard, Tisbury is named for the village of Governor Thomas Mayhew's birth, a sheep-raising community in Wiltshire, England. Before the incorporation of Tisbury in 1671 the early settlers on the Vineyard called it Middletown, because it covered the center of the island [an area also good for raising sheep]. In 1892, after growing disagreements on taxes, the farmers up-island successfully petitioned the General Court for the establishment of a new town, West Tisbury. The act of incorporation sharply restricted the area of Old Tisbury to lands extending from Vineyard Haven and Lagoon Pond to the areas not far west of Lake Tashmoo. The General Court gave West Tisbury the remaining lands stretching to Chilmark, more than three times as much in all. The Indians called a large section of this territory Takemmy, probably related to *touohkomuk* "the wilderness, the forest."

Tisbury Great Pond

The pond is half in West Tisbury, half in Chilmark, separated from the Atlantic by a beach barrier. In the 1940s the Quansoo Shellfish Farms, under the guidance of John Whiting, a Harvard anthropologist, had a channel cut through the barrier. The hope was that seawater would increase the salinity of the pond and lower its temperature sufficiently to enable oysters to grow. The experiment failed. Local fishermen take eels from the pond. At its upper reaches are necks the shape of fingers. A cove on the west end — Town Cove — is the mouth of the Tiasquam River. The Indians called the land near the cove Ukquieset, probably from *wequaé* 'end' + *es* 'little' + *ut* 'at' = "at the small end [of land]."

Tississa

Also called Sissa, this is a flat peninsula on Tisbury Great Pond. The Indians called it Kuppiauk, from Algonquian *kuppi* 'closed' + *aukup* 'cove' = "closed cove or harbor." Simon Athearn and his young bride Mary, not quite fourteen, were the first of the early settlers to buy land on the peninsula from the Indians.

Toad Rock

It is said that Michabo the Indian giant took his pet toad, just before he left the Vineyard for good, placed it near the head of Squibnocket Pond, and transformed it into a rock. Local Gay Head Indians, passing by the rock, would leave messages for one another in its eye.

Tower Hill

This hill in Edgartown near South Water Street and Katama Road once had a tower for sending messages by semaphore. It is also the oldest burial ground in the village and contains gravestones nearly three hundred years old.

Trapps Pond

For Thomas Trapp, who came to Edgartown in the 1600s and lived at the pond northeast of the village, near the Eel and Sengekontacket ponds. In the early days it was also known as Peter Mortals Pond, for a local sachem.

Turkeyland Cove

Turkeyland is a phrase for fields of turkey wheat, otherwise known as maize. It is also said that the owners of the land at the cove paid for it with turkeys. The cove is at the northeast end of Edgartown Great Pond.

Turn-around Hill

On the South Road just above Clam Cove, Nashaquitsa Pond, where drivers can park and on a clear day look across Menemsha and Lobsterville to the Elizabeth Islands. Midway up the slope of the hill is a group of boulders that some call a hog house and others a cromlech, supposedly built by Norsemen for their dead centuries ago.

U

Up-island and Down-island

Up-island refers to the western part of Martha's Vineyard, down-island to the eastern part. The terms are taken from the speech of navigators, who say of ships sailing eastward toward the prime meridian in Greenwich, England, that they are "running down longitude," whereas ships sailing west are "running up longitude."

V

Vineyard Haven and Vineyard Haven Harbor

Both so called since 1871 because villagers complained that the earlier name Holmes Hole [the oldest English name on Martha's Vineyard] was undignified and obscure. They thought *hole* was undignified because they had forgotten its old, geographical definition as a "body of water" or "inlet." No one remembered John Holmes, a blacksmith who had sailed on the *Mayflower* and had the task in later years of driving squatters from the Vineyard. There were, instead, anecdotes that Holmes was an Indian name, or a name for the holm oaks that once grew by a stream in the village. Others said that Holmes was an early settler who had either died in his hole or was a victim of Indians who had sunk his boat in Lagoon Pond while he was in search of fresh water. Vineyard Haven Harbor is also for some an unsatisfactory name because they say, "What is a haven but a harbor?" In the 1700s the village had the names East Tisbury and the West Side, because it is on the west shore of the harbor.

Vineyard Highlands

A locality developed in the 1860s by the Vineland Grove Company at the north end of Oak Bluffs. The Baptist church built a tabernacle at the Highlands that failed for lack of support. The locality overlooks Nantucket Sound from the highest ground on the Vineyard's east coast.

Violet Hill

So called because each spring blue and white violets cover this hill on South Road, Chilmark.

W

Wasque Point   ['wɪskwɪ]

The point at the southwest corner of Chappaquiddick on the Atlantic was also known as Wasqua Bluff, because the land rises about thirty feet from the beach to a watchtower. At ebb tide rocks offshore thrust up above the water line. Wasque may be related to *awwasse* 'on the farther side' + *auke* 'land' = "place beyond or on the farther side." Until the early 1800s humpback and finback whales were still in view during the spring in the waters south of the island. One of the rocks of Wasque Point is known as Blue Rock. Wasque Point is now a sanctuary for wildlife.

Wequobsque Cliffs
[ˌweˈkwabskwɪ]

Wequobsque is probably related to Algonquian *wehqu* 'at the end of' + *ompsk* 'standing or upright rock' + *ut* 'at' = "at the end of the cliffs." Below the cliffs are Boulder Point and Devils Den, clusters of glacial rock that sit on the Lucinda Vincent Memorial Beach, facing the Atlantic. Lucinda Mosher Vincent lived all her life in Chilmark on the family farm that included lands on the cliffs and beach. When she died in the 1960s she left the care of her property to the founders of the Chilmark Town Association, who have leased a good part of it to the town for recreational purposes. In the 1950s the villagers of Chilmark called the beach Jungle Beach, because of the thick undergrowth nearby.

Wesleyan Grove

So called because of the yearly Methodist camp meetings convened at this locality near Oak Bluffs Harbor in the mid-1800s. Jeremiah Pease, a lay preacher, drew hundreds of people each summer to his dais near the harbor. Within a generation the white tents of the congregations became cottages, and the dais a tabernacle. The summer is still a time for gathering at the Tabernacle and for celebrating Illumination Night, a closing ceremony adorned with Japanese lanterns glowing in the dark of the camp grounds. Before 1835 the camp grounds were a sheep pasture and a field known as Squash Meadow. In the 1600s the land was called Quasquannes, after a local Indian.

West Chop

At the north end of Tisbury. In 1817 the federal government built a lighthouse at West Chop to benefit ships on Vineyard Sound and in Vineyard Haven Harbor. Ten years later Reformation John Adams began the first of the Methodist revival meetings on the headlands of West Chop. In 1856 a telegraph cable to the Vineyard reached West Chop from Falmouth. And in 1889 West Chop became a village, after a group of Bostonians made it their home and began to design for themselves and for Vineyard Haven a water system with its sources in Tashmoo Spring.

Whiting Hill

For Henry L. Whiting, a federal surveyor of the 1800s, who lived on the Vineyard and published a description of Provincetown Harbor. The hill is near the Chilmark-West Tisbury bounds.

Witch Brook

The witch remains unknown, but the brook was once known as Looks Brook, for Thomas Look [1649-1725], a miller on the stream east of Whiting Hill, West Tisbury.

Z

Zacks Cliffs

East of the cliffs at Gay Head along the Atlantic near Long Beach. The cliffs are probably named for Zachary Howwoswee, who was the last preacher in the Church of the Standing Order [a church recognized in the 1700s as orthodox in Massachusetts], and was the last, also, to address his parishioners in the Wampanoag language. Of Zack it was said that "not many . . . understood him, but he could wring tears from his parishioners." According to tradition the Indian god Michabo and his wife Squantum walked along the sands on the beaches of Gay Head and Squibnocket until they disappeared in a huge hummock near Zacks Cliffs. In recent years the cliffs have been the setting for nude bathing.

Nantucket

A

Abrams Point

For Abram Quary, the last of Nantucket's male, native Indians, who lived near the point on Nantucket Harbor, northeast of Monomoy, until his death in 1854. While still an infant, Quary lost his father, who killed two men in 1769 and died on the gallows at Newtown Gate. The point is also known as Shimmo Point, for an Indian Village.

Academy Hill

So called because of a private school erected in 1800 on this hill in the north part of Nantucket Town.

Angola Street

So called for the west coast of Africa, the home of blacks who signed up on whalers and then settled on this street in the New Guinea section of Nantucket Town. In the 1920s, when whalers no longer sailed out, the name of the street temporarily became Angora. An itinerant painter of signs had mixed up his r's and his l's, as he was sprucing up the street markers.

Aurora Heights

A locality of Siasconset overlooking the ocean. It first opened in 1887, its name designed for summer people dreaming of dawn and the sun rising from the sea.

B

Bocochico   [ˌboko'čiko]

Once the name of a locality in Nantucket Town, bounded by Main, Federal, and Beach streets. A small creek in the vicinity may have prompted the name of the locality, since Portuguese boche-checo means "a mouthful of water." Some say a Dutch vessel, the Bochocheko [so called because it displaced a mouthful of water?], grounded on the east coast of Nantucket, also suggested the name. Bocca Chica was the site of a Spanish fort on the island of Hispaniola in the 1700s. Tobias Smollett describes an attack upon the fort in Roderick Random.

Brant Point

The point juts out into the harbor, not far north of Nantucket Point. Even in early years of settlement, the number of brants migrating to the point from the Arctic began to diminish. More and more wary of local gunners, they disappeared after the construction of a lighthouse on the point in 1746. From 1810 to 1843 the yards at the point were busy fitting out schooners and whalers.

C

Capaum Pond   [kə'pam]

Possibly from Algonquian kuppi-komuk "a close place or haven." The pond, two miles west of Nantucket Town, was actually a harbor on the sound until a storm in 1721 closed it. The first English settlers built their homesteads near Capaum in the 1600s.

Centre Street

One of the main thoroughfares of Nantucket Town. During the days of whaling in the 1700s and 1800s part of the street was known as Petticoat Row, because its shopkeepers were mostly women who earned their own livelihood. Their husbands were away sailing the seas in search of whales.

Chadwicks Folly

For William H. Chadwick, cashier of the Pacific National Bank in the late 1800s, who took funds to build houses for summer people at Squam Head on the east coast of Nantucket Island. But before Chadwick could complete construction, the bank's auditors exposed him and forced him to auction off the property in 1894.

Childrens Beach

A public beach in Nantucket Town just beyond the Yacht Club at Harbor View Way.

Cisco Beach

For John Jay Cisco, a banker from New York, who built a summer cottage in the 1860s at the beach at the end of Hummock Pond Road, southwest of Nantucket Town. In the 1600s and 1700s the beach, now open to the public, was a whaling station.

Clean Shore

So called because of its contrast to the shoreline east of Steamboat Wharf, where trying works rendered blubber in whaling days. The "clean shore" runs north of the wharf toward Brant Point.

Coatue Neck ['ko,tu] or [,ko'tu]

From Algonquian *kowaw* 'pine' + *tugk* 'wood' + *ut* 'at' = "at the pine woods." Early settlers found the neck on the north side of Nantucket Harbor overgrown with stands of wind-blown, salt-resistant pines. But nowadays it binds itself together with clusters of beach grass, plums, roses, and cedars. Coatue cactus also grows on the neck, a species that is green, spotted, and prickly. The inner shore of the neck is a scalloped coast of six headlands, ranging southwestward from Wyers Point to First Point. There are also a Second and a Third Point, but instead of a Fourth there is a Five Fingered Point, so called because it has three coves that divide the shore into five "finger tips." At the western edge of Coatue Neck is Coatue Point, opposite Brant Point, at the north edge of Nantucket Town.

Codfish Park

The beach at Siasconset, where fishermen returning in their dories would fillet and dry their catches of cod. Fishing for cod on the Atlantic took men out in all seasons. Once James H. Wood, a Siasconset fisherman, returned to Codfish Park in his dory in dead winter and found the beach crowded with his friends. "Cold?" he said when someone asked, "Sure I was cold. But I just stuck my mittens in the sea to keep'em unfroze." He was lucky, they said, that he hadn't died with the temperature five below and the harbor frozen over. Eventually fishermen abandoned the beach, and their ramshackle huts were taken over by squatters.

Coskata Beach and Pond [,ka'sketə]

Probably from Algonquian *kowaw* 'pine' + *htugk* 'tree' + *ut* 'at' = "at the pine trees." The beach and the pond, north of Wauwinet, were once the site of a whaling station.

The Creeks

A marshland southeast of Nantucket Town along the harbor. One of the creeks, Newtown Creek, is named for the Newtown Gate, constructed nearby in the 1700s to keep sheep off the road that goes from Nantucket Town to Siasconset. Not far from the Creeks and from the Newtown Gate was Gallows Field, the place of the few public executions on Nantucket before 1840.

D

Dionis Beach [ˌdaɪ'anɪs]

For Dionis Stevens Coffin, who in 1659 settled on Nantucket with her husband Tristram. The beach is on Nantucket Sound, just west of Capaum Pond. In the late 1880s some Nantucketers promoted an unsuccessful summer colony, which they called Dionis City.

E

Eat-fire Spring

One of the many springs on Nantucket, Eat-fire is near Polpis Harbor and is known especially for its cold water.

Eel Point

At the northwestern tip of Nantucket, it stands at the entrance to Madaket Harbor. More than 120 acres at the point are now set aside as a wildlife reservation.

Egypt

A residential section at the north side of the town. For some time it had too few street lights, and people complained that their neighborhood was as "dark as Egypt."

Esther Island

A narrow island westward from Madaket, so called because Hurricane Esther severed it completely from Nantucket in 1961. A few years earlier Hurricane Carol had cut a temporary channel across a narrow beach barrier from the Atlantic to Madaket Harbor.

F

Folger Hill

For the Folgers, an early family on Nantucket. Peter Folger came to New England in 1635, became Thomas Mayhew's business agent, and settled on Nantucket in 1663. He knew the Algonquian language and had the friendship of the Indians. Benjamin Franklin was his grandson. The hill is northeast of the pond named for John Gibbs, whose life Folger helped to save. Folger Marsh lies between Polpis Road and Nantucket Harbor.

Foot Ponds

In earlier days these ponds south of Shawaukemo Hills and north of Milestone Road were known as the Pout Ponds, possibly for the hornpouts that local fishermen would catch. But the word *foot* replaced *pout* [they look alike], because hornpouts are not on everyone's diet, and because the ponds have the shape of footprints.

Forked Pond Valley

So called because in the early days of settlement, when the south shore extended farther into the Atlantic, the valley and the water in it had a hooked shape, just like that of Hummock Pond. The valley runs north from the ocean, halfway between the Nantucket Airport and Tom Nevers Head.

G

The Glades

A large marsh running north from the Head of the Harbor. It was once an open plain located between the cedar trees on Coatue Point and Coskata Pond.

Gravelly Islands

So called because this cluster of small islands between Muskeget and Tuckernuck looked like rocks and gravel thrown into the sea. Dr. Samuel Gelston was possibly the first to name them, when in 1771 he defied the Quakers on Nantucket and built a smallpox hospital on the Gravellys. The next year the town bought Gelston out and promptly tore the hospital down. Since then the Gravellys have sunk deeper into the sea and have become a shoal.

Great Neck and Little Neck

Great Neck runs southeastward from Hither Creek to Long Pond; Little Neck runs northwestward toward Madaket Harbor.

Great Point or Great Head

At the end of a long, sandy strip, the point has the shape of a crab's claw and leans into Nantucket Sound from the northeast corner of the island. The Indians called the point Nauma, possibly related to *nam'e-auk* "fishing place." The point has a glacial core, but the hook of the claw is sand accumulated from headlands farther south on the east coast of Nantucket — Squam and Sankaty. The federal government erected a lighthouse on the point in 1818. It is also called Sandy Point.

Gull Island and Street

Gull Street is near the intersection of Centre, Chester, and Westchester streets, in Nantucket Town. In the 1800s Gull Island was actually a piece of upland not far from the swamps of Lily Pond, before they were drained.

H

The Haulover

A narrow strip of sandy beach that separates the Head of the Harbor from the Atlantic on the east coast of Nantucket between Great Point and the village of Wauwinet. Fishermen used to haul their boats over this stretch of sand and so saved themselves the trouble of sailing around Great Point, a distance of more than twelve miles. The Haulover has sometimes given way to the sea, as in 1896 when the tides broke through to the Head of the Harbor and formed a channel that remained open for twelve years.

Hidden Forest

So called because this low lying, wooded stretch near Polpis is sufficiently protected from the wind to enable trees to grow without suffering from the corrosive effects of sea salt. In the stands of Hidden Forest are clusters of oak, beech, and pine.

Hither Creek

So called because Hither Creek at the east end of Madaket Harbor was closer to Nantucket Town than Further Creek at the west end of the Harbor. Hither Creek still flows northeastward and is a herring run in the spring. It is linked to Madaket Ditch. Further Creek disappeared after Hurricane Esther blew a channel through the south shore of Madaket Harbor and so created Esther Island.

Hoicks Hollow [hɔɪks]

For a family of farmers at the hollow during the 1890s. But long before the Hoicks arrived, fishermen would haul up their dories from the sea onto what they called "the hollow," just south of Sesachacha Pond at the east end of the island.

Hummock Pond

This is the largest pond on Nantucket, shaped like a fish hook and located in the south central plains of the island. Hummock, here, is not a hill but rather a shortening of a sachem's name, Nanahumacke, who owned the neck on the pond. The Indians called the plains about the pond "the best on the island," Crèvecoeur says. The name for the plains was *tètoukèmah*, possibly related to Abnaki *teteba* 'level' + *kamighe* 'place' = "a level place or plain." Another early name is Starbucks Pond, for Edward Starbuck, a settler of the 1600s, and for his many descendants. Sheepherders used to call the plains Ram Pasture.

I

India Street

In the town of Nantucket, between North Liberty and Centre Streets. India Street was the address of shipmasters who sailed to the Carribbean and traded in the West Indies. It was also known as Pearl Street.

J

Jetties Beach

So called because this public beach on North Beach Street in Nantucket Town is near the West Jetty of the harbor. To keep a sandbar from closing Nantucket Harbor the federal government constructed East and West jetties at its mouth during the late 1800s.

John Gibbs Pond

South of Polpis Village, the pond is named for an Indian pastor, who studied briefly at Harvard and had a ministry among his people on Nantucket and Martha's Vineyard for twenty-five years. Metacomet, who led an Indian uprising in 1675, had ten years earlier threatened Gibbs for mentioning the name of his dead father Massasoit, a sacrilege to Algonquian belief. To rescue Gibbs, who was hidden in a swamp, the English on Nantucket paid Metacomet a ransom of eleven pounds. The swamp where Gibbs lay in hiding also bears his name.

L

Long Pond

East of Madaket, this narrow pond stretches southward from Eel Point Road to the beaches on the Atlantic. From North Head or the Gut [near the road] it tapers into a long needle with two barbs, the inlets of Jeremy and White Goose coves.

Long Woods

Also simply the Woods. For a large growth of trees long since cut over. In 1668 the settlers on Nantucket passed an early ordinance on conservation [with variances], forbidding anyone from cutting green wood from Long

Woods, except for making rails and fences. The Long Woods is now a marsh west of Hummock Pond; it is the same area as Ram Pasture [See Hummock Pond].

Low Beach

A broad beach at the southeastern corner of the island, between Tom Nevers Head and Siasconset. In 1895 some developers began a summer colony. In the 1950s the Coast Guard installed a loran station on the beach to assist navigators.

M

Macys Hill

For the Macys who came to Nantucket in the 1600s from Salisbury, Massachusetts, after the General Court in Puritan Boston fined them for giving shelter to Quakers. Atop the hill, just to the northwest of Gibbs Pond, is Altar Rock, where Nantucket town clerks have from time to time conducted marriage ceremonies. Few Nantucket boulders remain on the plains and hills because of the need for them in building.

Madaket ['mædəkɪt]

Possibly related to Algonquian *mat'uhtugk* 'without wood' + *auke* 'land' = "land without wood." When the Starbuck and Macy families and Isaac Coleman spent their first winter on Nantucket in 1659, they found the lands at Madaket treeless. In the spring they moved farther east to Capaum [not yet a pond]; the present village at Madaket took root many years later. Madaket Harbor, at the west end of the island, takes its name from the village. Madaket Beach is open for public bathing.

Madequecham Valley
[,mædəkɪ'čam]

Possibly related to Algonquian *metugquēmēs* "a small tree." The valley, southeast of the Nantucket Memorial Airport, is a long "crease" in the land running inland from the ocean. There was a Madequecham Pond, before the construction of the airport. And there was a Madequecham Fight in 1814, waged between the American privateer *Prince of Neufchatel* and the British frigate *Endymion*. The ships closed upon each other off Tom Nevers Head, where the American sailors overcame boats of British marines.

Maxey Pond ['mæksɪ]

There were Maxeys or Maxcys in Massachusetts in the 1700s and 1800s. Some lived on Nantucket, others in Attleborough and Charlestown. In 1823 Captain John Maxcy arrived in Nantucket aboard the *Factor*. In the 1600s it was known as Wyers Pond, for Nathaniel Wyer, an early settler. The pond is south of Capaum and Washing ponds, close to a large sheepshearing center of the nineteenth century.

Miacomet Pond [,maɪə'kamɪt]

Probably related to Algonquian *miyawéog* "they gather together." At the head of the pond on the west end of Surfside, the Praying Indians of the 1600s had their meeting place here. During the eighteenth and nineteenth centuries shepherds bathed and sheared their flocks at the pond and sometimes cut a channel from its south shore to the Atlantic to drain and purify the water. In 1901 a New Bedford tea man bought up eighty acres on the east side of the pond, cut them up into 2300 lots, and offered a "pound of tea" free with every purchase of a lot. Almost all the tea remained in the storehouse at New Bedford.

Mill Hill

So called because on the hill, near Cooper Street, stood the first windmill in Nantucket Town. Nathan Wilbur, back from Holland, built it in 1746. The Nantucket Historical Association owns the mill nowadays and keeps it running. The hill was once known as Swains Hill, for the early resident, Eliakim Swain.

Monomy ['manə,mɔɪ] or [,mane'mɔɪ]

Possibly related to Algonquian *munumuhkemoo* "there is a rush [of mighty water]." Although the waters of Nantucket Harbor off the shores of Monomoy are hardly as swift as the currents of the Atlantic near Monomoy in Chatham, still the tides that sweep up toward Head of the Harbor have been strong enough to carve out the scalloped edges of Coatue Neck. Monomoy on Nantucket, laid out in 1726, is at the southwest end of the harbor just below Monomoy Heights.

Mooers Lane [mʊrz]

For Captain William Mooers, who skippered ships for Rotch and Company. When in 1783 Mooers docked in London aboard the *Bedford*, the *Gentleman's Magazine* remarked that his was "the first vessel which has displayed the thirteen rebellious stripes of America in any British port." Mooers Lane is in Nantucket Town.

Muskeget [məs'kigɪt]

The westernmost island of Nantucket County, it has three hundred acres of beach and sand. Muskeget [from Algonquian *muskeg* 'grass' + *ut* 'at' = "at the grassy place"] has long since been cropped over by sheep. Nowadays terns and gulls breed on the island. In the 1880s sportsmen founded a club on Muskeget; in 1895 the General Court made part of the island into a park.

N

Nantucket and Nantucket Town

Possibly Nantucket is related to the idea of "far away land," but the likely source is Algonquian *naîan* 'point of land' + *tukq* 'tidal river' + *ut* 'at' = "at the point of land on a tidal river." The tidal stream suggested by the name may be the channel between Nantucket Island and Tuckernuck. Although the island was even in early years known as Nantucket, the town was first called Wesco, from Algonquian *woskechquett* "top of the rocks." The shores of the village were rocky, especially close to the moorings at what is now Straight Wharf. By 1673 the names Nantucket for the island and Wesco for the village had given way, until the year 1795, to the English name Sherburne. Sherburne was the homestead in England of John Gardner and his family. Gardner came to Nantucket in the 1660s, found himself limited by the first settlers to half a vote, and went to New York to seek the help of the island's governor, Francis Lovelace. Lovelace heard Gardner out, ordered an end to full and half votes on the island, and decided on the name Sherburne. But once the Revolution was over and the dispute between the Gardners and the old proprietors over the vote had become a matter of history, the islanders restored the name Nantucket to their town and county. The earlier names also remained for a time. Wesco Hill [also Quanaty Hill] rose from Main Street to Newtown on the south side of Nantucket Town, but is now levelled. Wesco Pond, then Lily Pond, is on the north side of town. And near the north shore of Nantucket Town are Sherburne Bluffs, overlooking the sound, and Sherburne Turnpike, off Cliff Road.

Nantucket, it is said, was the creation of the Indian giant Maushop. Some say that the island is actually the left moccasin of the giant, who once kicked it into the sea while shaking Cape Cod sand from his toes. Others say that Nantucket is an ash pile that Maushop knocked from his pipe after he had had a smoke. Still another legend says that Maushop gave Nantucket to an Indian girl who had no dowry, to marry a rich brave. After the wedding the bride and her husband paddled to the island and so began the large family of Nantucket Indians. And, lastly, after the English arrived, Maushop summoned his people together, acknowledged that he was no longer strong enough to protect them, and bid them worhip the Christian God. [See Maushop Village, Cape Cod.]

Nantucket Bluffs

On the north shore of the island, west of Nantucket Town. According to Starbuck this locality was the first, from 1873 on, "to interest those unfortunate people who were forced to live on the mainland. . . ."

Nantucket Harbor

The harbor extends about six miles northeastward from Nantucket Town toward Coskata Pond and Great Point. It is sheltered on the north by Coatue Neck and washes the shores of a few localities and villages on the south such as Monomoy, Quaise, and Polpis. During the many decades of active whaling the harbor was alive with artisans and sailors from the world over, from the South Seas, Africa, and the Azores, as well as New England. They rolled barrels of whale oil onto the wharves, took on new ropes and sails, delivered spermaceti and whalebone, and had their storerooms freshly stocked and their keels retarred. Many of the ships entering the harbor had to wait for a high tide to bear them over a sandbar at the entrance. But in 1842 Peter F. Ewer designed a floating drydock called a *camel*, to carry ships directly over the hump of the bar and into the harbor. Ewer's camel worked well; the first ship it brought in was the 318-ton whaler *Constitution*. The Harbor itself consists of three natural basins, formed by the whirling tides that sweep up from the entrance at Brant and Coatue points to Head of the Harbor. Each basin rises from the depths at its center to the shallows at its edges, as if the harbor, in all, contained three tubs of great size, one next to the other.

New Dollar Lane

Between Milk and Mill streets in Nantucket Town. A new dollar was a token for a ship safely returned with the riches of whale oil, spermaceti, and whalebone. Joseph Starbuck, who owned whalers in the 1800s, lived on New Dollar Lane. It was also known as Risdale Street.

New Guinea

A neighborhood near Pleasant and York streets in the town of Nantucket. During the 1700s and 1800s blacks and mulattoes lived in the neighborhood and sent their men to sea in whalers. In 1822 the whaler *Industry* is said to have been manned entirely by blacks.

Newtown ['nu,taʊn]

The first record of Newtown at the southeast corner of Nantucket Town appears in 1727-28. A gate was built at Newtown to keep sheep and other livestock off the road to Siasconset. Gallows Field, in use until the 1840s, was close by.

P

Pedee ['pidi]

Possibly related to Algonquian *petuckqui* "round." Pedee was an Indian camp during the fishing season, between Sesachacha and Sankaty Head at the east end of Nantucket Island.

Phillips Run

For Philip Quabe, an Indian who lived at the stream in the 1600s. The run flows from Gibbs Pond through a large cranberry bog to Tom Nevers Pond. Some say that Philip (or Metacomet), the leader of the Wampanoags, hurried with his men along the shores of the run toward their canoes after they had accepted a small ransom for sparing the life of John Gibbs. [See John Gibbs Pond.]

Plainfield

A tract of more than 2100 acres between Siasconset and Sesachacha that became involved in a suit brought by sheepherders on Nantucket before the Massachusetts Supreme Court. In 1813 the Court ruled that those who owned more than a hundred sheep could pasture them all in one place — Plainfield — rather than in different lots scattered throughout the island. Before 1813 the sheepherders had no land of their own, but held all pasturage in common. After the decision Nantucketers began to say that the way to acquire property was not to pay cash, but to purchase it with one's shares in the sheep commons on the island.

Pochick ['po,čɪk]

The two ridges of this reef probably suggested its Algonquian name *pohshâog* "where they divide in two." The reef lies south of Siasconset underneath a rip current, opposite a bluff also known as Pochick.

Pocomo Head ['pakəmo]

Possibly related to Algonquian *paug'un-auke* "a clearing," this head of land pushing into Nantucket Harbor lies opposite Bass and Five Fingered points on Coatue Neck. The first settler to own land at Pocomo was Stephen Hussey, who came from Lynn in the late 1600s, sold rum to the Indians, and induced them to grant him a deed for fifteen hundred acres. Hussey had a more difficult time manipulating the other settlers and found himself frequently in court to answer complaints for double-dealing.

Polpis and Polpis Harbor
['polpɪs]

Also spelled Podpis, this Algonquian name is probably related to Abnaki *podebag* "jutting [of the water inland]." Once an Indian settlement near Nantucket Harbor, it attracted settlers of the 1600s, who bought lands for their villages and farms. Not long after, they built fulling mills to clean and dress wool, evaporated water at the harbor to make solar salt, and dug peat for fuel. After the foundering of the *The British Queen* in Muskeget Channel, two emigrant survivors remained on Nantucket at Polpis as tenant farmers, among the first from Ireland. The village of Polpis now has a strong, new growth of oaks and beech, ferns and sassafrass.

Q

Quaise and Quaise Point [kwez]

Possibly a shortening of Algonquian *Wechquaesqueck* "the end of the marsh." Another name for this area on the south side of Nantucket Harbor, west of Polpis, is Masquetuck, from *mishasq* 'flags, reeds' + *auk* 'land' = "place of reeds." Indians and English settlers had villages at Quaise, and Thomas Mayhew kept about 370 acres of nearby land for himself after he had sold the remainder of his holdings on the island to the proprietors on Nantucket. Keziah Coffin, a Loyalist during the American Revolution and a prominent Nantucket businesswoman, lived at Quaise. Protected by ships of the British navy, her shipments from New York arrived without difficulty, enabling her to trade on Nantucket almost without competition. Within a few years she was able to buy a country house in Quaise and a town house in Nantucket Town, but she later fell into difficulties. Quaise also had an insane asylum until it burned down.

Quanata Beach [ˌkwaˈnetə]

Near this beach on the Atlantic, not far south of the Sesachacha sandbar, lies a hill that the Algonquians probably called *quin* 'long' + *adchu* 'hill' + *ut* 'at' = "at the long hill." The beach takes its name from the hill.

Quidnet [ˈkwɪdnɪt]

From Algonquian *aquidnet* "at the island," although the lands at Quidnet are no longer encircled by water. Quidnet, once a gathering of fishing huts and stages, is now a village on the eastern shore of Nantucket, just north of Sesachacha Pond.

S

Sankaty Head [ˈsæŋkɪtɪ]

At the southeastern corner of Nantucket Island, the head rises ninety-two feet above the Atlantic and supports a lighthouse, built in 1849, that rises more than seventy feet higher. The slopes of the head reveal glacial formations. The meaning of Sankaty is not clear; neither is a second Indian name for the head, Naphchecoy.

Sauls Hills and Ponds

For Old Saul, a leader of the Nantucket Indians in the 1600s. The hills, formed by glaciers, are four miles east of Nantucket Town. The highest of them are Macys and Folger hills. The ponds are west of the Town, near Crooked Lane.

Sesachacha Pond
[ˈsækəčə] or [səˈsækəčə]

At the east end of the island, Sesachacha is, next to Hummock, the largest pond on Nantucket. Indians had a village at the pond in the 1600s; fishermen had stages on its shore near the Atlantic in the 1700s. The village of

Quidnet is at the northeast corner of the pond. The Algonquian source of Sesachaca, commonly called Sachacha, is uncertain.

Shawaukemo and Shawaukemo Hills [šɔ'kimo]

Possibly related to Algonquian *k'chekomuck*, from *k'che* 'great' + *komuk* 'house' = "great house." Shawaukemo was a tract west of Quaise Point on the south side of Nantucket Harbor, where there may have been an Indian village. The hills are farther inland, south of the harbor and toward the Foot Ponds.

Shimmo [ˈʃɪmo]

Possibly from Algonquian *ashim* 'spring' + *ut* 'at' = "at the spring." Shimmo was once a settlement, also an Indian village, near Shimmo Road on the south side of Nantucket Harbor, a mile and a half east of Monomoy. There is also a Shimmo Creek and Shimmo Point. [See Abrams Point.]

Siasconset
[ˈskansɪt] or [ˌsaɪəˈskansɪt]

This community, planned in the late 1800s for summer people, is in the southeast corner of Nantucket. Crèvecoeur, in his *Letters from an American Farmer* [1782], describes the "Siasconèt lott" as "a very uneven track of ground, abounding with swamps." The name Siasconset is probably related to Natick *wososki* 'marshy, muddy' + *auk* 'place' + *ut* 'at' = "at the little muddy place." In the 1700s fishermen erected stages and huts on the coast for their hauls of cod and halibut. Thoreau arrived in 1854 to find "perhaps fifty little houses, but almost every one empty." In 1881 a railway connected the town of Nantucket with the new resort at Siasconset, "the Newport of the Nantucketoise." And actors of vaudeville and stage, such as Jo-

seph Jefferson, De Wolf Hopper, and Frank Gilmore, came for summer holidays. The village still draws visitors to its old houses and public beaches.

Smiths Point

For one of the early Smiths on Nantucket, either John Smith, a partner of Thomas Mayhew, or Richard Smith, an artisan who came in 1661. The point at the western end of Esther Island was called Nopque by the Indians, possibly related to *nunnob* 'dry' + *ohke* 'land' = "dry land" or to *noe* 'middle' + *pe* 'water' = "middle of the waters." It lies near the beach where the Indians would go ashore after crossing from Martha's Vineyard. The storms and currents at the point have made it the most unstable of all the lands within Nantucket County. In generations past the point was west of Tuckernuck; it is now just below the eastern edge.

Smooth Hummocks [ˈhəmɪks]

Possibly so called because this land between Miacomet and Hummock ponds was a fairly flat stretch of sheep pasture. In 1875 land speculators on the south shore advertised an unsuccessful sale of lots between Long and Hummock ponds under the name of Smooth Hummocks.

Snake Spring

Snakes are not nearly so common on Nantucket as they were in the 1700s, especially in the eastern end of the island, where the spring is. Snake Spring is not far west of the Sankaty Head Golf Course.

South Beach

On Washington Street in Nantucket Town. After 1812 a brass foundry made castings for several years near the beach. It is now one of the town's public beaches.

Squam Head [skwɔm]

Probably from Algonquian *Wanashqui-ompskut* "at the top of the rock." Squam Head is at the east end of the island, about a mile south of Wauwinet. Squam Pond is a half-mile farther on the way to Quidnet. French pirates in 1695 ransacked a household of the Bunkers, an old Nantucket family that lived at Squam Head. They took what they saw, but missed the gold that Captain Bunker had buried. Instead they made him pilot them through Nantucket and Vineyard sounds to Tarpaulin Cove. Although he went free, the pirates frightened the Captain so much that he could never remember where he had hidden the gold. For years the Bunkers dug holes all over Squam Head, but never found the family treasure. The region, once an Indian settlement, has been developed as a resort.

Sunset Heights

Although the heights are south of Siasconset Village and face the sun coming up from the Atlantic, the hotel keepers who first built on the locality in the late 1800s decided to name it for the sunset. Some say that they named the heights in the midst of a Nantucket fog and couldn't tell one direction from the other.

Sunset Hill

An open view lies westward from this hill near North Liberty Street in Nantucket Town toward Madaket. On the hill is the Horseshoe House, also known as the Coffin House. It is also called the Oldest House because it was built in 1686 by Jethro Coffin, the grandson of Nantucket's first settler. It is known as the Horseshoe House because its chimney bears a horseshoe designed to keep witches out. Horseshoes, like the blood on the doorposts in Egypt or the mezuza of Deuteronomy, are symbols designed to safeguard those within the house. In 1923 the Nantucket Historical Association acquired the house and began to restore it.

Surfside

On the south coast of Nantucket, east of Miacomet Pond, Surfside began in 1880 as an investment by Charles and Henry Coffin, two brothers who hoped to sell many building lots to their mainland relatives. The brothers succeeded in having the federal government run a railroad from Nantucket Town to their new locality, and they worked together with their kinsman, Squire Allen Coffin, to invite many descendants of the early Nantucketer Tristram Coffin to a family reunion. Over five hundred Coffins came, but few bought lots in the proposed community of Surfside. The Coffin brothers went bankrupt and the railroad was torn up in World War I to make tanks, but Surfside remained to become a favorite island beach.

Swain Hill

For Richard Swain, a Nantucket proprietor of the 1600s. Swain Hill is at the west end of Nantucket, near Madaket and Eel Point roads. Swains Neck, farther east, is at the village of Polpis on Nantucket Harbor, where John Swain purchased land from the Indians in 1680.

T

W

Tom Nevers Head

The head rises about sixty-five feet above the Atlantic in southeastern Nantucket. Tom Nevers was an Indian who lived near the head in the 1670s and watched for stranded whales. Some Islanders used to say during World War I that German U-boats anchored close to the head to take on supplies donated by sympathizers.

Trots Hill and Trots Swamp

Probably for John Trott, a settler on Nantucket in 1665. The hills lie west of Nantucket Town, southwest of Capaum Pond. Trots Swamp lies farther south.

Tuckernuck   ['təkər,nək]

In DeLaet's atlas of 1630, *Nieuwe Wereldt*, the name of the island appears as Pentockynock, possibly related to Natick *petukunneg* "a [round] loaf of bread." The island looks like a loaf, yet very few Indian place-names are metaphoric. Another possibility is that Tuckernuck is a form similar to Narragansett *tocekat'uck* "let us wade." Before 1900 farmers at South Point would drive their sheep at low tide across the channel to Tuckernuck, where they would graze. Since then grass has become sparse, but the island now has several dwellings.

Warren Landing

For Warren Ramsdall of Madaket, who moored his boat on the landing in Madaket Harbor.

Wauwinet   [wɔ'wɪnɪt]

A village on the east shore of Nantucket, near Head of the Harbor, named for a sachem of the 1600s who presided over most of the island's tribes. In the late 1800s it became a resort.

Weweeder Ponds   [wi'wɪdər]

Possibly from Algonquian *wewene* "round about or winding about," a description that once fitted these ponds on the south side of the island, just west of Surfside. The land between the ponds was known as Long Josephs Point, probably for an Indian of the 1600s. In the 1800s, before the ponds became a swamp, fishermen would dry their fish on stages constructed near them.

Selected Bibliography

Banks, Charles E. *The History of Martha's Vineyard, Dukes County, Massachusetts*. 3 vols. Boston: G. H. Dean, 1911-25.

Barbour, Harriot B. *Sandwich: The Town That Glass Built*. Cambridge, Mass.: Houghton Mifflin, Co., 1948.

Bingham, Amelia G. *Mashpee: Land of the Wampanoags*. Mashpee, Mass.: Mashpee Centennial Committee, 1970.

Bray, Ella W. *Early Days of Yarmouth in Plymouth Colony*. South Yarmouth, Mass.: Wayside Studio, 1939.

Burling, Francis P. *The Birth of the Cape Cod National Seashore*. Plymouth, Mass.: Leyden Press, 1978.

Chamberlain, Barbara Blau. *These Fragile Outposts: A Geological Look at Cape Cod, Martha's Vineyard, and Nantucket*. Garden City, N.Y.: American Museum of Natural History, Natural History Press, 1964.

Deyo, Simeon L., ed. *History of Barnstable County*. New York: H. W. Blake, 1890.

Douglas-Lithgow, Robert A. *Nantucket: A History*. New York: G. P. Putnam's Sons, 1914.

Elphick, Robert. *Falmouth Past and Present*. Falmouth, Mass.: Kendall Printing, 1960.

Federal Writers Project. *Massachusetts: A Guide to Its Places and People*. Boston: Houghton Mifflin, Co., 1937.

Forman, Henry C. *Early Nantucket and Its Whale Houses*. New York: Hastings House, 1966.

Freeman, Frederick. *The History of Cape Cod*. 2 vols. Boston: Geo. C. Rand and Avery, 1858, 1862.

Jennings, Herman A. *Provincetown, or Odds and Ends from the Tip End*. Yarmouth Port, Mass.: F. Hallett, 1890.

Keene, Betsey D. *History of Bourne from 1622 to 1937*. Yarmouth Port, Mass.: C. W. Swift, 1937.

Kittredge, Henry C. *Cape Cod: Its People and Their History*. 2nd ed. Boston: Houghton Mifflin, Co., 1968.

McCann, James A. *An Inventory of the Ponds, Lakes, and Reservoirs of Massachusetts: Barnstable County*. Water Resources Research Center, University of Massachusetts-Amherst, pub. no. 10-1, 1969.

Macy, Obed. *The History of Nantucket*. Boston: Hilliard, Gray, 1835.

Mayhew, Eleanor R., ed. *Martha's Vineyard: A Short History*. Edgartown, Mass.: Dukes County Historical Society, 1956.

New England Historical and Genealogical Register, 1847- New England Historic Genealogical Society.

Paine, Josiah. *A History of Harwich*. Rutland, Vt.: Tuttle, 1937.

Porter, Ruth S. "The Place-Names of the Elizabeth Islands," Master's thesis, University of Massachusetts-Amherst, 1967.

Pratt, Enoch. *A Comprehensive History, Ecclesiastical and Civil, of Eastham, Wellfleet, and Orleans*. Yarmouth, Mass.: W. S. Fisher, 1844.

Rich, Shebnah. *Truro, Cape Cod, or Land Marks and Sea Marks*. 2nd ed. Boston: D. Lothrop, 1884.

Sealock, Richard B. and Seely, Pauline A. *Bibliography of Place-Name Literature: United States and Canada*. 2nd ed. American Library Association, Chicago, 1967.

The Seven Villages of Barnstable. Barnstable, Mass.: Town of Barnstable, 1976.

Smith, William C. *A History of Chatham, Massachusetts*. 4 pts. Hyannis, Mass.: F. B. and F. P. Goss, 1909-47.

Starbuck, Alexander. *The History of Nantucket*. Reprint. Rutland, Vt.: Charles E. Tuttle, 1969.

Stevens, William O. *Nantucket: The Far-Away Island*. New York: Dodd, Mead & Co., 1936.

Stewart, George R. *American Place-Names: A Concise and Selective Dictionary for the Continental United States of America*. New York: Oxford University Press, 1970.

Swift, Charles F. *Cape Cod, the Right Arm of Massachusetts: An Historical Narrative*. Yarmouth, Mass.: Register Publishing, 1897.

Swift, Charles F. *History of Old Yarmouth*. Edited by Charles A. Holbrook. Yarmouth Port, Mass.: Historical Society of Old Yarmouth, 1975.

Thoreau, Henry David. *Cape Cod*. Edited by Dudley C. Lunt. New York: W. W. Norton, 1951.

Trayser, Donald Grant, ed. *Barnstable: Three Centuries of a Cape Cod Town*. Hyannis, Mass.: F. B. and F. P. Goss, 1939.

Trumbull, James Hammond. *Natick Dictionary*. Smithsonian Institution: Bureau of American Ethnology, Bulletin 25, Washington, 1903.

Vorse, Mary M. H. *Time and the Town: A Provincetown Chronicle*. New York: Dial Press, 1942.

Wilson, Harold C. *Those Pearly Isles: The Enchanting Story of the Elizabeth Islands*. Falmouth, Mass.: Kendall Printing, 1973.

Wood, Donald. *Cape Cod: A Guide*. Boston: Little, Brown & Co., 1973.

Index

This is an index to place-names found under the entries, not to the entries themselves.

Other Cape Cod-area books for your travelling pleasure

Guide to Martha's Vineyard

Guide to New England's Landscape

Guide to the Recommended Country Inns of New England

Nantucket: A Guide with Tours

Nantucket: The Other Season

Short Bike Rides on Cape Cod, Nantucket & the Vineyard

Short Walks on Cape Cod and the Vineyard

The New England Indians

Available at your bookstore, or order direct from the publisher. For a free catalogue of New England books, write:
> The Globe Pequot Press
> Old Chester Road
> Chester, Connecticut 06412